José E. Ramírez Kidd
Alterity and Identity in Israel

Walter de Gruyter
1749
250
1999
Berlin · New York

Beihefte zur Zeitschrift für die alttestamentliche Wissenschaft

Herausgegeben von
Otto Kaiser

Band 283

Walter de Gruyter · Berlin · New York
1999

José E. Ramírez Kidd

Alterity and Identity in Israel

The גר in the Old Testament

Walter de Gruyter · Berlin · New York
1999

∞ Printed on acid-free paper which falls within the guidelines of the ANSI
to ensure permanence and durability.

Die Deutsche Bibliothek — Cataloging-in-Publication Data

[Zeitschrift für die alttestamentliche Wissenschaft / Beihefte]
Beihefte zur Zeitschrift für die alttestamentliche Wissenschaft. —
Berlin ; New York : de Gruyter
    Früher Schriftenreihe
    Reihe Beihefte zu: Zeitschrift für die alttestamentliche Wissenschaft
    Bd. 283. Ramírez Kidd, José E.: Alterity and identity in Israel. —
    1999
Ramírez Kidd, José E.:
Alterity and identity in Israel : the "ger" in the Old Testament / José
E. Ramírez Kidd. — Berlin ; New York : de Gruyter, 1999
    (Beihefte zur Zeitschrift für die alttestamentliche Wissenschaft ; Bd.
    283)
    Zugl.: Hamburg, Univ., Diss., 1999
    ISBN 3-11-016625-9

ISSN 0934-2575

Printed in Germany
Printing: Werner Hildebrand, Berlin
Binding: Lüderitz & Bauer-GmbH, Berlin

To my daughter

Rebeca Ramírez Solt

Preface

This study was accepted as Dissertation by the Faculty of Theology of the Hamburg University in January 1999. I want to express my gratitude to Prof. Otto Kaiser for accepting it in the series BZAW. I am particularly indebted to my *Doktorvater* Prof. Hermann Spieckermann for his insightful comments. His constant encouragement took many forms all along these years. My gratitude to him goes beyond words. I am also indebted to Prof. Ina Willi-Plein who wrote the second *Gutachten*. She was also kind enough to read the first chapter of my manuscript at an earlier stage making several important suggestions.

To the colleagues of the Missionsakademie an der Universität Hamburg, especially to its director Dr. E. Kamhausen, I express my gratitude for their warm support. I would also like to record my appreciation to the personal of the Nordelbische Kirchenbibliothek for their significant contribution to the completion of my research.

Finally, I want to acknowledge the support of colleagues and friends, namely Dr. Adela Ramos who arranged everything for my *sejours* of research in Strasbourg, and who was always ready to attend my "urgent calls" asking for articles and other relevant material, Dr. Wendy Pradell who despite her advanced pregnancy took time to read the manuscript and suggested corrections corresponding to the different languages used in the dissertation, Dr. Kiran Sebastian and Dr. Sam Matthew read sections of the initial chapters and helped me to improve the style, and Selma Gomes helped me to elaborate the index of biblical references. The fellowship of my dear friend and colleague John Samuel Raj and his family was especially meaningful for me during these years. In our friendship I found the strength I needed to overcome the difficulties that are normally attached to the life away from home. The letters of my parents, José Ramírez and Felicia Kidd, were always comforting "like cold water to a thirsty soul" (Prov 25,25a).

Hamburg, March 1999   José E. Ramírez Kidd

"Was Israel im Umgang mit dem Fremden ... auszeichnet, ist die Entschlossenheit, die eigene identitätsstiftende Ursprungserfahrung und die Erfahrung des Fremden nicht beziehungslos nebeneinander stehenzulassen, sondern das eine nicht ohne das andere sein lassen zu wollen. Gerade in der Erfahrung des Fremden Gott wahrzunehmen, eröffnet Israel die Chance, das Fremde selbst weithin anders zu werten, als es die altorientalische Umwelt vorgelebt hat, und zugleich die eigene Erfahrungsvielfalt mit dem Fremden aus einem tieferen Zusammenhang heraus zu verstehen".

(H. Spieckermann, Die Stimme des Fremden im Alten Testament, PTh 83 p. 52.)

Table of Contents

Introduction

To gain a better idea about the present state of research on the theme of the גר,
it is appropriate to frame this subject in historical perspective. The first section
deals with some changes that have taken place in the *global approach* of the
research, and the second section considers some *specific issues* discussed in
the recent literature.

1. Survey of Past Research

1.1 Global approach

A comparison of the structure and the title of some studies written in the late
nineteenth century with later studies, shows clearly the way in which the
research has evolved. Let us consider two examples.

1.1.1 Lexica

A look at the entries for the noun גר in the lexica shows an important
increment in the number of legal references, and a significant improvement in
the structure of the entries. The evolution of this entry in Gesenius's
Handwörterbuch illustrates this well.[1] Ges[11] defines גר as: "Fremdling, von
Personen und ganzen Völkern gebraucht", and gives five references for this,
two of which are legal.[2] Ges[12] (the first revision from Buhl) substitutes for
this short definition the following reading:

"-Wanderer, Reisender ...
 -besonders: ein in einem fremden Lande sich aufhaltender, so
 -von den Patriarchen;
 -von den Israeliten in Ägypten;

---

1   Besides the editions of Gesenius quoted here, compare the entries to the noun גר in
    Ges[3] p. 166, Ges[14] p. 131-132; Zorell, Lexicon Hebraicum p. 158; Loewenstamm /
    Blau, Thesaurus II p. 247; Clines, DCH II p. 372-373 and the entries to גר and גור in
    the Thesavrvs Philologicvs criticvs lingvae hebraeae et chaldeae veteris testamenti,
    Tomi Primi, Lipsiae 1829 p. 273-275.
2   Gn 15,13; Ex 2,22; 18,3; 22,20; 23,9.

-von den geduldeten Ausländern im Lande;
-auch von Fremden, welche Israels Religion annehmen".

The entry contains 22 references, 13 of which are legal.[3]   A more differentiated definition of this noun is given in Ges[18], which contains the following complex scheme:

1. Schutzbürger, Fremdling, Gast
     a) allg.
     b) v. Israel i. Äg.
     c) (innerhalb Israels) volks- od. stammesfremder Schutzbürger
     d) übertr. (v. den Israeliten i. eigenen Lande)
               (v. dem leidenden Frommen)
2. Fremder, Gast.
3. Proselyt.

This entry includes sixty-five references, forty-five of them in the section "1. c)"; thirty four out of these forty five are legal texts.

This progressive complexity in the understanding of the noun גר in the lexica reflects a parallel process which has taken place in particular studies on this subject. Two examples illustrate this tendency in the research during the first half of this century:

1) T. Meek opens his article on the translation of גר in the Hexateuch with the following statement: "As is well known, a word does not necessarily mean the same wherever it is found.   In different contexts the same word may have decidedly different meanings, and in the course of time a word may change quite radically and in its later usage have a sense very different from what it had originally".[4] He suggests that the meaning of the term גר is: "immigrant" in the earlier references (JE); "resident alien" in the Covenant code and

---

3   The Brown-Driver-Briggs's *Hebrew and English Lexicon of the Old Testament*, based on Ges[10], enlarges the definition of גר as: "Fremdling, von Personen und ganzen Völkern gebraucht", with the following reading: "usually of gerîm in Israel (...); -dwellers in Israel with certain conceded, not inherited rights (...); -The ger is to share in Sabbath rest (...); -otherwise he is to have like obligations with Israel (...)" (p. 158).   It must be noticed that only in the explanation of the last point, this entry contains 25 legal references: "Ex 12,19.48.49; Lev 16,29 (all P) Lev 17,8.10.12.13.15; 18,26;   20,2; 22,18;   24,16.22 (all H); Num 9,14.14;   15,14.15.15.16.26.29.30;   19,10;   35,15 (all P)" (BDB p. 158).

4   JBL 49 p. 172.

Deuteronomy[5], and "proselyte" in the Holiness code and P.[6]   Earlier, the treatment of this noun in biblical commentaries was, usually, undifferentiated.[7]

2) There is also present in other studies a growing awareness of the legal nature of this noun: in his "Lehrbuch der Hebräischen Archäologie", for instance, Nowack discusses the term גר in the chapter on: "Rechtsverhältnisse" as "Politisches Recht"[8]; and I. Benzinger in his "Hebräische Archäologie", considers the גרים in the section of "Privatrecht" as "Personenrecht".[9] Weber, in his chapter on גרים in "Das Antike Judentum", speaks about "Rechtsverhältnis"[10]; and K.L. Schmidt describes this term as "eine rechtliche Kategorie eigener Art".[11] This distinction is, however, still absent in other important studies.[12]

1.1.2 Particular studies

A comparison of the titles of Bertholet's study (1896) and K.L. Schmidt's article (1945) on the alien, shows a fundamental difference in approach:

Bertholet: "Die Stellung der Israeliten und der Juden zu den Fremden".
Schmidt: "*Israels Stellung* zu den Fremdlingen und Beisassen
             und *Israels Wissen* um seine Fremdling- und Beisassenschaft".[13]

Each of these studies can be considered a classic example of a particular approach to this subject. Bertholet's book, influenced like other studies of his

---

5   The term "resident alien" became standard in the English literature. See for instance the recent study of Joosten, People p. 54.

6   This differentiated understanding of the noun גר is shown in Meek's own translation of the pentateuch in AT (after the second edition).   This version offers some other renderings as translation for גר: alien (Ex 20,10); foreigner (Deut 14,21); sojourner (2 Sam 1,13); stranger (Jer 14,8); guest (Ps 119,19).

7   See for instance Dillmann, Genesis p. 310; idem, Exodus und Leviticus p. 137; 581-582; 588; 612; Knobel, Genesis p. 178; idem., Exodus und Leviticus p. 126; 514-515.

8   Nowack, Archäologie I Chapter II § 62 p. 336-341.

9   Benzinger, Archäologie Chapter II § 54. A. p. 287-289.

10 The גר is: "ein Beisasse, der nicht nur unter dem privaten Schutz eines Einzelnen und dem religiösen des Gastrechts steht, sondern dessen Rechtslage von dem politischen Verband als solchem geregelt und geschützt wurde ... Dies Rechtsverhältnis wird bezeichnet mit dem Ausdruck 'ger ascher bisch'arecha'" (Judentum p. 39).

11 Judaica 1 p. 281.

12 It is interesting to note that Barrois and de Vaux do not consider this subject under the section of "Droit" but rather under "Évolution de l'organisation tribale" and "Les éléments de la population libre" respectively, see MAB II p. 42 and IAT I p. 116-118.

13 Judaica 1 p. 269-296, italics is ours.

time by the works of W. Robertson Smith[14], pays particular attention to the cultural and anthropological aspects of this subject.   This approach was common among most of the early works.[15]   In Schmidt's article, however, Israel's awareness of its own experience as גר turns into a viewpoint.   Israel had particular grounds to justify the laws on strangers in the fact, "daß es seine Existenz als ein Leben in der Fremdling- und Beisassenschaft verstanden hat".[16]

"Israel hat seine Volkwerdung in der ägyptischen Fremdlings- und Beisassenschaft begonnen und hat sich dieses Vorganges immer auch nach der Landnahme Kanaans erinnern müssen und sollen.   Eine ebenso einfache wie aber nun dringliche Verpflichtung ist im Bewußtsein Israel damit gegeben, daß Gott die ägyptische Sklavenexistenz seines Volkes als ein dauerndes Beispiel und Zeichen hingestellt habe".[17]

A similar approach is found in Spieckermann's recent article "Die Stimme des Fremdes im Alten Testament".   In this study "die Erfahrung, Fremde zu sein", becomes for Israel an hermeneutical key for the interpretation of its own traditions and for the understanding of its fundamental vocation.   As Spieckermann states at the end of this article:

"*Die Stimme des Fremden* im Alten Testament ist in dieser Studie auf ganz unterschiedliche Weise zu Gehör gekommen: zunächst als *die Stimme des israelitischen Selbstverständnisses,* das die Rettung aus der Fremdlingschaft in Ägypten als eigene Ursprungserfahrung festgehalten und ihr im Schutzrecht für den Fremdling (ger) ein würdiges Echo geschaffen hat ...".[18]

The lexicon entries and the particular studies show in sum:
• a progressive distinction of the different *levels of meaning* of גר,
• a better understanding of the *legal nature* of this noun,
• and growing awareness of the *theological dimensions* of this noun.
Apart from the specific works on the figure of the alien in the Old Testament, such as the articles of Amusin, Crüsemann, Albertz and Schwienhorst-Schönberger[19], we have also other more comprehensive word studies, which analyze the meaning of the noun גר in its historical development and its theological use, such as those of D. Kellermann, Martin-Achard and

---

14   See for instance Stellung p. 9; 11; 14; 15; 18; 21; 26; 27; 28; 45; 46; 47; 52; 53; 56; 57; 59; 62; 67; 69; 70; 71; 72; 73; 74.
15   See for instance: Bennett, Art. Stranger and Sojourner, in: EncB, IV, col. 4814-4818; Nödelke, Art. Fremde, in: BiL 2 p. 300
16   Judaica 1 p. 269.
17   Judaica 1 p. 269.
18   PTh 83 p. 66, italics is ours.
19   Amusin, KLIO 63/1 p. 15-23; Crüsemann, WuD 19 p. 11-24; Albertz, CTB 16 p. 61-72; Schwienhorst-Schönberger, BuL 63 p. 108-117.

Kuhn's triad in FJFr; TWNT and RECA.[20]   This last study, because of its scope and its sharp sociological and religious analysis, is particularly important.[21]

1.2 Specific issues

In his 1899 article: "Fremdlinge bei den Hebräern", P. Benzinger had already analyzed the term גר under the division: "Bundesbuch" => "Deuteronomium" => "Priestergesetz".[22]   With exceptions[23], this order has been maintained ever since, as the recent studies of Crüsemann, Albertz, Schwienhorst-Schönberger and van Houten show.[24]   Because of the number of references to the noun גר in the book of Deuteronomy and in the priestly writings, the attention focuses on these documents.

1.2.1 The גר in the book of Deuteronomy

The גר in Deuteronomy has been commonly identified as: "a foreigner, non-Israelite living within Israel".[25]   This idea has been challenged by two alternative suggestions: the first one, understands the גר as being part of the wave of immigrants coming from the northern kingdom after the fall of Samaria in 721 BC.[26]   According to Schwienhorst-Schönberger: "Vor diesem Hintergrund sind die besonderen Maßnahmen zum Schutz und zur Integration des Fremden zu verstehen, die sich im Buch *Deuteronomium* niedergeschlagen

---

20   D. Kellermann, Art. גור, in: TWAT I col. 979-991; Martin-Achard, Art. גור, in: THAT I col. 409-412; Kuhn, Art. Ursprung, FJFr 3 p. 199-234; idem, Art. προσήλυτος, in: TWNT VI, 1959 p. 727-745; idem, Art. Proselyten, in: RECA Supp IX, 1962 col. 1248-1283.

21   See also Cardellini, RivBib 40 p. 129-181; Schreiner, BiKi 42 p. 50-60.

22   Benzinger, Art. Fremdlinge bei den Hebräern, in: RE VI p. 263.

23   According to Bultmann: "Das Schutzgebot für den *ger* stellt keinen vordtn Bestand des Bundesbuchs dar, sondern ist von einer generalisierenden nomistischen Tendenz in der späteren Wirkungsgeschichte des dtn Gesetzes her zu verstehen" (Der Fremde p. 169). Joosten in his recent study on the Holiness Code states: "We are led to the conclusion that the historical conditions addressed by H are those of the pre-exilic period. It seems likely that the real audience of H should have lived under these same conditions, i.e. before the exile" (People p. 90).

24   See footnote 19 and van Houten, Alien p.22.

25   Mayes, BEThL 68 p. 323.   According to van Houten: "the laws of Deuteronomy consistently treat the alien as a non-Israelite" (Alien p. 107); von Rad takes him as "ein ... Individuum nicht-israelitischer Herkunft" (TB 48 p. 53-54); Buis-Leclercq as "un des anciens habitants de Palestine" (Deutéronome p. 179); Meek as "the indigenous population of Palestine conquered by the Hebrews" (JBL 49 p. 173); Barbiero thinks that: "Effetivamente il ger (in Deut) non è un 'fratello'" (L'asino p. 201).

26   Broshi, IEJ 24 p. 21-26; idem, RB 82 p. 5-14.

haben".[27]   Cardellini (who shares the same opinion) states, therefore, that
these גרים are "fratelli nella stessa fede".[28]   Despite several isolated critics[29],
this thesis has received general acceptance.[30]   The second proposal is that of
Bultmann: the figure of the גר can be explained as result of an internal social
differentiation in Juda.   Next to the class of the local, well established farmers,
there is in the Judean population a subclass of free, landless people, temporary
workers at the service of these farmers from whom they also receive charitable
support in order to survive.[31]   The גר is here neither a foreigner nor an
immigrant.[32]

Schwienhorst-Schönberger and Otto have contributed to the understanding
of the origin of the גר - legislation in Deuteronomy.   They have pointed out the
social changes which took place in Israel during the VIII century BC.[33], and
indicate that in Deuteronomy the laws for the protection of the *personae miserae*
are no longer based on genealogical but on religious principles.   It is this
transition which makes possible the solidarity with the גר, circumscribed before
(i.e. the solidarity) to the limits of one's own kinship.

1.2.2 The גר in the Holiness Code and P

There is consensus among some authors that the noun גר in (the late
references of) the priestly writings, designates a religious type of non-Israelite
origin, i.e. a foreigner who seeks integration in the religious community of

---

27   Schwienhorst-Schönberger, BuL 63 p. 112.

28   Cardellini summarizes his position in this way: "È probabile che nelle disposizioni
     umanitarie l'attenzione particolarissima del Deuteronomio per il *gér* ... sia dovuta al
     fatto che questi *gérîm*, o un consistente numero fra essi, non siano altro che fuggiaschi
     israeliti del nord" (RivBib 40 p. 149 and footnote 33).

29   Lang, Art. Fremder, in: NBL 1 col. 701-702; Bultmann, Der Fremde p. 44; 213-214.

30   See for instance: H. Weippert, Palästina II/1 p. 588-589; Welten, Art. Jerusalem I, in:
     TRE 16 p. 596; idem: FS R. Mayer p.132; Smith, Parties p. 178; de Vaux, IAT I p.
     118; Gonçalves, L'Expédition p. 67; Osumi, Kompositionsgeschichte p. 165;
     Schwienhorst-Schönberger, BuL 63 p. 112; D. Kellermann. TWAT I col. 984-985;
     Weinfeld, DDS p. 90-91; Crüsemann, Bundesbuch p. 34; idem: WuD 19 p. 16.

31   Next to this class of the local farmers: "steht eine andere Schicht von einzelnen, freien,
     besitzlosen Personen, die darauf angewiesen ist, daß diese Bauern ihre Arbeitskraft
     beanspruchen oder, dem Religionsgesetz gehorchend, ihnen in ihrer Notlage gewisse
     Begünstigungen bei der Beschaffung ihres Lebensunterhalts gewähren" (Der Fremde p.
     214).

32   Bächli thinks "daß er sowohl israelitischer Volksgenosse als auch Fremder sein kann"
     (Israel p. 128).

33   Schwienhorst-Schönberger makes particular reference to the wave of immigrants coming
     from the northern kingdom after the fall of Samaria in 721 BC. (BuL 63 p. 112-113).
     Otto makes reference to the growing process of social differentiation (Ethik p. 103-104;
     idem, OH 3 p. 135-161).

Israel.[34] Who these people are, and to what extent they can be identified with the later proselytes, remains open. On the issue of the identity of the גר, there is a wide spectrum of opinions. They have been identified with Israelite exiles after their return to Palestine[35]; with Israelites who remained in the land and joined the community of the returnees[36]; with persons who, coming from outside, wanted to become part of the religious community[37]; with Jews from the Dispersion coming to Jerusalem for the celebration of the feasts[38]; with members of the Samaritan leading classes[39]; with the nationals of Northern Israel submitted to Judean control, especially after the downfall of Samaria[40]; and with foreigners who have settled in the land of Israel, and have been assimilated culturally and religiously.[41]

The question of whether the גר in the Holiness code can be identified with the later proselyte or not, is obviously related to the question of the date of composition of this document. Since the chronology of the documents (i.e. J, E, D and P), was already established by Wellhausen, the identification of the גר with the proselyte in the priestly writings was simply a corollary of this idea and, therefore, a commonplace in the nineteenth century. Bertholet titles the section V. 5 of his study: "Das endgültige Resultat: Der Ger = der Proselyt".[42] This idea has been maintained until the present.[43] For Y. Kaufmann, on the contrary, who takes this document as preexilic and rejects the possibility of religious conversion in the Old Testament: "The ger of P is a free man, a foreigner who has settled in the land of Israel and has been assimilated culturally and hence religiously"[44]; this view is shared by other Jewish authors.[45] Among the recent studies, Ohana, Crüsemann and Joosten also

---

34 Bertholet, Stellung p. 155; 174f; Smith, Parties p. 178-182; Driver, Deuteronomy p. 165.
35 Cazelles, VT 4 p. 131.
36 Van Houten, Alien p. 156.
37 Bultmann, Der Fremde p. 216.
38 Grelot, VT 6 p. 178.
39 Vink, OST XV p. 48.
40 Cohen, RHR 207 p. 131. According to Cohen the גר is "un ressortissant de l'Israël septentrional soumis à la domination judéenne". This definition of גר is valid "non seulement dans le code sacerdotal mais également dans le Deutéronome". The difference between them is ideological: "D aurait adopté à l'égard des *gerim*, i.e. des Ephraïmites de l'après-Samarie, une attitude ségrégationniste, P, au contraire, une attitude intégrationniste" (p. 156-157).
41 Kaufmann, Religion p. 206. This opinion is shared by Joosten, People p. 54-58 and Weinfeld, DDS p. 228ff.
42 Stellung p. 152ff. See also Meyer, Entstehung p. 230-234.
43 Horst, Art. Fremde, in: RGG³ II col. 1126; D. Kellermann, TWAT I col. 988; Mathys, Liebe p. 40.
44 Kaufmann, Religion p. 206.
45 Weinfeld, DDS p. 228f; Milgrom, JBL 101/102 169ff.

opposed -with different arguments-, the identification of the גר with the proselyte.[46]

1.3. Specific studies on the גר

1.3.1 "The Alien in Israelite Law": C. van Houten

According to this author, M. Weber made a lasting contribution to biblical research on the alien: "by drawing attention to the way the definition of the alien changed as the definition of the people of Israel changed" (p. 14). In a diachronic study she pursues, therefore, an examination of the legal treatment of the גר in the Book of the Covenant, Deuteronomy and the Priestly laws, and a reconstruction of the historical identity of the alien throughout Israel's history. Van Houten concludes that: "the legal status of the alien has changed dramatically over time" (p. 164). The results of her study can be summarized as follows:

• The identity of the alien in the pre-monarchical period is defined in terms of clan; the alien thus is someone from another tribe, whether Israelite or non-Israelite. The laws pertaining to the alien in the *Book of the Covenant* are requirements dealing with charity, equity and cultic activity. Behind this legislation stands the custom of hospitality, formulated here as a law. The transition from a moral norm to a written legal tradition is a significant step.

• There are two kinds of references to the alien in *Deuteronomy*: (1) those of the law code (12-26), which treat the alien as a non-Israelite and deal with cultic matters and social justice (these laws created a permanent support system which would prevent the "alien, widow and orphan" from becoming poor); and (2) those of the legal code in which the aliens are second class citizens who have entered into a legal relationship with Israel, such as the case of the Gibeonites in Deut 29.

• In the *Priestly laws* there are two levels of redaction: the primary level reflects an ancient (pre-exilic) tradition. Unlike the deuteronomic laws which established a support system to avoid poverty, these laws simply require from the Israelites to be charitable; the second level reflects a post-exilic situation: the aliens were those who were considered impure by the returnees and who must go through a purity ritual before being considered members of the confessional community.

---

46   Ohana rejects with strong arguments the idea of religious conversion in the Old
      Testament (Biblica 55 p. 320-323). Joosten maintains the same basic position of
      Kaufmann, Weinfeld and Milgrom (People p. 54-58); Crüsemann denies the existence of
      such forms of proselytism at this time in Israel: "So etwas wie Proselytismus gab es
      noch nicht" (Concilium 29/4 p. 343); he also states: "Ein Hauptproblem dieser Epoche
      war die ... sogenannten Mischehen zwischen Juden und Frauen der umliegenden Völker
      ... Der Grundsatz, sich von den Völkern abzusondern (vgl. etwa Esr 10,11), steht in
      dieser Zeit neu auf dem Spiel ... Darum geht es, es geht gerade nicht um so etwas wie
      Proselytismus!" (WuD 19 p. 23).

On the basis of these results and "because the laws pertaining to the alien are typical of the laws in each of these collections" (p. 158), she claims to be in the position of describing "the development of law in general in Israel", and "to characterize the ethical development that has occurred in this body of literature" (ibid.). The critical problems involved in such an enterprise are, of course, far more complex than the simplified version presented in van Houten's arguments[47], and the conclusions (p. 165ff.) exceed, by far, the nature of the study.

1.3.2 "Der Fremde im antiken Juda": C. Bultmann

Bultmann's study opens with a question which will resound again in different chapters, that is: "ob die Bezeichnung *ger* (גר) im Alten Testament einen Fremden meint, der nicht-israelitischer Herkunft ist, ..." (p. 9). The author states that there are two lines of use of this noun in the Old Testament; in the deuteronomic source: "Der ger ist fremd an dem Ort seines Aufenthalts". Nothing in these references suggests that "der ger eine Gestalt nicht-israelitischer Herkunft wäre" (p. 213). He states, then: "Mit dem Wechsel des Bezugsrahmens ... hängt der wortgeschichtliche Bedeutungswandel zusammen" (p. 216); and explains concerning the priestly source: "Der Fremde ist nicht-israelitischer, d.h. nicht-jüdischer Herkunft" (p. 216).

The leading question of this study surprises because the notion that the גר in the Old Testament can represent *either* an Israelite *or* someone of a non-Jewish origin, was already stated in 1869 by Nödelke[48] and repeated ever since by different authors.[49] Bultmann, who seems to be aware of this, states that the central question of his study "ist offenkundig wenig umstritten, aber auch wenig geklärt" (p. 12). The study does not make clear, however, in which

---

47 See for instance the criteria used to determine the redactional levels in the book of Deuteronomy, Alien p. 78ff.

48 Nödelke, Art. Fremde, in: BiL 2 p. 300.

49 See for instance: Benzinger, Art. Fremdlinge bei den Hebräern, in: RE VI p. 263; Weber, Judentum p. 40; Pedersen, Israel I-II p. 40; Löhr, SKG.G 7/3 p. 189; Meek, JBL 49 p. 172ff; Bächli, Israel p. 128; Michaeli, Exode p. 108; Spina, FS D.N. Freedman p. 323; Crüsemann, WuD 19 p. 14; Joosten, People p. 54-55; 61; Ges[14] p. 131; Ges[18] p. 227. Although the גר is taken either as a *stranger* (Robertson Smith, Religion p. 75 and Lods, Israël p. 229), or as a *foreigner* (Bertholet, Stellung p. 101; Driver, Deuteronomy p. 126; Meek, JBL 49 p. 172; Horner, ATR 42 p. 49; Spencer, Art. Sojourner, in: ABD VI p. 103), the aspect of *origin* plays only a marginal role in the definition given by important studies such as those of Kuhn, Art. Proselyten, in: RECA Supp IX, col. 1255-1256; Martin-Achard, Art. גור, in: THAT I col. 410; Dion, Universalismo p. 186; D. Kellermann, TWAT I col. 983-984; Crüsemann, WuD 19 p. 14 and Joosten, People p. 55.

sense the clarification of a point on which there is such a consensus might contribute to a better understanding of this subject in the Old Testament.[50]

2. Proposal

The use of the noun גר in the Old Testament alternates between the reference to the *individuum* and the reference to *Israel.* This noun, used originally in the laws to refer to the stranger, is used later by the Israelite community as self-designation in prayers. The translation of the noun גר in the Septuagint (προσήλυτος/πάροικος), and the later use of this Greek version in the Jewish and Christian communities, gave this term dimensions that went beyond the meaning of the original Hebrew noun. The present study attempts: (1) to determine other uses of this noun besides that of "גר as individuum" and to acknowledge their theological relevance, (2) to describe the semantical transformations that this noun underwent within the Old Testament, and in its transition from the Hebrew Bible to its Greek translation. This is, then, not a study about *the* גר *in ancient Israel,* but about *the use of the noun* גר *in the Old Testament.*

The publication of J. Barr's Semantics of Biblical Language in the early sixties, opened a debate on some methodological aspects of the word studies.[51] As a result of this discussion, the role played by *verbal roots* and *sentences* in the study of nominal forms was reconsidered. Taking into account some aspects of this discussion:

• we give priority to the semantic value of the גר noun in its actual context, rather than to etymological associations. The initial chapter reconsiders, therefore, the relationship between the verb גור and the noun גר.

• the noun גר is studied in some relevant constructions: a study of the word-groups draws attention to the deuteronomic triad "גר, orphan, widow" and to the priestly pair "גר - אזרח"; a study of the formulas "גרים in the land of

---

50   On the other hand, Bultmann points out that there are two lines of use of this word in the Old Testament: "Das deuteronomische Gesetz" and the "Heiligkeitsgesetz". There are, consequently, *two* different notions of גר: the social and the religious one. But, if there is such a differentiation in the nature of the sources, it is methodologically not clear, how we can have *one and the same* leading question for both of them. See also Crüsemann, Concilium 29 p. 343-344.

51   J. Barr, The Semantics of Biblical Language, 2. Ed., Oxford 1962; idem, Semantics and Biblical Theology - a contribution to the discussion, SVT 22 p. 11-19; idem: Semitic Philology and the Interpretation of the Old Testament, in: G.W. Anderson (Ed.), *Tradition and Interpretation*, Oxford 1979 p. 31-64. In reaction to Barr's initial work see Boman, TLZ 87 p. 262-265; Friedrich, TLZ 94 p. 801-816; and idem, KuD 16 p. 41-57.

Egypt" and "גרים before Yahweh", draws attention to the role of this noun in
the deuteronomistic and priestly theology.

Since the majority of the references to this noun refers to the גר as
individuum, most of the studies on this term follow a historical approach. As
the titles of van Houten's and Bultmann's studies show, they concentrate on
the individual גר in ancient Israel.[52]   The present study attempts to draw
attention to the transition that takes place in the Old Testament between
speaking *about the* גר and speaking *as a* גר. We give attention, therefore, to
the use of this noun not only as *figura iuridica* in the laws (i.e. the גר as
individuum), but also to its use as *figura theologica* (i.e. the Israelites as גרים).

In the last two chapters, we present an overall view of the theological
development of this noun in three moments: (1) the elements of continuity and
discontinuity between Israel and the surrounding cultures in relation to their
attitude towards strangers, (2) the transition from the legal to the metaphorical
use of this noun in religious language of the Old Testament, i.e. the notion of
human existence as a pilgrimage, (3) the transformation that the noun גר
underwent as a result of the Greek translation of the Hebrew Bible, and its later
impact in the Jewish and Christian communities. The comprehensive approach
of this study takes for granted the discussion of some specific issues
concerning the גר in the Old Testament, and which have already been discussed
in van Houten's and Bultmann's studies.

---

52   C. van Houten, The Alien in Israelite Law, JSOTSS 107, 1991; C. Bultmann, Der
      Fremde im antiken Juda, FRLANT 153, 1992.

Part 1

The noun גֵר as *figura iuridica*:
the גֵר as *individuum*

1. The emergence of the noun גֵר as a legal term

Specific studies and lexicon entries of the term גֵר usually share two basic premises: (1) the understanding of the גֵר as a "*person* " who, in order to protect his life and family, looks for a new home, and (2) the semantic equivalence of the verb גור and the noun גֵר.[1] HAL's definition of the noun גֵר illustrates this well:

"גֵר ist e. Mann, der allein od. m. Familie wegen Krieg 2S 4³ Js 16⁴, Hungersnot Rt I¹, Seuche, Blutschuld usw. Dorf u. Stamm verlässt u. anderwärts Zuflucht u. Aufenthalt sucht, wo s. Recht auf Grundbesitz, Ehe u. Teilnahme an Rechtsprechung, Kult u. Krieg verkürzt ist".[2]

Following this definition one could expect that the persons who went through such circumstances (i.e. "Krieg, Hungersnot, Seuche, Blutschuld usw.") be designated in the Old Testament by the noun גֵר. But those who on account of such misfortunes had to leave their original dwelling place and seek dwelling at another place, are not normally designated by the noun גֵר. When the Old Testament speaks about persons who went through such circumstances, it uses rather a combination of different verbs[3]:

---

1   See for instance: Martin-Achard, THAT I col. 410; Muntingh, NGTT 3 p. 549ff; de Vaux, IAT I p. 117f.

2   HAL 1 p. 193. KBL had basically the same definition: "die Leute v. בְּאֵרוֹת fliehen nach נְתִים u. bleiben dort als גֵרִים 2S 4³; e. Hungersnot lässt e. Mann mit Frau u. Söhnen von Bethlehem nach Moab ziehen u. dort als גֵר bleiben Rt I¹; die aus e. Land Versprengten נִדָחִים werden anderwärts גֵרִים Js 16⁴. גֵר ist e. Mann, der allein (oder mit seinen Leuten) wegen Krieg, Unruhen, Hungersnot, Seuche, Blutschuld, e. Unglück Dorf und Stamm, zu denen er gehört, verlässt u. anderwärts Zuflucht und Aufenthalt sucht, wo er in seinem Recht auf Grundbesitz, Ehe u. Teilnahme an Rechtsprechung, Kult u. Krieg verkürzt ist" (p. 192). Note that no references for "Seuche, Blutschuld" are given. This definition is cited in Muntingh, NGTT 3 p. 549; Zimmerli, Ezechiel p. 303 and Wildberger, Jesaja p. 1303. See also Bultmann, Der Fremde p. 11 note 15.

3   See also Jud 11,3: "Then Jephthah fled (וַיִבְרַח) from his brothers and lived (וַיֵשֶׁב) in the land of Tob", and 1 K 11,40: "Solomon sought therefore to kill Jeroboam; but Jeroboam promptly fled (וַיָקָם ... וַיִבְרַח) to Egypt ... and remained (וַיְהִי בְמִצְרַיִם) in Egypt until the death of Solomon".

"Then Jotham ran away (וַיָּנָס) and fled (וַיִּבְרַח), going to Beer (וַיֵּלֶךְ), where he remained (וַיֵּשֶׁב) for fear of his brother Abimelech" (Jud 9, 21).

Cases which correspond to HAL's definition of גֵר but in which the noun גֵר is not used are for instance: Jud 11,3;   1 Sam 21,11;   22,20;   27,4;   2 Sam 4,3;   13,34;   1 K 11,17.23.40.

The motive of a journey abroad in order to avoid a famine is a common one. The people mentioned in these stories, however, were never called גֵרִים:

	X escaped	motive	went from .. to	protected by
1. Gen 12,10f.	Abraham	hunger	Canaan > Egypt	Pharaoh
2. Gen 26,1f.	Isaac	hunger	> Gerar	Abimelek
3. Gen 47,4f.	Jacob/fam.	hunger	Canaan > Egypt	Pharaoh
4. Ruth 1,1f.	Elimelech	hunger	Judah > Moab	–
5. 1K 17,1f.	Elijah	drought	Israel > Sidon	widow
6. 2K 8,1f.	Shunammite	hunger	Shunem > Philistia	–[4]

All these cases, in all of which the verb גוּר is used, deal with "Israelites" going abroad. No reference is found to non-Israelite people coming to Israel under similar circumstances.

1.1 The supposed semantic equivalence of the verb גוּר and the noun גֵר

According to HAL's definition 2 Sam 4,3, Ruth 1,1 and Is 16,4 illustrate the meaning of the noun גֵר.[5]   These three references are, however, cases of the verbal form גוּר, not of the noun גֵר.[6]   The question to be addressed here is whether the meaning of the verb גוּר and the noun גֵר are really equivalent, as it is assumed in this definition, or not.   With this purpose in mind we will compare in the following section different aspects of the forms גוּר and גֵר.

---

4   There are other examples: the people who in case of need escaped to Egypt (1 K 11,40; 12,2;   Jer 26,20-23;   41,15-18;   42,4-7) and that of Jacob (Gen 27,43).   See also 2 Sam 15,14;   Jon 1,3;   Gen 11,31.

5   The semantic equivalence of the verb גוּר and the noun גֵר is usually taken for granted by the majority of the authors, see for instance: D. Kellermann, ThWAT I p. 984; Kloppers, NGTT 23/3 p. 130-141;   de Vaux, Institutions I p. 116;   Crüsemann, Tora p. 214 notes 373-375.   See also p. 33 note 133.

6   The form found in 2 Sam 4,3 is the participle plural; in Ruth 1,1 the infinitive form and in Is 16,4 the imperfect 3 plural.

1.2 *The non-legal use of* גּור *vs. the legal use of* גֵּר

The verb גּור is used mainly in narrative *non-legal texts:* the story of the patriarchs[7], the story of Moses[8], the deuteronomistic history[9], the Chronistic narrative[10] and the narrative in the book of Jeremiah.[11]

This verb is used to describe specific events in the life of concrete characters.[12] We are told about particular events regarding the sojourn of Lot in Sodom (Gen 19,19); and that of Sarah and Abraham in Egypt (Gen 12,10) and in Gerar (Gen 20,1), that of Abraham in Beer-sheba (Gen 21,23) and Isaac in Gerar (Gen 26,3); the long sojourn of Jacob with Laban (Gen 32,5); the story of Joseph's family in Egypt (Gen 47,4) or that of Elimelech and his family in Moab (Ruth 1,1); the Levite living in the house of Micah in Ephraim (Jud 17,7-9); the story of the Levite's concubine (Jud 19,1ff.); the sojourn of Elisha with the Shunammite woman (2 K 8,1-2); or the discussions of Jeremiah with the Israelites who wanted to migrate to Egypt (Jer 42,15.17.22). In these stories we can identify particular persons by their names and concrete circumstances in their lives. The verb גּור is commonly used in dialogues.[13]

The noun גֵּר, instead, is used mostly in *legal texts:*

1. Covenant Code: 4 times.[14]
2. Deuteronomy: 20 times.[15]
3. Holiness Code: 18 times.[16]

---

7   Gen 12,10; 19,9; 20,1; 21,23.34; 26,3; 32,5; 35,27; 47,4.
8   Ex 3,22; 6,4.
9   Jud 17,7.8.9; 19,1.16; 2 Sam 4,3; 1 K 17,20; 2 K 8,1.2.
10   2 Chron 15,9; Ezra 1,4.
11   Jer 35,7; 42,15.17.22; 43,2.5; 44,8.12.14.28.
12   The verb גּור is used mainly in narrative texts (33x out of 58 references): Gen 12,10; 19,9; 20,1; 21,23.34; 26,3; 32,5; 35,27; 47,4; Ex 3,22; 6,4; Jud 5,17; 17,7.8.9; 19,1.16; 1 K 17,20; 2 K 8,1.2; Jer 35,7; 42,15.17.22; 43,2.5; 44,8.12.14.28; Ez 14,7; 47,23; Ezra 1,4; the participial form גֵּר (25x) is used 7x in narrative texts: Ex 3,22; Jos 20,9; Ez 47,22; 2 Sam 4,3; Jer 35,7; 1 Chron 16,19; 2 Chron 15,9.
13   Gen 19,19; 21,23; 26,3; 32,5; 47,4; Jud 17,9; 1 K 17,20; 2 K 8,1; Is 33,14; Jer 42,15.17.22; 43,2. The verb גּור is also used frequently in Yahweh's speeches: Is 52,4; Jer 44,8.12.14.28; 49,18,33; 50,40, and in the narrative connections of story telling: Gen 12,10; 20,1; 21,23; 35,27; Jud 17,7.8; 19,1.16; 2 Sam 4,3; 2 K 8,2; Jer 43,5; Ruth 1,1.
14   Ex 22,20; 23,9.9.12.
15   Deut 1,16; 5,14; 10,19; 14,21.29; 16,11.14; 23,8; 24,14.17.19.20.21; 26,11.12.13; 27,19; 28,43; 29,10; 31,12. Without Deut 10,18 (parenetical text) and 10,19b (plural form).
16   Lev 17,8.10.12.13.15; 18,26; 19,10.33.34; 20,2; 22,18; 23,22; 24,16.22; 25,35.47.47.47, without Lev 19,34b and 25,23.

4. P: 16 times.[17]
5. Others: 3 times.[18]

In these legal texts the noun גר is used as an anonymous figure in theoretical situations.   Unlike the references of the verb גור, no name nor personal events are attached to this noun.[19]   The גר carries out no action[20] and says no word. He has only "eine Art literarisches Dasein".[21]   The noun גר refers in these cases not to a "*person*" but to the "*legal status*" of a man within the community where he presently lives.[22]   That means, this status grants to the person specific rights such as: the rest during the day of atonement (Lev 16,29); the right not to be oppressed (Ex 22,20); the right to gather fallen grapes (Deut 24,21); the right to benefit from the communal meal during the offering of the first fruits (Deut 26,11); the right to make use of the cities of refuge (Num 35,15); the right to receive the protection of the law (Deut 1,16); the right to benefit from rest during the Sabbath (Deut 5,14); the right to receive free meat (Deut 14,21) and the tithe of the third year (Deut 14,29).   Unlike the verb גור, the noun גר is seldom used in dialogues.[23]

The verb גור I appears 81 times in the Old Testament.[24] Only in three cases is this verb, by itself, used in legal texts.[25]   In these cases the verb גור simply gives additional specification to a noun[26]:

---

17   Ex 12,19.48.49; Lev 16,29; Num 9,14.14   15,14.15.15.16.26.29.30; 19,10; 35,15 and Jos 20,9; without Gen 23,4 .

18   Ex 20,10; Jos 8,33.35.

19   Gen 23,4 and Ex 2,22 (= 18,3) are the only exceptions to this.

20   There are some cases in which the noun גר is used as subject of a verb: he may come and eat from the tithe of the third year (בוא: Deut 14,29);   during the covenantal ceremony he may hear, learn to fear the Lord and to observe his law (למד, שמר, שמע, ירא: Deut 31,12); he may celebrate the Passover (פסח עשה: Ex 12,48) and present an offering made by fire (עשה אשה ליהוה: Num 15,14).

21   Greger, BN 63 p. 30.

22   The specific legal nature of this term has been already noticed by several authors: Briggs states that this noun is used in general "with technical sense" (BDB p. 158); Smith sees in the noun גר "a new legal status" (Parties p. 178) and Weber a "Rechtsverhältnis" (Judentum p. 39); Schmidt describes this term as "eine rechtliche Kategorie eigener Art" (Judaica 1 p. 281); for Driver the "term is really a technical one" (Deuteronomy 126); Nowack discusses the term as "Politisches Recht" (Archäologie I p. 336-341) and Benzinger as "Personenrecht" (Archäologie p. 287-289).

23   The noun גר is used in dialogues with another human being (Gen 23,4 and 2 Sam 1,13); with Yahweh (Gen 15,13; Job 31,32) and in prayers (Ps 39,13; 119,19).

24   Qal 80x: Gen 12,10; 19,9; 20,1; 21,23.34; 26,3; 32,5; 35,27; 47,4; Ex 3,22; 6,4; 12,48.49; Lev 16,29; 17,8.10.12.13; 18,26; 19,33.34; 20,2; 25,6.45; Num 9,14; 15,14.15.16.26.29; 19,10; Deut 18,6; 26,5; Jos 20,9; Jud 5,17; 17,7.8.9; 19,1.16; 2 Sam 4,3; 2 K 8,1.1.2; Is 5,17; 11,6; 16,4; 23,7; 33,14.14; 52,4; Jer 35,7; 42,15.17.22; 43,2.5; 44,8.12.14.28; 49,18.33; 50,40;   Ez 14,7; 47,22.23; Ps 5,5; 15,1; 61,5; 105,12.23; 120,5; Job 19,15; 28,4;   Ruth 1,1; Lam 4,15; 1 Chron 16,19; 2 Chron 15,9; Ezra 1,4.   Htpol. 1x: 1K 17,20. Including Jud 5,17 (Ges[18], Lisowsky, HAL, DBHE, BDB, DCH); without Is 54,15b

1) the law of the sabbatical year in Lev 25,6 leaves the crop that grows by itself to the male and female slaves, and to the hired (שָׂכִיר) and bound (תּוֹשָׁב) labourers "who *live* with you (הגרים עמך)".

2) the law of the levitical year in Lev 25,45 allows the Israelites to acquire male and female slaves among the תושבים *residing* with them (הגרים עמכם).

3) the law of the rights of the levitical priests in Deut 18,6: "If a Levite leaves any of your towns, from wherever he has been *residing* in Israel (גר שם)".[27]

There are 19 additional references in which the verb גור is used in laws. It must be noted, however, that these references *all occur in function of the noun* גר. That is, these references occur in phrases which give additional specification to the noun גר, either with the construction "הגר הגר"[28], with the construction "הגר אשר־יגור"[29] or with "וכי־יגור אתך גר".[30]

The noun גר, on the other hand, also appears 81 times in the Old Testament.[31] In 61 of these cases the noun גר is used in legal texts. There are, in addition, six other references which are similar to them. These references depend on the deuteronomic triad: Jer 7,6; 22,3; Ez 22,7.29; Zech 7,10; Mal 3,5. We can summarize the statistics of these two forms as follows:

(גור Q[2] DCH, Mandelkern, Ges[18], BDB); Hos 7,14 (יתגודדו BHS) and Jer 30,23 (מתחולל BHS).

25   The prayer pronounced on the occasion of the presentation of the first fruits at the central sanctuary in Deut 26,5, although part of the deuteronomic code, is not taken as a legal text.

26   See the participle plural masculine (הגרים) in Lev 25,6.45 and the perfect 3 singular masculine (גר) in Deut 18,6.

27   On this text see Abba, VT 27 p. 257ff. and Bettenzoli, RSLR 22 p. 4-8; 19-23.

28   Ex 12,49; Lev 16,29; 17,10.12.13; 18,26; 19,34; 20,2; Num 15,15.16.26.29; 19,10; Jos 20,9.

29   Lev 17,8.

30   Ex 12,48; Lev 19,33; in the plural form וכי־יגור אתכם גר in Num 9,14; 15,14. In two cases (Num 9,14b; 15,15b) the noun גר is used in the formula "there shall be one law for both of you the גר and the native of the land (אזרח)" and it is not used, therefore, with verb. In only two occasions the verb גור is used together with גר in a non-legal text: Ez 14,7; 47,22. In Ez 47,22 the verb גור is used together with the plural form גרים.

31   Without the plural form גרים.

		Non-legal:	56x.[32]
	גור alone: 59x		
		Legal:	3x.[33]
Verb גור total: 81x			
		Non-legal:	3x.[34]
	גר + גור: 22x		
		Legal:	19x.[35]
		Legal:	60x.[36]
Noun גר total: 81x			
		Non-legal:	21x.[37]

1.3 The transit character of גור vs. the punctual character of גר

The verb גור is often associated with verbs of movement. First of all, with those verbs which imply *the departure* or initial movement from the home town to the new one:

Gen 20, 1: "Abraham *journeyed* ... and *sojourned* in Gerar"   ויסע ... ויגר

2 K 8, 1: "Elijah said *depart* ... and *sojourn* wherever you can"   לכי ... וגורי

In eighteen cases the infinitive construct גור with ל appears as a continuation of a previous finite verb which (with only one exception), is always a verb of movement, mostly בוא.[38] In these cases the verb גור conveys the idea of the final intention or purpose of the movement[39]:

---

32   Qal 55x: Gen 12,10; 19,9; 20,1; 21,23.34; 26,3; 32,5; 35,27; 47,4;   Ex 3,22;
      6,4;   Deut 26,5;   Jud 5,17;   17,7.8.9;   19,1.16;   2Sam 4,3;   2K 8,1.1.2;   Is 5,17;
      11,6;   16,4;   23,7;   33,14.14;   52,4;   Jer 35,7;   42,15.17.22;   43,2.5;   44,8.12.14.28;
      49,18.33;   50,40;   Ps 5,5;   15,1;   61,5;   105,12.23;   120,5;   Job 19,15;   28,4;   Ruth
      1,1;   Lam 4,15;   1 Chron 16,19;   2 Chron 15,9;   Ezra 1,4.   Htpol. 1x: 1K 17,20.

33   Lev 25,6.45;   Deut 18,6.

34   Ez 14,7; 47,23. In Ez 47,22 we have the plural form גרים.

35   Ex 12,48.49;   Lev 16,29;   17,8.10.12.13;   18,26;   19,33.34;   20,2;   Num 9,14;
      15,14.15.16.26.29;   19,10;   Jos 20,9.

36   Ex 12,19.48.49;   20,10;   22,20;   23,9.9.12;   Lev 16,29;   17,8.10.12.13.15;   18,26;
      19,10.33.34;   20,2;   22,18;   23,22;   24,16.22;   25,35.47.47.47;   Num 9,14.14;
      15,14.15.15.16.26.29.30;   19,10;   35,15;   Deut 1,16;   5,14;   10,19;   14,21.29;
      16,11.14;   23,8;   24,14.17.19.20.21;   26,11.12.13;   27,19;   29,10;   31,12;   Jos
      8,33.35;   20,9.

37   Gen 15,13;   23,4;   Ex 2,22;   18,3;   Deut 10,18;   28,43;   2 Sam 1,13;   Is 14,1;
      Jer 7,6;   14,8;   22,3;   Ez 14,7;   22,7.29;   47,23;   Zech 7,10;   Mal 3,5;   Ps 39,13;
      94,6;   119,19;   Job 31,32.

38   ירד: Gen 12,10; Is 52,4; בוא: Gen 19,9; 47,4; Jer 42,15.17.22; 43,2;
      44,8.12.14.28; הלך: Jud 17,8.9; Ruth 1,1; יבל: Is 23,7; שוב: Jer 43,5. In Lam

Gen 19, 9: "this fellow *came to sojourn* and he would ... judge!" בא לגור

Gen 47, 4: "They said: 'we have *come to sojourn* in the land'" לגור ... באנו

Gen 12, 10: "Abraham *went down to Egypt to sojourn* there" וירד ... לגור

Ruth 1, 1: "a man of Bethlehem ... *went to sojourn* in ... Moab" וילך ... לגור

Is 23, 7: "your city ... whose feet *carried her to settle afar* ?" יבלוה לגור

The noun גר, instead, is associated with expressions which point not to the initial move, but to the actual residence of the person in his new home, i.e. "the גר *among* you".[40] The following chart shows the different associations of the verb גור and the noun גר:

The transit character of גור	versus	the punctual character of גר
Verb of movement + גור		Noun גר + preposition ב
Ruth 1,1: וילך ... לגור[41]		Ex 12,49: הגר בתוככם
Jer 42,17: לבוא לגור[42]		Lev 19,33: גר בארצכם
Gen 12,10: וירד ... לגור		Lev 22,18: הגר בישראל
Gen 20,1: ויסע ... וינר		Deut 14,29: הגר אשר בשעריך
Is 23,7: יבלוה ... לגור		Deut 29,10: גרך אשר בקרב מחניך

It is important to note that *in the cases in which the verb* גור *appears associated with the noun* גר[43], *the idea of move disappears and instead, a punctual expression such as* "*the* גר *among you*"[44] *or* "*the* גר *with you*" *appears.*[45]

The verb גור is associated not only with verbs of movement but also with the reasons behind such a move. When the verb גור is associated with verbs which indicate movement out of Palestine, the main reasons involved are

---

4,15b we have: "they shall stay here no longer" (לא יוסיפו לגור). Note, however, that in 4,15a we have the verbs נצו ... נעו ("they became fugitives and wanderers").

39 See Soisalon-Soinenen, VT 22 p. 82-90; Joüon-Muraoka, Grammar § 124.1 and GK § 114 p.

40 והגר אשר בקרבך (Deut 11,1622) and with the participle הגר (Ex 12,49; Lev 17,12; Nm 15,26).

41 See also the construction לכי ... וגורי in 2 K 8,1 ("Elijah said ... depart ... and sojourn wherever you can").

42 See also Gen 19,9: "this fellow came to sojourn (בא לגור) and he would play the judge!" and Gen 47,4: "They said to Pharaoh: 'we have come to sojourn in the land' (לגור .. באנו)".

43 הגר בתוככם הגר (Lev 16,29; 17,8.10.12.13; 18,26).

44 Lev 17,8.

45 Num 15,14.

famine[46], war[47] or personal danger.[48]   The movements within Palestine are
related with the material need of the Levites.[49]   The references to the noun גֵר,
on the contrary, do not mention the reasons which led the person to become גֵר.
The silence of the texts about this matter is significant, it shows that the גֵר-
references stress rather the present situation.   The fact that the גֵר appears
integrated in the deuteronomic code, suggests that he had already lived for some
time in the community.[50]

1.4 The "emigrant" character of גור vs. the "immigrant" character of גֵר

The verb גור, as we said before, is often associated with verbs of
movement, such as the case of those verbs which denote the idea of *departure*.
We must add to this that, in about half of the fifty-nine cases in which the verb
גור appears independently from the noun גֵר, this move has a specific direction:
it goes out of the limits of the "Israelite territory".   The persons of whom this
verb is used follow the direction: centre (Israel) => periphery (abroad).   In
this way, we find *Israelites* sojourning in:

1. Moab: Ruth 1,1
2. Philistia: Gen 21,33
3. Phoenicia: Jud 5,17
4. Egypt: Gen 12,10
5. Mesech: Ps 120,5
6. Persia: Ezra 1,4
7. and the nations: Lam 4,15

We find also people sojourning specifically in the cities of:

1. Sodom: Gen 19,9
2. Gerar: Gen 20,1

---

46   Gen 12,10; 26,3; 47,4;   Ruth 1,1;   2 K 8,1.2;   Jud 5,17 is probably related to
     economic needs of the Danites; and Ps 120,5 to the theme of the enemies in the book of
     Psalms.
47   Jer 42,15.17.22; 43,2.8.12.14.28;   Lam 4,15. See also Jer 39,1-10.
48   Personal danger is mentioned in relation to Esau's journey to his uncle Laban. See Gen
     32,5 and 27,43.   Bertholet, Stellung p. 13, mentions under "Verfolgung" the cases of
     Cain: Gen 4,16; Moses: Ex 2,15; Absalom: 1 K 11,17 and the fugitive slaves in Deut
     23,17.
49   Deut 18,1;   Jud 17,7.8.9;   19,1.9. Cf. Jud 17,8: לגור באשר ימצא, with 2 K 8,1:
     וגורי באשר תגורי.
50   The גֵר is mentioned in connection to the feasts of Shebuôt (Deut 16,11) and Sukkôt
     (Deut 16,14); the tithes (Deut 14,29; 26,12-13) and the harvest (Deut 24,19-21). In
     several cases the noun גֵר is used in context in which the author refers to the future of
     the community: Is 14,1; Ez 47,22.

3. Sidon: 1 K 17,20
4. Haran: Gen 32,5
5. and Babylon: Ez 20,38

In a few cases, the verb גור is associated with verbs which denote movement *within* the Israelite territory[51], with an extended meaning[52] or in prophetic speeches.[53]   If we take into account the fact that the noun גר is used in many cases to speak about foreigners living in Israel[54], the direction followed initially by these persons was contrary to that of the verb גור, that is: periphery (abroad) => centre (= Israel).[55]

The use of the verb לוה niphal in Is 14,1 helps us to understand the reason of this particular direction.   According to Is 14,1: "The גר will be *joined* (ונלוה) to Israel".   He is one of the נלוים.[56]   That is, one of the non-Israelites who after the exile[57] expected to join Israel[58] and Yahweh[59] in the line suggested by Ez 47,22-23.   The גר (Is 14,1), the בן נכר (Is 56,3.6) and *even* the גוים (Zech 2,15) are expected to join (לוה) the Lord and his people as part of the pilgrimage of the nations towards Israel.   This general *movement towards Israel* is described in Zech 8,22 with a beautiful image: "In those days ten men from nations of every language shall take hold of a Jew, grasping his garment and saying, 'Let us go with you, for we have heard that God is with you'".

The direction followed by the verb גור (centre => periphery), explains why the verb גור is sometimes associated with the theme of *exile:*

1) the exile in general: Is 16,4; Ruth 1,1; Ps 120,5

---

51   This is the case of a Levite in Ephraim: וילך ... לגור (Jud 17,8); ואנכי הלך לגור (Jud 17,9). See also the cases of Levites living in Ephraim (Jud 19,1) and Gibeah (Jud 19,16).

52   This is the case of texts that speak about sojourning: "with the devouring fire ... with the everlasting flames" (Is 33,14); in Yahweh's temple (Ps 5,5) and in Yahweh's tent (Ps 15,1; 61,5).

53   Jer 49,18.33; 50,40; Is 11,6; 23,7.

54   This is the case, for instance, of the noun גר in the Holiness Code and P (35x), where the noun גר, with a few exceptions, is used of a non-Israelite. See for instance Kilian, Untersuchung p. 171 and Bultmann, Der Fremde p. 176.

55   There are a few non-legal references in which the גר is received "in the land of Israel" (2 Chron 2,16; 1 Chron 22,2); "in Israel" (Ez 47,22); "in Israel tribes" (Ez 47,23); "in the House of Jacob" (Is 14,1). See also 2 Chron 30,25: aliens in the Jerusalem of Hezekiah's times; and Gen 23,4: Abraham among the sons of Heth.

56   Is 56,3; Esth 9,27. See Donner, Aufsätze p. 81-95; Bardtke, Esther p. 680-681 and especially Petit-Jean, Oracles p. 139.

57   In 9 cases (out of 11 total references), the verb לוה is post-exilic: Num 18,2.4; Is 14,1; 56,3.6; Jer 50,5; Zech 2,15; Esth 9,27; Dan 11,34;   Exceptions to this are probably Gen 29,34 and Ps 83,9.

58   Is 14,1; Esth 9,27. See also Dan 11,34.

59   Is 56,3.6; Zech 2,15. See also Jer 50,5.

2) the theme of Israel's forefathers in Egypt: Deut 26,5; Is 52,4; Ps 105,23
3) the dispersion after 587 BC.: Lam 4,15; Ezra 1,4; Ez 20,38[60]

Since the sojourning abroad was forced by external circumstances, the *return* to the homeland always remained as a natural longing. Jacob, for instance, escaped to Haran in order to protect his life but later on, he urged Laban: "Send me away, that I may go to my own home and country!" (Gen 30,25). This explains why the verb גור is often associated with verbs which imply the return from the place in which the persons sojourned temporarily, to their original (Israelite) home towns:

גור	שׁוב
A woman went to sojourn in Philistia (2 K 8,1)	and returned (2 K 8,3)
Israelites went to sojourn in Egypt (Jer 42,15)[61]	and returned (Jer 44,28)
Naomi went to sojourn in Moab (Ruth 1,1)	and returned (Ruth 1,6-7)
Israelites went into exile (Ezra 1,4)	and returned (Ezra 2,1)[62]

גור	עלה
Abram went to sojourn in Egypt (Gen 12,10)	and returned (Gen 13,1)
Jacob went to sojourn in Egypt (Gen 47,4)	and returned (Gen 50,7-9)

It is not surprising then, to see that the verb גור is commonly used at the beginning of a story, as a narrative device to set in motion the plot of the story which is often related to God's providence.[63]   In these stories the idea of a *return* is of paramount importance, as in the case of Ruth (Ruth 1) and Jacob (Gen 31).

Nothing of all this, usual in the case of the verb גור, is mentioned in the case of the noun גר. Nothing is told about the subject's original hometown nor of an eventual return, nothing about the reasons which led him to be a גר.[64] Even the twenty-two references in which the verb גור appears associated with the noun גר, make no reference either to foreign lands or cities.[65] These twenty-two references of the verb גור follow the pattern of the noun גר and are, therefore, also situated "in Israel".

---

60   The verb גור is also related to the remnant (שׁארית) of Judah: Jer 42,15.22; 43,5; 44,12.14.28.

61   Jer 42,15.17; 43,2.5; 44,8.12.

62   See also the case of Jacob who went to sojourn with Laban (גרתי: Gen 32,5) and was commanded to return (שׁוב: Gen 31,3; ושׁוב ... קום צא: Gen 31,13).

63   Gen 12,10; 20,1; 26,3; Ruth 1,1; Jud 17,7-9; 19,1ff.; 2 K 8,1-2.

64   That is why HAL's definition of גר seems to correspond more appropriately to the participial form גָר than to the noun גֵּר. See for instance the references in 2 Sam. 4,3 and 2 Chron 15,9.

65   Ez 47,23, which is framed in the context of the Babylonian exile, might be considered an exception to this.

1.5 The different subjects used in relation with גּוּר and גֵּר

As shown in the previous paragraph, the verb גּוּר is frequently used in relation with persons who go to sojourn abroad. The point of departure of these persons was an Israelite town or city, i.e. these persons were Israelites. A significant difference between the verb גּוּר and the noun גֵּר has to do, then, with the subjects involved in each case. The verb גּוּר is mostly used in association with *Israelites* who go to sojourn out of their towns.[66] Among those "Israelites" sojourning (mostly) abroad we find:

1. In Egypt: Abraham (Gen 12,10), Jacob[67], the forefathers (Gen 47,4)
2. In Gerar: Abraham (Gen 20,1; 21,23), Isaac (Gen 26,3)
3. In Philistia: Abraham (Gen 21,34), the Shunammite woman (2 K 8,1.2)
4. In Phoenicia: the Danites (Jud 5,17)[68]
5. In Haran: Esau (Gen 32,5)
6. In Moab: a Bethlehemite (Ruth 1,1)
7. In Meshech: the Psalmist (Ps 120,5)
8. In Sodom: Lot (Gen 19,9)
9. In Sidon: Elijah (1 K 17,20)

The verb גּוּר is also mentioned in relation to the lands of:

1. Egypt: Is 52,4; Jer 42,15.17.22; 43,2; 44,8.12.14.28
2. Babylon: Ez 20,38
3. Persia: Ezra 1,4[69]
4. and the nations: Lam 4,15

The noun גֵּר is often used, especially in the priestly writings, to speak about foreigners living in Israel.[70] Since the majority of the references to the noun גֵּר are legal, they are situated "in Israel". For this reason, the גֵּר in the laws is portrayed as someone welcomed "in Israel"[71] or simply "in your land within your towns".[72] A similar situation is found outside the Pentateuch, where the גֵּר is received "in the House of Jacob"[73], or "in the land of Israel".[74] The גֵּר is not portrayed, however, as being גֵּר in non-Israelite cities or territories.[75] And

---

66 Exceptions to this are: Is 16,4 in which the verb גּוּר is used to described the sojourning of Moabite refugees in Juda, and Jer 43,5 in which the remnant returned (שָׁב) to settle (לָגוּר) in the land of Judah from all the nations to which they had been driven.

67 Ps 105,23: Jacob in Ham (= Egypt); Deut 26,5.

68 See Donner, Geschichte p. 136.

69 אֲשֶׁר הוּא גָר־שָׁם (Ezra 1,4).

70 See Ges[18] p. 227; Loewenstamm, Thesaurus II p. 247 and note 54.

71 Lev 22,18.

72 Deut 24,14.

73 Is 14,1. See also 2 Sam 1,13; Ez 47,23.

74 1 Chron 22,2; 2 Chron 2,16, both with the plural form גֵּרִים.

75 Gen 23,4 and Ex 2,22 are the only two exceptions. The late plural form גֵּרִים is used in both ways: (1) the motive clauses of Ex 22,20b; 23,9b; Lev 19,34b and Deut

this is so because in the Old Testament *someone is* גר *before the law;* to be more precise, before the *Israelite* law.

The comparison established so far shows that in different aspects the relationship between the forms גור and גר, is one of difference rather than one of equivalence.   Before paying attention to some external aspects of this comparison, we want to draw attention to some additional distinctions found in the Old Testament in relation to the forms גור and גר.

In sum, we can say that: in similar circumstances of need and misfortune, both Israelites and non-Israelites looked for a place of refuge out of their home towns.   The verb גור and the noun גר were not used, however, in the same circumstances.   The verb גור was used, mostly, in association with those (Israelites) who left their original towns and *went* to sojourn temporarily abroad.   It is associated with the idea of emigration.   The noun גר, on the contrary, designates the legal status granted to those (strangers and foreigners[76]) who *came* to sojourn and were ruled by the internal regulations of an Israelite community.   It expressed rather the idea of immigration.[77]

It is interesting to note that the noun גר does not occur at all in the book of Ruth, a story which fits perfectly with HAL's definition of this noun.   The noun גר is neither used for Elimelech and his family during their sojourn in Moab nor for Ruth during her sojourn in Bethlehem.   This story illustrates well what we have stated: the meaning of the verb גור and that of the noun גר are not equivalent.   The book opens with the verb גור, it tells a story of Israelites abroad (i.e. *emigration*).   This excludes, consequently, the use of the noun גר which presupposes the Israelite law.   The noun גר *could* have been used in the case of Ruth during her sojourn in Bethlehem (a Moabite coming to Israel) but the noun גר designates a legal status and is, therefore, restricted to *men,* (see p. 28).   Ruth introduces herself, therefore, as נכריה (2,10).   It must be noted,

---

10,19b, speak about the Israelites as having been גרים abroad: because you were גרים in the land of Egypt;   (2) 1 Chron 22,2;   2 Chron 2,16 speak about people of non-Jewish origin as having been גרים "in the land of Israel"; and Ez 47,22 speaks about the גרים "among the tribes of Israel" .

76   The idea that the גר can be either a stranger or a foreigner was formulated already by Th. Nödelke in 1869: "Im allgemeinen haben die Vorschriften des Pentateuchs hauptsächlich nichtisraelitische Fremdlinge im Auge ... Aber auch der Israelit kann bei einem andern Stamm seines Volks oder einer andern israelitischen Gemeinde als Fremdling leben" (Art. Fremde, in: BiL 2 p. 300). See p. 9.

77   The term "immigrant" was one of the translations suggested by Meek (JBL 49 p. 172); and used in his rendering of texts like: Gen 15,3;   23,4;   Ex 2,22;   18,3; see AT. Cf. also Dion, Israël p. 223 and Spina, Israelites p. 323. See, however, Spieckermann, PTh 83 p. 54 and Bultmann, Der Fremde p. 22.

finally, that the idea of a *return,* which is of paramount importance in this story[78], is also related to the verb נור, not to that of the noun גֵּר.

The *semantic distance* between the verb נור and the noun גֵּר can also be illustrated by the construction "הַגֵּר הַגָּר", which specifies the meaning of the noun "הַגֵּר" by means of the participle "הַגָּר".[79] If the noun גֵּר designates, as the HAL definition suggests: a man who on account of misfortunes had to leave his original place and seek dwelling at another place, why should biblical authors see the need of explaining this noun by means of the participle "הַגָּר" which results in a totally redundant construction?[80]

It must also be noted that, although the forms "גָּר" and "גֵּר" (perfect and participle) are identical in a non punctuated text, the Masoretes distinguish them consistently, so that constructions such as: "וְכִי־יָגוּר אִתְּךָ גֵּר"[81] or "אֲשֶׁר־יָגוּר הַגֵּר"[82], were used naturally with the noun but not with the participial form. And this makes sense, because the additional specification of the participial form גָּר with the phrase "אֲשֶׁר־יָגוּר ...", for instance, would be unnecessarily redundant. Interestingly enough, it was not seen like that in the case of the noun גֵּר.

It is worth mentioning that the distinction between the noun גֵּר and the verb נור seems to have been clear also for the translators of the LXX, a fact which is reflected in the different renderings of the corresponding nominal and verbal forms. A comparison of גֵּר with the participial form גָּר illustrates this clearly: while the term προσήλυτος renders the noun גֵּר sixty-eight times out of

---

78 The verb שׁוּב appears in Ruth 1,6.7.8.10.11.12.15.15.16.21.22.22; 2,6; 4,3.15. The paradox is clear: coming from "House of Bread (בֵּית לֶחֶם)" they have to *emigrate* due to famine (!) When Naomi heard that Yahweh had considered her people and had given them food, she decided to *return.*

79 Lev 17,10.12.13; 18,26; 19,34;   20,2. The peculiarity of this construction had already been pointed out by W. Gesenius in his Thesavrvs Philologicvs criticvs lingvae hebraeae et chaldeae veteris testamenti, Tomi Primi, 1829 p. 274; Ges[15] makes also reference to this distinction: "Pt. גָּר versch. v. (s.d.) גֵּר הַגֵּר הַגָּר בְּתוֹכְכֶם Ex 12,49 u.ö." (p. 133). Interestingly enough in the second edition of his Wörterbuch, Gesenius explained the form גֵּר as "גֵּר m. (part. von נור w.m.n.) Fremdling" (Handwörterbuch, 2. Aufl. 1823 p. 155), and so does Winer, Lexicon p. 178.

80 The noun תּוֹשָׁב is also specified with the construction הַגֵּר, Lev 25,6.45.

81 Ex 12,48; Lev 19,33; cf. also the plural form וְכִי־יָגוּר אִתְּכֶם גֵּר in Num 9,14 and 15,14.

82 Lev 17,8.

eighty-one instances[83], it renders the participial form גָּר only *one* time out of twenty-five instances.[84]

The relationship of the גֵּר with the Levites also illustrates the distinction between these two forms. The verb גּור is used of the Levites several times.[85] The Levite has in common with the גֵּר the fact of being landless. They are sometimes mentioned together among other poor people[86], and sometimes by themselves[87], but they are never confused with each other. The Levite is said, for instance, to have sojourned (גָּר pf.) in a town, but he is *never* called גֵּר. The fact that the Levite *sojourned* in a new town did not make of him a גֵּר.[88]

1.6 גּור *and* גֵּר*: presence and absence of synonyms*

The idea of a temporary sojourn of someone away from home is a common element between the verbs גּור, יָשַׁב (Q "to dwell, to live") and שָׁכַן (Q "to settle"). Because of this, there are several references in the Old Testament in which the verb גּור finds a semantic equivalent in the verbs יָשַׁב and שָׁכַן.

1.6.1 Synonyms of the verb גּור

In his oracle against Edom, in which Yahweh compares the fate of this nation with that of Sodom and Gomorrah, the verbs גּור and יָשַׁב are used in synonymous parallelism:

---

83   The noun גֵּר (81x) is translated sixty-eight times by προσήλυτος: Ex 12,48.49; 20,10; 22,20; 23,9.9.12; Lev 16,29; 17,8.10.12.13.15; 18,26; 19,10.33.34; 20,2; 22,18; 23,22; 24,16.22; 25,35.47.47.47; Num 9,14.14; 15,14.15.15.16.26.29.30; 19,10; 35,15; Deut 1,16; 5,14; 10,18.19; 14,29; 16,11.14; 24,14.17.19.20.21; 26,11.12.13; 27,19; 28,43; 29,10; 31,12; Jos 8,33.35; 20,9; Jer 7,6; 22,3; Ez 14,7; 22,7.29; 47,23; Zech 7,10; Mal 3,5; Ps 94,6; ten times by πάροικος: Gen 15,13; 23,4; Ex 2,22; 18,3; Deut 14,21; 23,8; 2 Sam 1,13; Jer 14,8; Ps 39,13; 119,19; two times by γ(ε)ιώρας: Ex 12,19 (γειώρας); Is 14,1 (γιώρας) and once by ξένος: Job 31,32.

84   In 2 Chron 15,9 the participial plural form גָּרִים is translated by the construction: τοὺς προσηλύτους τοὺς παροικοῦντας. There are only two cases in which the participial form גָּר is translated in the LXX by a nominal form: Ex 3,22, συσκήνου "tentmate, fellow lodger" (GELS II p. 463) and Job 19,15, ἀλλογενὴς "foreign, stranger" (GELS I p. 20). In Is 5,17 the LXX reads גָּרִים instead of גָּרִים, see Duhm, Jesaja p. 37; Wildberger, Jesaja p. 178 and Vermeylen, Isaïe p. 173.

85   Perfect: Deut 18,6; Jud 17,7; 19,1; infinitiv: Jud 17,9.

86   Deut 14,29; 16,11.14; 26,12.13.

87   Deut 26,11.

88   There is no single case in the Old Testament of someone who, after having sojourned somewhere (גּור), is called גֵּר because of this.

"no one shall live (לא־ישב) there,
nor shall anyone settle (ולא־יגור) in it" (Jer 49,18.33; 50,40).
In the words addressed by Jeremiah to the Rechabites, he said: "you shall *live*
(תשבו) in tents all your days, that you may live many days in the land where
you *sojourn* (גרים)" (Jer 35,7).
In Gen 47,4 Jacob says to Pharaoh "We have come to *sojourn* (לגור) in the
land because the famine is severe..".   Pharaoh then says to Joseph "... *settle*
(הושב) your father and your brothers in the best part of the land, let them *live*
(ישבו) in the land of Goshen ..." (Gen 47,6).
In the dialogue between Micah and the Levite in Jud 17, the Levite says: "I am a
Levite of Bethlehem in Judah, and I am going to *sojourn* (לגור) wherever I can
find a place".   Then Micah said to him, "*Stay* with me (שבה עמדי)" (Jud
17,9b-10a).
In a similar situation Laban invites Jacob to stay with him and uses exactly the
same expression used by Micah in the previous example: "*Stay* here with me
(שבה עמדי)" (Gen 29,19).[89]   Later, Jacob himself describes his stay with
Laban in the following terms: "I have been *sojourning* (גרתי) with Laban"
(Gen 35,5).   There are other similar constructions between גור and ישב:

Ruth 1,1:	וילך ... לגור	≈	Jud 1,16:	... וילך וישב
Gen 19,9:	בא לגור	≈	Gen 11,31:	... ויבאו ... וישב
Gen 12,10:	וירד ... לגור	≈	Num 20,15:	וירדו ... ונשב
Gen 20,1:	ויסע ... ויגר	≈	2 K 19,36:	ויסע ... וישב

The verbs גור and שכן are also used in parallelism, Psalm 120,5 states:
"Woe to me that I sojourn (גרתי) in Meshech,
that I live (שכנתי) among the tents of Kedar!".
The Psalmist asks: "who may sojourn (יגור) in your sanctuary,
who may dwell (ישכן) in your holy hill?" (Psalm 15,1).
There are also examples in which the verbs גור, ישב and שכן appear
together.   In Gen 26 Yahweh appears to Isaac and says:
"Do not go down to Egypt; dwell (שכן) in the land which I shall tell
you of: 'sojourn (גור) in this land' ...
and Isaac dwellt (וישב) in Gerar" (Gen 26,2.6).
In Jud 5,17 these verbs are used in parallelism[90]:
"Gilead stayed (שכן) beyond the Jordan ...
Dan, why did he sojourn (יגור) with the ships?
Asher sat (ישב) still at the coast ...
settling down (ישכון) by his landings".

---

89   In Gen 29,14b we have a similar sentence: "and he (Jacob) stayed with him ..". Here the
text has וישב עמו. We find the same request in Jud 17,10 where Micah says to the
Levite שבה עמדי. Compare this with the request of Abimelech to Isaac in Gen 26,3
גור בארץ הזאת.
90   In V. 17a we have גור - שכן, and in 17b ישב - שכן.

1.6.2 The exclusive character of the noun גר

Unlike the verb גור in its relation with the verbs ישׁב and שׁכן, there are no cases in the Old Testament in which the noun גר finds a semantic equivalence in other nouns. It is commonly stated that the terms גר, זר and נכרי designate the different kinds of strangers in Israel.[91] It must be noted, however, that the terms זר and נכרי are never used as synonyms of the noun גר. There are, on the contrary, basic differences between them. First of all, feminine forms are attested only for נכרי and זר:

זר		נכרי	
זרה	8x.[92]	נכריה	12x.[93]
זרות	2x.[94]	נכריות	12x.[95]

The term גר, *instead, is restricted to its use as a masculine noun.*[96] The references which have suffixes are found in legal texts and have, consequently, only masculine singular forms: גרך[97] and גרו.[98]

In connection with this point it must be noted that the verb גור, being a *non legal term,* is used in relation with women[99] and also with families.[100]

Secondly, the terms זר and נכרי are used with adjectival value in a wide range of contexts. The term נכרי, for instance, is used in relation with very different subjects:

נכרי used for people: 1. of a man: Deut 17,15; Eccl 6,2, אישׁ נכרי
                         2. of a woman: Ruth 2,10, אנכי נכריה
                         3. of women: 1 K 11,1.8; Gen 31,15, נשׁים נכריות
                         4. of a people: Ex 21,8, עם נכרי
                         5. as t.t. in Prov for harlot: 2,16; 5,20; 6,24, נכריה

---

91   Cardellini, RivBib 40 p. 140-154; Block, Art. Sojourner, in: ISBE, 4 p. 561- 564; Lesètre, Art. Étranger, in: DBV, X/2 col. 2039-2042; van den Born, Art. Fremde, in: BL col. 494.

92   Ex 30,9; Lev 10,1; Num 3,4; 26,61; Prov 2,16; 5,3.20; 7,5.

93   Ex 2,22; 18,3; Is 28,21; Jer 2,21; Prov 2,16; 5,20; 6,24; 7,5; 20,16; 23,27; 27,13; Ruth 2,10.

94   Prov 22,14; 23,33.

95   Gen 31,15; 1 K 11,1.8; Ezra 10,2.10.11.14.17.18.44; Neh 13,26.27.

96   Eighty one references are masculine singular. 2 Sam 1,13 (אישׁ גר) is the only case in which גר is used in apposition; see p. 29 note 102.

97   Ex 20,10; Deut 5,14; 24,14; 29,10; 31,12.

98   Deut 1,16.

99   מגרת: partic. sing. fem. const. Ex 3,22; תגורי: impf. 2 fem. 2 K 8,1; תגר: impf. 3 fem. 2 K 8,2; גורי: imper. fem. 2 K 8,1.

100   Sarah and Abraham in Egypt: Gen 12,10; Sarah and Abraham in Gerar: Gen 20,1; Joseph's family in Egypt: Gen 47,4; Elimelech and his family in Moab: Ruth 1,1.

נכרי used for things:	1. of a land: Ex 2,22, אֶרֶץ נכריה
	2. of a city: Jud 19, 12, עיר נכרי
	3. of a house: Prov 5,10, בית נכרי
	4. of wine: Jer 2,21, הגפן נכריה
	5. of clothing: Zeph 1,8, מלבוש נכרי

| נכרי used for the body: | 1. of a bosom: Prov 5,20, חק נכריה |
| | 2. of a tongue: Prov 6,24, לשון נכריה |

| נכרי used for God: | 1. of God's deeds: Is 28,21, נכריה עבדתו |

The participle זר is also used with adjectival value in a similar wide range of contexts:

זר in realm of the family:	1) of a man: Deut 25,5; Lev 22,12, אִישׁ זר
	2) of children: Hos 5,7, בנים זרים
	3) of a woman (i.e. harlot): Prov 2,16; 5,3; 7,5, אשׁה זרה

זר in realm of religion:	1) of a god: Ps 44,8.21; 81,10, אל זר
	2) of Yahweh's work: Is 28,21, זר מעשׂהו
	3) of incense: Ex 30,9, קטרת זרה
	4) of fire: Lev 10,1; Num 3,4; 26,61, אשׁ זרה

| זר used of things: | 1) of waters: 2 K 19,24; Jer 18,14, מים זרים |
| | 2) of a vine-branch : Is 17,10, זמרת זר[101] |

Unlike זר and נכרי, *the term גּר is never used with adjectival value.*[102] These differences between "נכרי - זר" and גּר are due to the fact that זר and נכרי are *ordinary terms.* The noun גּר, instead, is a *technical term* which designates not a person but a legal status. Its use is, therefore, restricted to the nominal masculine singular form, which is the form used in legal texts. The difference in the relationship between the Israelite and these two groups of people (i.e. "נכרי - זר" and "גּר"), becomes clear by the fact that it is only in the case of the גּר that suffixes are attached to the word: גרך and גרו.[103] The reason for this lies in the fact that it is only with the גּר with whom the Israelite enters into mutual relationships. The זר is basically an enemy[104], and with the נכרי there is never *communio in sacris.* The only relationships expected with him (i.e. with the נכרי), are commercial relations and this "at arm's length"![105]

---

101 Used figuratively of a strange god.
102 In two occasions the noun גּר is used in apposition. But here also, the noun is restricted to a masculine form: singular in 2 Sam 1,13 (אִישׁ גּר) and plural in 2 Chron 2,16 (האנשׁים הגירים).
103 גרך: Ex 20,10; Deut 5,14; 24,14; 29,10; 31,12; גרו: Deut 1,16.
104 "ein זר ist ein צר" (G. Stählin, TWNT V, 8); van den Born, Art. Fremde, in: BL col. 494; Snijders, TWAT II col. 559-562.
105 Dion, Israël p. 222.

It must also be noted that the plural form גרים seldom appears. A look at
the frequency of the singular and plural forms of זר, נכרי and גר shows that,
while the relation of the singular and plural forms of זר and נכרי is
proportional, the plural form גרים[106] represents only a small percentage of the
גר-references:

	זר	נכרי	גר
singular	37	13	81
plural	33	16	11

The reason for this difference lies again in the legal character of the noun גר.
This noun was used originally (i.e. in the Covenant Code and the deuteronomic
code), with a restricted legal sense.[107] Since the majority of the גר-references
are laws, formulated like the laws in general[108] in singular form[109], no plural
form was needed. The plural form גרים is found in post-exilic references and
used either in non-legal contexts[110] or in the motive clauses of legal texts.[111]

1.7 גור and גר: derivation versus denomination

The verb גור has sometimes been taken as a denominative verb.   C.
Westermann, for instance, thinks that "Von גר = Fremdling ist גור = als
Fremdling (Gast) leben abgeleitet".[112] It is true that in the Rabbinical Hebrew
of the Hellenistic world the meaning of גר as "converted foreigner" came to be
so well established, that the verb גייר II (Piel "to make a Proselyte", Hithp. and

---

106 For גרים see: Ex 22,20; 23,9; Lev 19,34; 25,23;   Deut 10,19; Ps 146,9; 1 Chron
     29,15; 22,2; 2 Chron 2,16; 30,25; Ez 47,22.
107 Compare for instance the sharp difference between the status of the נכרי with that of the
     גר in the book of Deuteronomy. When they appear together (Deut 14,21), there is a
     clear difference in treatment: the נבלה is *given* to the גר and *sold* to the נכרי. When
     the גר appears alone, he appears in texts in which he is *included* in the community (Deut
     24,19-21). When the נכרי appears alone, he is *excluded* from communal benefits like
     the law of remission, or the loan without interest (Deut 15,3; 23,21).
108 Liedke, Gestalt p. 29-39; 138-148.;   Boecker, Recht p. 129-149;   168-180;
     Gerstenberger, Wesen p. 65-88.
109 Note the interesting example of Deut 29,10 where the singular form גר is mentioned
     after plural forms: טפכם נשיכם וגרך.
110 1 Chron 29,15; 22,2; 2 Chron 2,16; 30,25; Ez 47,22; Psalm 146,9, is also a late
     text, see note 118.
111 Ex 22,20b; 23,9b; Lev 19,34b; Deut 10,19b and Lev 25,23b.
112 Westermann, Genesis p. 190. See also Procksch "Von גר, einem alten Nomadenwort,
     ist גור 'als גר leben' abgeleitet ..." (Genesis p. 100); Bennet, Art. Stranger and
     Sojourner, in: EncB IV col. 4814; and HAL's entry on גור: "ja. ᵗᵍ denom. v. גֵּר,
     Proselyt werden" (1 p. 177).

Niph. "to become a proselyte") was formed from it.[113]   In the Old Testament, however, this does not seem to have been the case.

The idea of denomination has been suggested on the basis of a possible cultic origin of the term גר.[114]   A look at the book of Psalms, where the use of the verb גור seems to be older than that of the noun גר, does not speak in favour of this possibility.   The verb גור is related in Ps 5,5; 15,1 and 61,5 with the idea of asylum, i.e. the protection which comes from being the guest of a deity.   This is a very ancient idea common to the near Eastern religions.[115] The references to the noun גר in the Psalms are, instead, later. Ps 94,6, where the גר is mentioned in relation to the orphan and the widow, depends clearly on the triad of *personae miserae* ("גר-orphan-widow"), mentioned for the first time in the deuteronomic code.[116]   The reference to the גר in Ps 39,13 depends on Lev 25,23b[117], and Ps 119,19 is clearly a late reference.[118]   This means that the references to the verb גור in the book of Psalms are older than that of the noun גר.

The idea that the use of the noun גר in Psalms depends on the legal tradition and not vice versa[119], may be considered valid for other Old Testament references.   The earliest and vast majority of references to the noun גר are legal references.   Non-legal references, both in the prophets and in the Qetubîm, are either dependent on the deuteronomic triad[120] or late references.[121]

Although the noun גר appears for the first time in the Book of the Covenant, the גר becomes an important element only in the deuteronomic code.[122]   This is not surprising because the emergence of this term required a certain degree of

---

113 See Levy-Fleischer, Wörterbuch, I p. 327 and Schürer, History III/1, p. 170 note 78. See also the active form התיהד "to make a Jew" denominative form of יהודי: Esth 8,17 (מתיהדים Hitp. pt.).

114 See below p. 103 and Wildberger, EvTh 16 p. 418.

115 See de Vaulx, DBS 9, col. 1480-1510, especially the section: "Le droit d'asile dans l'antiquité non biblique" (p. 1483-1489); Auffarth, Numen XXXIX/2 p. 193-214.

116 Deut 14,29; 16,11.14; 24,19.20.21; 26,12.13; 27,19.

117 Lev 25,23 is discussed in p. 102ff.

118 In Ps 146,9 we have the plural form גרים, and just as in Ps 94,6, the mention of גרים יתום ואלמנה in V. 9a depends also on the deuteronomic triad.   On the late date of Ps 146 see Kratz, ZThK 89 p. 1-40, espec. p. 19ff.

119 The fact that cities of refuge might have been inspired by the idea of the religious asylum of the sanctuaries, does not mean that the status of the גר derives from the condition of the Psalmist in Yahweh's temple.   In the Psalms no reference to the noun גר is related to the idea of asylum.

120 Ps 94,6; 146,9; Jer 7,6; 22,3; Ez 22,7; Zech 7,10; Mal 3,5.

121 Job 31,32; Ps 39,13; 119,19; Is 14,1.

122 Together with אח, אב and איב, the noun גר is among the most frequent nouns used in Deut besides terms designating family relationships.   With the exception of the legislation on Civil and Religious Authorities (Deut 16,18-18,22), this noun is attested in all sections of the book from the earliest to the late additions (introduction, final address and appendix): Deut 1,16; 5,14; 10.18.19; 14,21; 16,11.14; 23,8; 24,14.17.19-21; 26,11-13; 27,19; 28,43; 29,10; 31,12.

differentiation in Israel's religious ideas.[123]   The counter position גר -
Israelite[124] presupposes a certain consciousness of one's own "peoplehood",
i.e. a particular notion of common origins and traditions, which in Israel are the
result of a later development in which "historical facts" were arranged according
to particular theological interests.[125]

The religious measures taken during the deuteronomic reform, which should
be understood within the larger framework of the Assyrian domination of
Palestine[126], created a new sense of national unity and identity which is at the
base of this counter position.[127]   It is not surprising, therefore, that the pair
"גר-אזרח", which crystallizes this counter position in its classical form, is
found in the priestly literature[128], a legal corpus in which the identity of Israel
is so well defined.[129]

In other words, the simple presence of resident aliens in Israel did not
provide the origin, automatically, to the noun גר.   During the early monarchy
people who resided temporarily in a town different from their own, were
usually referred to as: "Jezreelite", "Sharonite", "Bethlehemite", i.e. with a
gentilicium.[130]   These specific designations define the person from *the point of
view of their own origin.*   The noun גר, instead, is a generic term[131] which
defines the person from *the point of view of the Israelites,* for whom the גר
was a new element in their midst.   Being גר means *being perceived as* גר.   The
Israelite spoke, therefore, of the גר in "their towns", in "their midst".

---

123 It must be noted that the pre-exilic laws on behalf of the גר do not have sanctions. This
       means that they presuppose already a *differentiation* of law and ethos, which took place
       during the VIII century BC.; see Otto, Ethik p. 103-104.

124 Cf. the terms אח-גר in Deut 1,16;   24,14; and cf. the terms אזרח-גר in the Holiness
       Code: Lev 17,15; 18,26.

125 The tradition of "the conquest" for example, belonging originally to Benjamin, was
       generalised and nationalised later and made a tradition of the "whole Israel". For the use
       of the name "Israel" in relation to the pre-monarchichal traditions see Zobel, FS G.
       Sauer p. 109-117, espec. p. 11-12.

126 According to Perlitt: "Für Entstehung und Erfolg dieser religiösen Bewegung und ihrer
       Theologie war die *politische Situation konstitutiv*" (Israel p. 55), and according to
       Donner: "Die Kultusreform ist mithin auch Ausdruck der Emanzipationspolitik, die Josia
       gegenüber Assyrien betrieb" (Geschichte p. 379).

127 The atmosphere in relation to foreigners at this time, can be deduced from references like
       Zeph 1,8 and Jer 30,8-9, where the foreign fashion (מלבוש נכרי) is criticised and the
       restoration promised to Israel and Judah presupposes that they will not serve strangers
       (זרים) anymore.   On this theme see Bertholet, Stellung p. 70-90 and Dion,
       Universalismo p. 85ff; 173ff.

128 Ex 12,19.49;   Lev 16,29;   17,15;   18,26;   24,16.22;   Num 9,14;   15,29.30;
       Jos 8,33.

129 See for instance Hayes-Prussner, Theology p. 275.

130 For instance Bethlehemite: 1 Sam 16,1; Jezreelite: 1 K 21,7; Sharonite: 1 Chron
       27,29; Gileadite: 2 Sam 17,27; Beerothite: 2 Sam 4,5.

131 See for instance the transition from מצרי in Deut 23,8 to גר in Deut 10,19.

Although a complex issue such as the problem of derivation or denomination of the noun גֵּר cannot be settled on the basis of these general considerations, the derivation of the noun גֵּר from an original root גּוּר I seems to be, however, more likely.   The term גֵּר is then, a verbal noun.[132]   This does not mean, however, that we can turn automatically to the verb גּוּר in order to establish the meaning of the noun גֵּר, as has usually been done.[133]   It can not be taken for granted that the "root meaning" is automatically impregnated in all the words belonging to the same pattern.[134]   The meaning of a word can not be established by an individual study of the term alone.   For this reason, the weight assigned to the "root meaning" in the definition of the noun גֵּר, should not be given to the detriment of the semantic value of this noun in its actual context.[135]   The *legal context* in which the noun גֵּר is systematically used needs, therefore, to be rescued in the task of establishing the meaning of this noun.

---

132 TWAT I col. 980-983;   BDB p. 158;   DCH I p. 336;   DBEH p. 155;   Baentsch, Exodus-Leviticus p. 99;   Ravasi, Salmi I, 276 and Joosten, People p. 54.   The ē in גֵּר is result of contraction, characteristic of verbal nouns derived from a עׁיׁ root, the same as in: נֵר "lamp"; שֵׁר "bracelet"; מֵת "corpse"; עֵד "witness"; see König, Lehrgebäude II p. 82-83;   Bauer / Leander, Grammatik p. 464;   Stade, Grammatik p. 149.

133 This is what Barr called "the root fallacy": "It seems to be commonly believed that in Hebrew there is a 'root meaning' which is effective throughout all the variations given to the root by affixes and formative elements, and that therefore the 'root meaning' can confidently be taken to be part of the actual semantic value of any word or form which can be assigned to an identifiable root" (Semantics p. 100).   In the first chapter of his book Bultmann, for instance, discusses: "Die Bezeichnung *ger* im alttestamentlichen Hebräisch" (Der Fremde p. 17-22).   Despite the title of this section, the discussion is based on seven references of the verb גּוּר and two references of the noun גֵּר (!).   Moreover, one of these גֵּר-references (Ex 2,22) is theologically so coloured, that it can hardly be used to decide any historical matter in relation to the study of the גֵּר.   See Siebert-Hommes, ACEBT 10 p. 16-20.

134 Schökel summarizes Barr's notion of the root fallacy in the following terms: "se toma la raíz como una realidad lingüística, dotada de una significación radical, presente en todas las palabras que participan de la misma raíz, y que permite una impregnación mutua entre las palabras de la misma raíz" (Biblica 43 p. 219).

135 This is a point with which Friedrich, in his answer to Barr, agreed upon, see ThLZ 94 p. 812.

Part 2

The use of the term גר as legal status

2. The triad "גר - orphan - widow"

The noun גר appears twenty-one times in Deuteronomy: eleven times as part of the triad "גר-orphan-widow" and ten times independently of this triad.[1] Although these two groups of references are used indistinctly in the studies about the גר in the book of Deuteronomy[2], they are different in several aspects.

The triad references:

a) are found mainly in the deuteronomic code. Nine out of eleven triad-references are found in Deut 12-26.[3]

b) are clustered around the theme of *food*. Out of the eleven references, eight deal with eating-measures.[4] The unity of this cluster of references is underlined by the fact that the first and the last reference to this triad, form a sort of inclussio in the deuteronomic Code: 14,29 - 26,12-13 (the law of the tithe).[5]

c) although it is difficult to date all the references to the noun גר in Deuteronomy, there is consensus that the references dealing with eating measures are part of the deuteronomic reform and, therefore, earlier than the references dealing with legal and cultic measures.[6]

d) The triad references use the Egypt-עבד formula (i.e. "Remember that you were a *slave* in the land of Egypt" Deut 24,22), which corresponds to the older

---

1   גר in the triad: Deut 10,18; 14,29; 16,11.14; 24,17.19.20.21; 26,12.13; 27,19. גר apart from the triad: Deut 1,16; 5,14; 10,19; 14,21; 23,8; 24,14; 26,11; 28,43; 29,10; 31,32. There is, besides, one reference to the plural form גרים in Deut 10,19b.

2   There are five studies about the גר in the book of Deuteronomy: Bertholet, Stellung p. 105-122; Kloppers, Fax Theologica 6/2 p. 1-44; Dion, Israël p. 211-233; van Houten, Alien p. 68-108 and Bultmann, Der Fremde p. 34-120.

3   Deut: 14,29; 16,11.14; 24,17.19.20. 21; 26,12.13. The only two exceptions are Deut 10,18 and 27,19. Deut 10,18 is not properly a triad reference, instead of the appositive pattern "גר-orphan-widow", this verse juxtaposes two different sentences: "orphan-widow" + עשה משפט and גר + ואהב . Deut 27,19, on the other had, is a late reference based on the pre-exilic triad. See Krapf, VT XXXIV, 1 p. 89 and note 11.

4   Deut 14,29; 16,11.14; 24,19.20.21; 26,12.13. In the law of the tithe (Deut 14,29; 26,12), the גר appears related to the statement "eating and being sated".

5   Crüsemann, Tora p. 241.

6   Preuß, Deuteronomium p. 53; 58; Braulik, Deuteronomium p. 10; 12-13; Rose, 5. Mose p. 32-35; 52; 55; 201-204; 363; Steuernagel, Deuteronomium p. 6-10.

strata of Deuteronomy. The model of argumentation of this motive clause is introduced with the verb זכרת, and is used to support commands even when the term עבד does not appear in the main clause (Deut 24,17-18.19-22).[7]

The גר references on the contrary:

a) are found mainly in the introduction and the appendixes to the deuteronomic Code.[8]

b) deal mainly with legal and cultic matters.[9]

c) are mainly exilic and post-exilic references.

d) use the Egypt-גר formula (i.e. "for you were a גרים in the land of Egypt" Deut 10,19). This clause is introduced in each case by the particle כי and is used to support גר commands.[10]

Besides, the triad "גר-orphan-widow" is a *collective subject* which has a particular function as a fixed formula in the humanitarian laws of the book of Deuteronomy. The גר mentioned in this triad is part of that group of helpless and marginalised people of the late pre-exilic Israel for whose material well-being the deuteronomic code was concerned. The גר out of this triad, instead, is an *individual subject*, not necessarily poor (Deut 28,43), and connected more with the matters of religious integration.

2.1 The deuteronomic expansion of the traditional pair "widow-orphan"

The association of the noun "גר" with the pair "widow-orphan" in a triad is a novelty of the deuteronomic code. It is convenient, therefore, to study first the circumstances which gave rise to this combination.

In the ancient near Eastern literature the pair "widow-orphan" appears either alone or in relation with other elements like "the poor, the humble, the hungry". In the Egyptian literature, for instance, there are two major categories of underprivileged people: (1) the "hungry-thirsty-naked" and (2) the widow and the orphan. An example of the first group is found in the 125th chapter of the book of the Dead:

"I have done that which men said and that with which gods are content.
I have satisfied a god with that which he desires.
I have given bread to the hungry, water to the thirsty,
clothing to the naked, and ferry-boat to him who was marooned".[11]

---

7   Schwienhorst-Schönberger, Bundesbuch p. 346-353.

8   Deut 1,16; 5,14; 10,19; 28,43; 29,10; 31,12.

9   Deut 1,16; 14,21; 29,10; 31,12.

10   Ex 22,20; 23,9.12; Lev 19,34; Deut 10,19.

11   Translation: J.A. Wilson, ANET p. 36. The last phrase of this quotation became a stereotyped element in the ideal biographies and appeared frequently in the inscriptions of the New Kingdom, see Havice, Concern p. 30.

The second group "widow-orphan", is an old fixed form found for instance:
a) in biographical inscriptions:

"I announced the needs of the humble,
the widows and the fatherless likewise".[12]

b) in hymns:

"Mon coeur (désire) te voir,
mon coeur est dans la joie, Amon,
protecteur du pauvre!
Tu es le père de celui qui n'a pas de mère
l'epoux de la veuve".[13]

c) and in the wisdom story of The Eloquent Peasant:

"Because thou art the father of the fatherless,
the husband of the widow, the brother of the divorcee,
and the apron of him that is motherless".[14]

The pair "widow-orphan" is frequently found also in the Mesopotamian
literature:
a) in inscriptions:

".. (finally) Urukagina made a covenant with Ningirsu
that a man of power must not commit an (injustice)
against an orphan or widow".[15]

b) in legal codes:

"The orphan was not delivered up to the rich man;
the widow was not delivered up to the mighty man;
the man of one shekel was not delivered up to the man of one mina".[16]

c) in hymns:

"Schamasch wenn du aufgehst, / werden die Weltufer erhellt!
Die Waise, die Witwe, / ... (und) die Freundin
erwärmen sich bei deinem Aufgang /
(wie) alle Menschen!".[17]

---

12   This text from the inscription of Mentuhotep (11th Dynasty), is found in Janssen, Autobiografie p. 100; translation: Havice, Concern p.31.
13   Hymn to Amon # 71, VIII 1-3, translation: Barucq / Daumas, HPEA p. 204-205.
14   The eloquent peasant to the Chief Steward N° 60; translation: J.A. Wilson, ANET p. 408.
15   Votive inscription from the cones of Urukagina of Lagash, in: Kramer, Sumerians p. 319.
16   Translation: J.J. Finkelstein, in: ANET, p. 524.
17   Hymn to Shamash # 57, translation: Falkenstein / von Soden, SAHG p. 323.

It is found also in the Ugaritic literature:
a) in the description of the king's function:

"he will uphold the case of the widow,
  will do justice to the orphan".[18]

b) in the legend of king Kereth:

"You do not judge the cause of the widow
  You do not try the case of the importunate
  You do not banish the extortioners of the poor
  You do not feed the orphan before your face
  (nor) the widow behind your back".[19]

c) in the story of Aqhat:

"He judged the cause of the widow,
  tried the case of the orphan".[20]

The comparison of these texts (see Appendix, p. 134), shows that the pair "widow-orphan" appears frequently along with other characters:

In Egypt:[21]

Text 8:	widow	fatherless	poor	
Text 1:	widow	fatherless	humble	
Text 6:	widow	fatherless	citizen	
Text 4:	widow	fatherless	fearful	poor
Text 2:	widow	fatherless	one-who-has-nothing	
Text 3:	widow	fatherless	motherless	divorcee
Text 5:	widow	fatherless	prisoner	poor	sick one

In Mesopotamia:

Text 1:	orphan	widow		
Text 3:	orphan	widow	weak	
Text 6:	orphan	widow	widower	
Text 5:	orphan	widow	abused	deprived
Text 2:	orphan	widow	man of one shekel	
Text 7:	orphan	widow	poorest	refugee	weak

In Ugarit:

Text 1:	orphan widow

---

18   KTU 1,19. I:23-25 quoted in Weinfeld, Deuteronomy p. 439.
19   Kereth 16.VI.46-50, in Gibson, Myths p. 102.
20   Aqhat 17,ii,v,8, in Gibson, Myths p. 107. See also Aqhat 19,1,24 "(he) judged (the case of the widow), (tried) the case (of the orphan)" (Gibson, Myths p. 114).
21   The number of the texts are those of the Appendix.

Text 3:   orphan widow   poor oppressed[22]

It must be noted that among the characters mentioned together with the pair "widow-orphan", the stranger is not mentioned.   This absence is not extraordinary.[23] The inclusion of the other characters (poor, weak, deprived, hungry and others), is based on the fact that these were pyramidal societies in which each member had a particular place, even the underprivileged.[24] In the hierarchical structure of the Egyptian society, for instance, those who were in a superior position had the duty of beneficence to those who were below them. But this was a closed society and the principles of solidarity applied primarily to its members. This may explain why, although the protection of the weak was a common policy in the legal and wisdom tradition of the ancient near Eastern societies[25], the stranger was very seldom mentioned among them.

In relation with the triad "גר-orphan-widow" in the Old Testament, it is important to note that we have *pre-deuteronomic* references of the pair "widow-orphan" (Is 1,23; Ps 68,6). In Is 1,17 for instance, this pair appears together with the oppressed (חמוץ)[26], and in Is 10,2 with the poor (עני) and the needy (דלים).[27]

The deuteronomic code replaces these elements (i.e. "oppressed - poor - needy") with the גר, creating in this way the typical deuteronomic formula "גר-orphan-widow".[28]

---

22   Gibson translates 'qsr nps' by "importunate" (Myths p. 102), Olmo Olete by "oprimido" (Mitos p. 620).

23   See below p. 114 and Liverani, Art. Nationality, in: ABD, IV p. 1031ff. The instruction of Amen-em-opet (XXVIII) mentions the widow, the stranger and the poor, see Anet p. 424.

24   Bolkestein, Wohltätigkeit p. 54. Although the list could be enlarged, there are two major categories of underprivileged people: the "hungry-thirsty-naked" and the "widow-orphan". The statement of concern for the needy in the three-member form, appears in Egyptian biographical inscriptions of the eleventh dynasty: "I gave bread to the hungry, water to the thirsty, clothing to the naked" (Havice, Concern p. 30).

25   Weiler, Saeculum 31 p. 168-173; Lohfink, TS 52 p. 34-38; Patterson, BS 139 p. 223-234; Fensham, JNES XXI p. 129-139; Zobel, FS Boecker p. 33-38.

26   In a different context Is 9,16 mentions the pair "orphans-widows" in relation to the term "young people" (בחורין).

27   Koch states: "Es ist aber bezeichnend, daß Jesaja seine Gegenwartskritik nicht auf das Schicksal der kleinen Bauern beschränkt, sondern die grundbesitzlosen Witwen und Waisen mit einbezieht (auch 1,17.23). Jesajas Kritik ist also allgemeiner, zielt nicht mehr bloß auf die Benachteiligung einer bestimmten soziologischen Gruppe wie bei Amos und Micha" (Koch, FS von Rad p. 580). The גר is, however, omitted in Isaiah's critic. On Amos see Koch's remarks on page 575 of the same article. An interesting variant of this form is the double pair found in Zech 7,10: do not oppress widow-orphan / alien-poor.

28   Speaking about Deuteronomy Schwienhorst-Schönberger states: "Wir haben die altorientalische Trias der personae miserabiles Witwe, Waise, Armer nun israelitisch erweitert zur Vierergruppe: Fremder, Witwe, Waise, Armer" (BuL 63 p. 112b). In the Old Testament there is only one reference to this 'Vierergruppe', Zech 7, 10. In this

There are other references of the pair "widow-orphan" which are *later* than those of the deuteronomic triad "גר-orphan-widow".[29]   This means that the deuteronomic triad "גר-orphan-widow" had an independent existence from that of the previous formula "widow-orphan".

2.2 The triad " גר-orphan-widow" as collective subject

It must also be noted that the triad "גר-orphan-widow" is not unique.   There are other triads similar to this one in the book of Deuteronomy.   These triads show clearly that they deal with a *collective subject,* not with any specific member of the group.

The triad "grain and wine and oil"[30], for instance, behaves very much like that of the triad "גר-orphan-widow":

1) The word order follows a distinct pattern "grain > wine > oil": Deut 7,13; 11,14; 12,17; 14,23; 18,4; 28,51; just like the pattern: גר > orphan > widow.

2) Two of these terms (grain and wine[31]), are often used together out of Deuteronomy: Gen 27,28.37; Is 36,17; 62,8; Hos 2,11; 7,14; Zech 9,17; Ps 4,8; just like the pair widow - orphan.

3) The apposition can include the three elements: "grain-wine-oil" (Deut 11,14), just like "גר-orphan-widow" (Deut 24,19-21); or include only two of them with an additional sentence including the third element: "grain-wine ... + olive" (2 K 18,32); just like "orphan-widow ... + גר" (Deut 10,18).

4) The triad "grain - wine - oil" is found *in Deut* 7,13; 11,14; 12,17; 14,23; 18,4; 28,51, as well as *out of Deut* : Num 18,12; Deut 28,51; 2 K 18,32; Hos 2,10.24; Joel 1,10; 2,19; Hag 1,1; Neh 5,11; 10,40; 13,5.12; 2 Chron 31,5; 32,28; just like the triad "גר-orphan-widow".

These references show that in the triad "grain - wine - oil" it is not an individual element such as "the grain" which matters.   It is the triad as such, with its *collective meaning* of agricultural products, which is used as a symbol of abundance.[32]

---

case the four members are arranged also in two pairs עני - גר - יתום - אלמנה.   Two other similar references are Jer 22,3: triad + partc. from גזל, and Mal 3,5: triad + שכיר.

29   See for instance Job 24,3-4: יתומים אלמנה; Job 29,12-13: יתום אלמנה; Job 31,16-17: אלמנה יתום; Lam 5,3: אלמנות יתומים.

30   The phrase דגנך ותירשך ויצהרך appears 6 times in Deuteronomy: 7,13; 11,14; 12,17; 14,23; 18,4; 28,51.   This triad is found also in the Ugaritic literature, see Gordon, UT 126 III 13ff.

31   On the use of the pair "grain and wine" in Ugaritic, Phoenician and Mesopotamian religious literature see examples given by Weinfeld, Deuteronomy p. 373.

32   The triad "grain - wine - oil" has been called the "Formelgut des Dt" (Wolff, Hosea p. 44).

This idea of the triad as a *group*, not as the simple juxtaposition of three independent subjects, can be seen even more clearly with the triad "Abraham, Isaac and Jacob". The names of the patriarchs, which form a later addition[33], often appear in apposition to the collective term "fathers":

לאבתיך לאברהם ליצחק וליעקב	Deut 6,10; 9,5; 29,12
לאבתיכם לאברהם ליצחק וליעקב	Deut 1,8
לעבדיך לאברהם ליצחק וליעקב	Deut 9,27
לאברהם ליצחק וליעקב	Deut 34,4

1) Just as in the case of the previous triad, the word order also follows a distinct pattern "Abraham > Isaac > Jacob" : Deut 6,10; 9,5; 29,12; 30,20; 1,8; 9,27; 34,4; just like the pattern "גר > orphan > widow".
2) Two of these terms (Abraham and Jacob) are used together out of Deut: Gen 32,10; 28,13; 48,15.16[34]; just like the pair "widow-orphan".
3) The triad "Abraham-Isaac-Jacob" is found *in Deut* 6,10; 9,5; 29,12; 30,20; 1,8; 9,27; 34,4, as well as *out of Deut*: Gen 31,53; 32,9; 35,27; Ex 3,16; Lev 26,42; 2 K 13,23; Jer 33,26; just like the triad "גר-orphan-widow".

The comparison with other triads shows that the triad "גר-orphan-widow" is a collective subject. This *group of personae miserae* is the real subject of the triad.[35] The גר mentioned in this triad is not to be seen or dealt with on individual basis, nor is he individualised in any form. He is simply a *subspecies* of this group.[36] This triad does not deal, properly, with "<u>the</u> גר in

---

33   See van Seters, VT 22 p. 452 and Römer, Väter p. 234.

34 . In 1 K 18,36; 1 Chron 29,18 and 30,6 this pair appears together with "Israel".

35   See the plural form אכלו in the laws of Deut 14,29; 26,12. Van der Leeuwen's designation for the laws concerning the triad as: "Les droits des pauvres" (Développement p. 176), is appropriate. See also Maarsingh, Onderzoek p. 82-89, especially p. 87-89. According to Lohfink there is a sort of specialisation of the terms for poor in Deuteronomy. We have two different groups: "עני - אביון" and "גר - orphan - widow". The poor properly belongs to the first group, the triad "גר - orphan - widow" belongs to the second, see BN 51 p. 30-31; 33.

36   It must also be taken into account that the information contained in the triad references is sometimes valid for larger groups. The feast of the Weeks for instance, is equally prescribed for the sons, daughters, male and female slaves and Levites, Deut 16,11. In these references there is, therefore, nothing specific about the גר. It is true that in Deuteronomy the גר outside the triad is also mentioned among other characters, but there are differences between these two groups of references: (a) the גר in the triad "גר-orphan-widow" is mentioned among others in virtue of what is common to all of them, their poverty. The mention of the גר in these texts is not surprising; (b) the גר out of the triad, on the contrary, is not mentioned among *equals*, but mostly among others who like the Israelite, were in a better position than his. The גר is mentioned for instance, with איש and אח in Deut 1,16; with לוי and אתה in Deut 26,11; 28,43; with טפכם and נשיכם in Deut 29,10; and with האנשים, והנשים, והטף in Deut 31,12. The issue in these texts is no longer related to the economic status of its

Israel", but specifically with the group of *personae miserae* in the late VII century BC.

2.3 Beyond the limits of a genealogical ethics

It is important to note that eight out of the eleven references to the triad in the book of Deuteronomy are related to eating measures:

1) Two verses refer to the festivals of Weeks and of Tabernacles (Deut 16,11.14). During these times the "גר-orphan-widow" should "rejoice before the Lord", that is, they may take part of the communion meal.

2) Three references enjoin the Israelites to bring the tithes of the produce so that: "the גר, the orphan and the widow may come and eat their fill" (Deut 14,29; 26,12.13).

3) Three references enjoin the Israelites to leave what is left from the harvest of the fields, from the olive-trees and from the grapes of the vineyard for the "גר - orphan - widow" (Deut 24,19-21).[37]

Note that in contrast to these previous references:

• the reference to the גר in Ex 22,20a and to the pair "widow-orphan" in Is 1,17.23; 10,2 (all *pre-deuteronomic*), are not related to *eating* measures but with *legal* matters:

Ex 22,20:	You shall not oppress the גר.
Is 1,17:	Conduct the case of the widow! ... help the orphans to their rights!
Is 1,23:	The widow's cause do not come before ...
	they don't help the orphans to their rights.
Is 10,2:	... to turn aside the needy from justice and to rob the poor ... of their right,
	you spoil the widows! ... you make the orphans your prey!

• the *post-deuteronomic* references to the triad "גר-orphan-widow" are, again, related only to *legal* matters not with *eating* measures:

Jer 22,3:	Do not oppress the גר, the orphan and the widow.[38]
Zech 7,10:	Do not oppress the גר, the widow, the orphan and the poor.
Mal 3,5:	... those who oppress the orphan, the widow, the גר and the poor.

---

members. It is not a common need which brings them together here but rather a common opportunity: all have the right to take part in the assembly of the community, *even* the גר.

37   The three additional references to the triad are Deut 10,18; 24,17; 27,19.

38   On the verbs for oppression in these texts see Pons, L'Oppression p. 67ff.; 85ff.

These references show clearly that *the association of the triad "גר-orphan-widow" with eating measures is circumscribed to the deuteronomic code.*[39] This conclusion is confirmed by:
• the mention of the verbs "eating and be sated"[40] and "rejoice (during the communal meals)"[41],
• the use of the expression: "to give to the גר"[42],
• the frequent reference to agricultural products, which should be given or left on the field for them.[43]   All these elements are absent in the post-deuteronomic references of the triad.

2.4 Support measures on behalf of the triad

The reasons behind the eating measures on behalf of the triad "גר-orphan-widow" are to be sought in the effort to counteract the growing poverty of the population due to the process of urbanisation[44], and to the emergence of large numbers of immigrants in Israelite society during the VIII century BC.[45]

The book of Deuteronomy, unlike the Covenant Code, reflects an urban situation.[46]   As a result of this we witness in the book of Deuteronomy the modification of some basic family traditions:

---

39   Some laws on behalf of the triad are a theological adaptation of old pre-Israelite agrarian customs. Deut 24,19-22 for instance, can hardly be taken as an original law; similar prescriptions are already found in Sumerian texts, see Kramer, Sumerians p. 341. This text is the adaptation of the ancient custom of leaving behind a portion of the harvest as an offering to the gods of fertility, see v. Gall, ZAW 30 p. 91-98. By sowing, the integrity of the earth was violated. The tithe was "ein Tribut der Angst" that aimed to restore this violated integrity (Rose, ZB 5/1 p. 202). Israel preserved the rite but gave it a new interpretation: it was taken as an offering to Yahweh in the person of the poor. See Buis-Leclerq, Deutéronome p. 163.

40   ואכלו ושבעו (Deut 14,29;   26,12).

41   שמח (Deut 16,11.14;   26,11).

42   נתן ל ... (ואכל) (Deut 14,21;   26,12.13).

43   Deut 14,28-29;   16,9-11.13-14;   24,19-21;   26,11-13.

44   On the general theme of this section see especially Otto, Ethik p. 103-104 and idem, OH 3 p. 135-161.

45   In the period between the fall of Samaria and the reign of Josiah, the Neo-Assyrian kings carried more mass-deportations than in the entire previous history of the empire. In his annals (wall inscription from his palace in Chorsabad), Sargon II claims to have deported thousands of people: "Am Anfang meiner Regierung, in meinen ersten Regierungsjahre ... belagerte und eroberte ich Samaria. [27290 Leute, die in ihr wohnten], führte ich weg" (Galling, TGI N° 28 p. 53-54). He did likewise in Hamath and Ashdod, see ANET, p. 284-286 and Oded, Deportations Chap. II.

46   The גר is presented as "living in the cities" Deut 5,14;   14,21.29;   16,14;   24,14. The monetary system is introduced, allowing the substitution of the tithe in kind for money, Deut 14,24-26.

• Deuteronomy limits the authority of the father in the case of the rights of the first son (21,15-17). The father is not permitted to treat the son of the loved woman any better, as if he were his firstborn.

• Deuteronomy also limits the authority of the father to the right over life and death of his children (21,18-21; 22,13-21).

• Even more important, the father loses his priestly functions. Originally all slaughter was a sacrifice but with the centralisation, the slaughtering of animals became something secular (Deut 12,13-16). According to Causse this measure, which undermined the domestic culte, "ébranlait gravement le fondement traditionnel et religieux de la solidarité familiale".[47]

These measures modified essentially the traditional and religious foundations of family solidarity.[48]   With urbanisation began the substitution of the old forms of solidarity for individualism.   As van Leeuwen explains:

"on peut s'imaginer que la position des veuves et des enfants sans père était supportable, aussi longtemps que les liens de parenté étaient ressentis comme une véritable attache, au point que la maison paternelle de la femme garantit la protection et les soins de la veuve et de l'orphelin. Plus tard, cette assistance de la parenté est supprimée par le développement social au cours duquel les sentiments de groupe reculent de plus en plus devant un individualisme croissant. Ainsi du temps des prophètes les veuves et les orphelins manquent de leur appui naturel. Les jeunes gens, qui perdent leur père, ne pouvant pas se fier à un fort pouvoir d'état, sont souvent sans aucun appui, Job 29,12".[49]

The poor did not appear with urbanisation[50], but the care for the underprivileged became a problem only with the fragmentation of clan bonds.[51] In this new situation, the law of levirate, for instance, was not longer as imperious as before.   The refusal of this responsibility, although disapproved, was allowed (Deut 25,5-10).[52]   By transferring the responsibility of the material well-being of the needy directly to the people (i.e. not depending any more on their families), laws like Deut 24,19-22 acknowledged a situation which existed *de facto* long before: the bankruptcy of the ancient solidarity

---

47   Causse also states: "Le développement des sanctuaires urbains, et d'autre part le mouvement d'épuration et de centralisation du culte avaient contribué à la décadence des anciens groupes sociaux" (RHPR 13 p. 292). See also Albertz, Religionsgeschichte p. 329-330.

48   See Causse, RHPR 10 p. 24-60.

49   Van Leeuwen, Développement p. 30.

50   Sicre, Pobres p. 49-72.

51   See Havice, Concern p. 205-206.   In his analysis of the "segmentäre Solidarität", Kippenberg comes to the conclusion: "daß je näher die Verwandtschaft, um so größer die Solidarität ist" (Entstehung p. 35).

52   De Vaux explains that in this new situation: "L'exercice de la vengeance du sang est limité par l'existence d'une justice d'État et par la législation sur les villes de refuge, Nb 35,9-29; Dt 19,1-13" (IAT I p. 43).

system.[53]   As solidarity decreased, widows and orphans lost the natural support of their families and became helpless.[54] Since unity and togetherness could hardly be based on kinship when these bonds have been disolved by the gradual process of social differentiation, a new foundation was needed for this. As Otto explains: "Das Ethos nimmt dort, wo bislang das Normensystem tragende Solidarität aus genealogischer oder lokaler Nähe durch die zunehmende Heterogenität der staatlichen Gesellschaft in die Krise kommt, seinen Ausgangpunkt.   Die theologische Rechtsbegründung ist in sozialhistorischer Perspektive die Reaktion auf die Krise der Gesellschaft und damit der Begründung des Rechts aus der Gesellschaft".[55]

The emergence of the גר as part of the deuteronomic triad "גר-orphan-widow" in the deuteronomic code is, on the other hand, the combined result of different circumstances.   Among the external factors, we must count with the Assyrian domination of Palestine.[56]   The archaeological studies of M. Broshi[57] concerning the expansion of Jerusalem at about 700 BC., lead to think that this growth can hardly be independent from the wave of immigrants coming from the northern kingdom after the fall of Samaria in 721 BC.[58]   This expansion cannot be explained by mere demographic or economic growth, nor was it a gradual process.[59]

---

53   "Wenn jemand aus dem verwandschaftlichen Netz herausfällt, fällt er zugleich aus dem sozialen Netz heraus" (Schwienhorst-Schönberger, BuL 63 p. 110).

54   "Le sentiment de la solidarité s'amoindrit et la personne se dégage peu à peu du groupe familial. Le principe de la responsabilité individuelle est posé dans Dt 24,16 ... mais aussi, le devoir d'assistance entre parents est négligé et les prophètes doivent plaider la cause de la veuve et de l'orphelin, Is 1,17; Jr 7,6; 22,3" (de Vaux, IAT, I p. 43).

55   Otto, Ethik p. 104.

56   Schreiner, BiKi 42 p. 52-53.

57   Broshi, IEJ 24 p. 21-26; idem: RB 82 p. 5-14; H. Weippert, Palästina II/1, 589.

58   In opinion of Welten: "Diese Erweiterung ist kaum zu trennen vom Fall des Nordreichs und den Flüchtlingen in seinem Gefolge" (Art. Jerusalem I, in: TRE 16 p. 596); and Crüsemann states: "Historisch hat, nach allem, was wir archäologisch und aus den Texten wissen, erst der durch den Untergang des Nordreichs ausgelöste Flüchtlingsstrom nach Juda ein massives gerim-Problem ausgelöst" (Bundesbuch p. 34).   This possibility has been related to the thesis of the northern origin of the deuteronomic code: Levites and scribes from the north brought the core-Deuteronomy to Jerusalem. See for instance Alt, KS II p. 270-275 espec. 273-274 and Gese, Studien p.11.

59   There is a wide consensus among archaeologists and biblical scholars about this point, see: H. Weippert, Palästina II/1, 588-589; Welten, Art. Jerusalem I, in: TRE 16 p. 596; idem: FS R. Mayer p.132; M. Smith, Parties p. 178; de Vaux, IAT I p. 118; Gonçalves, L'Expédition p. 67; Osumi, Kompositionsgeschichte p. 165; Schwienhorst-Schönberger, BuL 63 p. 112; D. Kellermann, TWAT I col. 984-985; Weinfeld, DDS p. 90-91; Crüsemann, Bundesbuch p. 34; idem, WuD 19 p. 16.   Bultmann rejects Broshi's thesis on the basis of the lack of historical value of 2 Chron 30,25 (Der Fremde, p. 44; 213-214), but the recourse to this text is unnecessary as de Vaux, Smith and D. Kellermann's discussion of this thesis proves.

The emergence of the noun גר as a legal term in the deuteronomic code, attempts to preserve Israel's identity in situations of political turmoil, in which immigrants were to be accepted as having similar rights and duties as those of the native citizens. The legal term גר functioned, on the one hand, as an internal boundary between the native members of the Israelite community and those newly accepted and, on the other hand, as a sort of external boundary of the community in relation to immigrants, whose religious practices were commonly perceived as a threat to their own material security and religious purity.[60] During the Josianic period, we witness a new sense of national unity and identity in which foreign elements were seen with suspicion and criticised (Zeph 1,8).[61] The restoration promised to Israel and Judah presupposed that they will not serve strangers anymore (Jer 30,8-9).[62] These circumstances make unlikely the possibility that the גר in Deuteronomy is a non-Israelite.[63]

2.5 Conclusion

The combination of the noun גר with the pair "widow-orphan" in the triad "גר-orphan-widow" is a novelty of Deuteronomy which brings together persons who are in a similar situation of need. The reason behind their misery is, however, different in each case. The reference to the widow and the orphan can be explained in relation to internal factors of Israelite society (i.e. the problem of increasing urbanisation and the emergence of large numbers of immigrants in Israelite society of the VIII century BC.). The emergence of the גר is a partial consequence of the Assyrian presence in the region. The relationship of the triad "גר-orphan-widow" to *eating* measures, which are

---

60   According to Gonçalves: "Si Juda veut éviter le sort d'Israël, la purification de sa religion, qui est elle aussi canaanisée, s'impose de toute urgence" (L'Expédition p. 100).

61   See for example the military speeches (Deut 20), and rallying cries in the book of Deuteronomy (7,24: לא יתיצב איש בפניך; 7,21: לא תערץ; see Weinfeld, DDS p. 45-48). The religious measures taken during the deuteronomic reform may be understood within the larger framework of the Assyrian domination of Palestine; see Donner, Geschichte p. 379 and Perlitt, Israel p. 55.

62   The use of the term אח in Deut expresses the nationalistic focus of the book, and makes clear that the laws are designed for Israelites who are brothers: "non-Israelites who may be living within the borders of Israel are specifically referred to when anything that may affect them (i.e. the Israelites) is mentioned" (Mayes, Deuteronomy p. 124). See also Driver, Deuteronomy p. 175 and Weinfeld, DDS p. 229. Note the sharp contrast between the release owed to the "fellow" or "brother" and the attitude towards the נכרי in Deut 15,2. Particularly interesting here is the presence of the pair: גוים - נכרי in Deut 15,2.6.

63   For examples of this see Introduction footnote 25. According to Dion: "Pour la pensée deutéronomique proprement dite, l'étranger n'avait guère d'intérêt qu'en fonction de l'élection et de l'alliance" (Israël p. 232). See also Bächli, Israel p. 11-13.

circumscribed to the deuteronomic code, warns us against rapid generalisations about "the גר in Israel" on the basis of some triad references.   The noun גר appears as part of the triad in less than 20% of the cases.

The justification of laws on behalf of the גר with religious arguments (Deut 24,17-22 for instance), represents the transition from *kinship* to *ethos* as foundation for the protection of the *personae miserae* in Israel.   This is an important development in the laws of the Old Testament because solidarity based on a genealogical principle, rules out the possibility of solidarity with the גר.[64]

We cannot ignore the fact that, whatever the possible origin of the noun גר may have been, it was in post-exilic times that the term acquired particular relevance in Israel's life.   The vast majority of the references to the noun גר in the Old Testament (including those of the triad out of the book of Deuteronomy), are later than the deuteronomic references to the triad.   The specific conditions which gave rise to the triad "גר-orphan-widow", are not always valid for the גר mentioned out of the triad (Deut 28,43).   In the sociological and religious setting of the post-exilic period, the noun גר was used in connection with religious matters which were far beyond the original and restricted meaning of the *sociological* גר as *persona misera*.[65] While the triad "גר - orphan - widow" always refers to a social category of helpless and marginalised people, the references to the גר sometimes convey the idea of temporality but not necessarily of poverty.[66]

Although the גר in Deuteronomy initially appears in laws dealing with protective measures on behalf of the triad "גר - orphan - widow", it became in its later development, an independent subject related more to cultic and legal matters. The pair orphan-widow appears i Deuteronomy only in relation to the גר (i.e. as part of the triad).   In later stages of development the term גר appears, instead, alone.[67] In P for example, there is no longer any reference to the triad.[68]   The role of the triad as source for the study of the גר should not be, therefore, overestimated. The triad-references in Deuteronomy shed light, properly, on other triad-references[69] and on the term גר in the first stages of its development.

64   Schwienhorst-Schönberger, BuL 63 p. 110-111 and Otto, Ethik p. 84f.

65   See for instance Is 14,1; Ez 47,22-23; Ps 39,13; 119,19; Lev 25,23.

66   Job 31,32   Jer 14,8. This nuance is shown in modern translations of the Bible, see for example the BP. The social status of the גר as a *persona misera* cannot be generalised, cf. Ex 12,48; Lev 25,47; Deut 28,43.

67   Is 14,1; Ez 14,7; 47,23.

68   The mention of the pair גר-עני in Lev 19,10 is due to the synthetic character of Lev 19 which combines laws of the Book of the Covenant with laws of the deuteronomic code, see Otto, FS H. Graf Reventlow p. 65-80.

69   An identical structure to that of the deuteronomic triad is found only in Jer 7,6 and 22,3. A modified form of the triad is found in: Ez 22,7; Zech 7,10 and Mal 3,5; Ps 94,6 has the plural form יתומים and Ps 146,9 the plural form גרים.

3. The pair "גר - אזרח" in the Holiness Code

The noun גר appears eighteen times in the Holiness Code.[1]   In each case it appears together with another noun such as אזרח[2]; תושב[3]; עני[4]; with the expressions בית ישראל[5] or בני ישראל[6]; with prepositions plus suffix such as אתך[7] or עמך[8]; or qualified by a verbal form[9] such as וכי־יגור גר[10] or הגר הגר.[11]   The noun גר is used in casuistic laws with the patterns: "כל־נפש..."[12], "...איש איש"[13] or "...וכי־".[14]   The noun is used also in a few apodictic laws.[15]   Out of these eighteen references to the גר in the Holiness Code:

• in four cases we have the re-formulation of a previous law:

Lev 19,10   =>   old pre-Israelite agrarian custom[16]
Lev 19,33   =>   Ex 22,20[17]

---

1   Lev 17,8.10.12.13.15; 18,26; 19,10.33.34; 20,2; 22,18; 23,22; 24,16.22; 25,35.47.47.47.   We have, besides, the plural form גרים in Lev 25,23 and the pronoun אתו in Lev 19,33b which refers to the גר in 19,33a.

2   Lev 17,15; 18,26; 19,34; 24,16.22.

3   Lev 25,35.47.47.

4   Lev 19,10; 23,22.

5   Lev 17,8.10; 22,18.

6   Lev 17,12.13; 20,2.

7   Lev 19,33.

8   Lev 25,47.

9   Note that in the pattern הגר הגר, the noun גר appears consistently with article, while in the pattern וכי־יגור גר without it. In Lev 17 we find the three kind of patterns: (a) without verbal qualification (v. 15); (b) with the pattern: וכי־יגור גר (V. 18), and (c) with the pattern: הגר הגר (V. 10.12).

10   Lev 19,33. In Lev 17,8: הגר אשר־יגור.

11   Lev 17,10.12.13; 18,26; 19,34; 20,2.

12   כל־נפש מכם ... והגר (Lev 17,12). See page וכל־נפש באזרח ובגר (Lev 17,15); כל־נפש מכם ... והגר (Lev 17,12). See page 56.

13   For the pattern איש איש מבית ישראל ומן־הגר, see Lev 17,8.10; 22,18; for the pattern איש איש מבני ישראל ומן־הגר, see Lev 17,13; 20,2. The construction איש איש without the noun גר appears in: Lev 15,2; 18,6; 22,4 (with מזרע אהרן); 17,3 (with מבית ישראל) and 20,9 (with כי־איש איש).

14   וכי־יגור גר (Lev 19,33); וכי־ימוך ... גר (Lev 25,35); וכי־תשיג ... גר (Lev 25,47).

15   Lev 18,26; 24,16.22.

16   According to Faley: "The charitable motivation given this procedure is an early Heb adaptation of a pre-Israelite custom of leaving something of the harvest to honour the deity responsible for the soil's fertility, a motive clearly excluded by the concluding affirmation in 10b" (Leviticus p. 79). See also Beer, ZAW 31 p. 152; v. Gall, ZAW 30 p. 91-98 and Cholewiński, Heiligkeitsgesetz p. 49 notes 21-22.

17   See Elliger, Leviticus p. 250 and Cholewiński, Heiligkeitsgesetz p. 50-51 notes 25-30.

Lev 19,34   =>   Deut 10,19[18]
Lev 23,22   =>   Lev 19,10[19]
• in four cases the noun גר is found in Lev 25.[20]   These are laws concerned with the impoverished Israelite brother and in which the noun גר is used as a term of comparison.   From the ten remaining references, nine cases are prescriptions about matters which affect the sanctity and purity of the congregation[21]; one reference is related to criminal law (Lev 24,22).

3. 1 The noun גר in the Holiness Code

3.1.1 The supposed status of the גר in the Holiness Code

The idea that the גר, being subject to "the same laws as the Israelite", has a status similar to the one held by proselytes during the post-exilic period, has exerted an enormous influence in the basic approach of later studies on this subject.

In his commentary on Deuteronomy (1895), S.R. Driver describes the development from the גר - laws in Deuteronomy and those in P in the following terms:

"In P the גר is placed practically on the same footing as the native: he enjoys the same rights (Num 35.15, cf. Ez 47.22), and is bound by the same laws, whether civil (Lev 24.22), moral and religious (18.26 20.2 24.16, cf. Ez 14.7), or ceremonial (Ex 12.19 Lev 16.29 17.8.10.12.13.15. 22.18 Num 15.14.26.30. 19.10): the principle, 'One law shall there be for the home-born and for the stranger' is repeatedly affirmed (Ex 12.49 Lev 24.22 Num 9.14 15.15.16.29)".[22]

In his commentary on Leviticus (1904), Driver speaks about "the complete equalisation" of the גר and the native Israelite.[23]

In his study "Die Stellung der Israeliten und der Juden zu den Fremden" (1896), A. Bertholet states that the גר in P

"ist ganz und gar ein religiöser Begriff geworden. Es bezeichnet den Nichtisraeliten, der unter Israel wohnt und in seine religiöse Verfassung zum allergrössten Teil oder sogar (durch

---

18   See Bultmann, Der Fremde p. 177-178; Martin-Achard, THAT I col. 412; Mathys, Liebe p. 42; 134; Cholewiński, Heiligkeitsgesetz p. 50-51 notes 25-30.
19   See Elliger, Leviticus p. 250 and Cholewiński, Heiligkeitsgesetz p. 94.
20   Lev 25,35.47.47.47. On the problems involved in the formation of this chapter see Cortese, Riv Bib 18 p. 395-401 and Kilian, Untersuchung p. 121-148. For the analysis of specific differences between Lev 25 and the rest of the book, see Joosten, People p. 155 note 77.
21   Lev 17,8.10.12.13.15; 18,26;   20,2; 22,18;   24,16.
22   Driver, Deuteronomy p.165.
23   Driver, Leviticus p. 87.

Annahme der Beschneidung) vollständig aufgenommen ist. In diesem letzteren Falle ist es schon so viel als Proselyt", and he adds later: "In der Zeit zwischen P und dem Chronisten hat sich also der Schritt vollzogen: רג hat den spezifischen Sinn bekommen, in dem es später in die thalmudische Literatur übergegangen ist; es braucht nicht mehr der in der jüdischen Gemeinde sich aufhaltende Fremde zu sein, es ist der Fremde überhaupt, der ihre Religion angenommen hat. In einem Worte: Der רג ist der Proselyt geworden".[24]

This *developmental* conception of the רג, common among nineteenth century authors[25], understood the רג references in the Old Testament as an evolutionary process which began with the protective measures of the Book of the Covenant and ends with the final "religious" stage of the רג in the Priestly writings. This approach lies behind the major recent studies on this subject. A few examples will suffice to illustrate this point. F. Horst in his RGG article "Fremde" (1958), gives some references to describe the position of the רג in the priestly laws[26], and concludes: "So wird aus dem Schutzbürger der *Proselyt*, der unter derselben Gottesweisung wie der Angestammte leben darf (Ex 12,49; Lev 24,22; Num 9,14 u.a.)".[27] K.G. Kuhn, in his TWNT article "προσήλυτος" (1959), speaks about the line of *development* between Deuteronomy and P:

"Im Priesterkodex ist der רג, in Fortführung der mit dem Deuteronomium angebahnten Entwicklung, so gut wie ganz in die jüdische Religionsgemeinschaft mit hineingenommen. Für ihn gelten grundsätzlich dieselben religiösen Rechte und Pflichten wie für den israelitischen Vollbürger ... Im religiösen Sinne kommt also der Begriff dem spätjüdischen "Proselyt" schon recht nahe".[28]

And in his TWAT article "גור" (1973), D. Kellermann not only states: "daß in späten Schichten von P der רג der voll integrierte Proselyt ist" but also that: "Für diesen Teil von P darf man dann alle Gesetze als ebenfalls für den רג gültig ansehen, auch dann, wenn er nicht ausdrücklich genannt ist".[29]
L. Schwienhorst-Schönenberger summarizes his article "...denn Fremde seid ihr gewesen im Land Ägypten" (1990) in the following way:

"Die soziale und rechtliche Stellung des Fremden (ger) -so können wir hier zusammenfassend feststellen- hat sich im Lauf der Geschichte Israels gewandelt: vom Schutz vor wirtschaftlicher Ausbeutung in den ältesten Texten des Bundesbuches über ein umfassendes Reformprogramm zur wirtschaftlichen und sozialen Integration im 8. und 7. Jahrhundert, der

---

24   Bertholet, Stellung p. 174; 178.
25   See for instance Benzinger, Art. Fremdlinge, RE, VI, p. 262-265, espec. p. 264.
26   See for instance Ex 12,19.48; Lev 18,26; 24,16; 20,2; 17,15; Num 9,14;
      15,14.26; 19,10.
27   Horst, F., Art. Fremde, in: RGG³ II col. 1126.
28   Kuhn, TWNT VI p. 729.
29   D. Kellermann, TWAT I col. 988. According to Mathys: "Bei P wurde der Fremde
      endgültig zum Proselyten" (Liebe p. 40).

Zeit des Deuteronomium, bis hin zur völligen Gleichberechtigung in der exilisch-nachexilischen Gemeinde".[30]

3.1.2 The addresses of the Holiness Code

The difference between the priestly and the deuteronomistic attitudes towards the גר is probably not a result of historical development, but rather one of definition of status.[31] The alleged evolution from the position of the גר in the Book of the Covenant to that of P is disputable.[32]

A study of the introductory formulae to the laws in the Holiness Code shows that these laws are either instructions for the community or instructions for the priests *exclusively*. No mention whatsoever is made of the גר. The introductory formulae of the different sections of the Holiness Code have two elements:

1) the first part is the phrase: וידבר יהוה אל־משה לאמר.[33] There are a few variations on this pattern.[34] In the Holiness Code, unlike P, only Moses is mentioned.[35]

2) the second part is the transmission command (Weitergabebefehl[36]). In two instances the introductory formula appears, however, without the transmission command (Lev 22,26; 23,26). This second part of the formula, which describes the real addressees of the laws, is the principal one.[37]

The addressees are, as throughout the book:

a) the sons of Israel:[38]

דבר אל־כל־עדת בני־ישראל ואמרת אלהם   Lev 19,2[39]

---

30 Schwienhorst-Schönberger, BuL 63 p. 114.

31 Weinfeld, DDS p. 225-232. According to Joosten: "The peculiar status accorded to the *gér* in priestly legislation derives from the priestly theology and world-view, not from changed historical conditions or from a different meaning of the term *gér*" (People p. 57-58).

32 On the matter of "Entwicklungstendenzen" in biblical exegesis and in the reconstruction of Israel's religious history see Perlitt, Vatke p. 80-83; 173-185.

33 Lev 17,1; 18,1; 19,1; 20,1; 21,16; 22,1.18.26; 23,1.10.23.26.34; 24,1.13; 25,1.

34 Lev 19,2 introduces, for instance, the expression כל־עדת. In Lev 21,1, instead of the usual וידבר, we have ויאמר.

35 In P Moses and Aaron are addressed in Ex 12,1.43; Lev 11,1; 13,1; 14,33; 15,1; Num 19,1; and Aaron alone in Lev 10,8 and Num 18,20. See Rendtorff, Gesetze p. 66-70.

36 Rost, Studien p. 16.

37 See Cortese, Riv Bib 29 p. 140-141.

38 Lev 1,2; 4,2; 7,23.29; 11,2; 12,2; 15,2; 18,2; 20,2; 23,2.10.24.34; 24,2; 25,2; 27,2.

39 The usual pattern in the Holiness Code has in the second part of the transmission's command, the formula ואמרת אלהם. Variations of this formula are found: in Lev

בני ישראל ואמרת אלהם	דבר אל־	Lev 18,2[40]
בני ישראל לאמר	דבר אל־	Lev 23,24.34
בני ישראל תאמר	ואל־	Lev 20,2

b) Aaron and the priests:

דבר אל־אהרן לאמר	Lev 21,17
דבר אל־אהרן ואל־בניו	Lev 22,2[41]
אמר אל־הכהנים בני אהרן	Lev 21,1

c) In two cases Aaron and Israel are addressed together[42]:

דבר אל־אהרן ואל־בניו ואל כל־בני ישראל	Lev 17,2
דבר אל־אהרן ואל־בניו ואל כל־בני ישראל	Lev 22,18

The גר appears in no single case in the entire Holiness Code as addressee of the laws.   He is referred to in the text of the law[43], but never in the introductory formulae. We must distinguish between the original introductory formula and the inclusion clause גר-אזרח which is introduced later.[44]

The distinction made between "the people of Israel" and "the גר" is particularly clear in Lev 19 where the law is addressed to "the *whole* community (כל־עדת)"[45], which is enjoined to be holy (v. 2), and to keep the statutes (v. 19). Here again, the גר is not included among the addressees.   It is true that he is mentioned twice in appendices[46], but in 19,10 the noun גר is introduced with the preposition ל (ולגר), which makes of him just the *beneficiary* of the law; and in 19,33a the גר is mentioned in the protasis, which introduces only, the *circumstance* of the law mentioned in 19,33b.[47]

The גר in the Holiness Code often appears in later additions: Lev 17,15; 18,26; 24,16; 24,22[48] and, as was already mentioned in the introduction (p.

21,16; 23,24.34 (with לאמר instead ואמרת), and in Lev 20,2 (with תאמר instead ואמרת). Note also that in Lev 24,2 , instead of the usual דבר, we have צו.

40   Lev 23,1.10;   25,1.
41   See also Lev 6,2.
42   In Lev 21,24 the introduction formula וידבר יהוה אל־משה לאמר has been changed to וידבר משה אל־אהרן, and the laws are addressed "to Aaron and to his sons and to all the people of Israel" (אהרן ואל־בניו ואל־כל־בני ישראל).
43   These references appear always together with another noun: גר-אזרח, גר-עני or גר-תושב.
44   See p. 54 and 56.
45   Lev 19,2: דבר אל־כל־עדת בני־ישראל ואמרת אלהם.
46   Lev 19,10.33. See Kilian, Untersuchung p. 65 and Milgrom, Holiness p. 73.
47   See Waltke-O'Connor, Syntax § 38.2.d.4-5.
48   On Lev 17,15 see Elliger, Leviticus p. 218-219. 222; Cholewiński, Heiligkeitsgesetz p. 27 note 42 and p. 40 note 19; Kornfeld, Studien p. 69. On Lev 18,26 see Kornfeld, Studien p. 69; Elliger, Leviticus p. 234; Noth, Leviticus p. 115. On Lev 24,16 see Kilian, Untersuchung p. 121; Elliger, Leviticus p. 331; Cholewiński,

48), in reformulations of older laws.   One could argue that the גר is not explicitly mentioned in the second part of the introductory formulae (i.e. the transmission command) because, being part of the people, he is already assumed under the בני־ישראל.   But this is certainly not the case.   Different expressions in the Holiness Code such as: "the גר among you"[49] and "the גר in Israel"[50], distinguish clearly between those who *are the people* and those who *live among them* .   Even more, the distinction made:

"between *the House of Israel*   and the גר"[51] and

"between *the sons of Israel*   and the גר"[52],

makes quite clear that in the eyes of the author, the גר does not originally belong to any of these two groups.[53]   Finally, it must be noted that the noun אזרח is opposed to or distinguished from the noun גר eleven times in the Holiness Code.

3.1.3 The development of the Israelite legal system

Some references to the גר in the Holiness Code might lead to think of the later proselyte, for instance: Lev 17,8; 22,18.[54]   In order to get an appropriate perspective of the גר in the Holiness Code, we have to see him within the broader context of the development of the Israelite legal system and the perspective of the spatial notion of holiness in the Holiness Code.

During the post-exilic period different measures were taken in order to complete "the Sinai laws" in those aspects in which these laws were insufficient

---

Heiligkeitsgesetz p. 96-100.   On Lev 24,22 (probably taken from v. 16), see Kilian, Untersuchung p. 121; Elliger, Leviticus p. 332; Cholewiński, Heiligkeitsgesetz p. 96-100.

49   הגר בתוכם (Lev 17,10.13); בתוכם ... הגר (Lev 17,8.12) and in Lev 18,26: הגר ... בתוככם.

50   הגר ... בישראל (Lev 20,2);   הגר בישראל (Lev 22,18).

51   מבית ישראל ומן־הגר (Lev 17,8.10;   22,18).

52   מבני ישראל ומן־הגר (Lev 17,13; 20,2).

53   It is true that in Lev 24,16a.γ the term כל־העדה is explained with the expression כגר כאזרח (24,16.b.α).   This phrase (which function as a merism here, see Krašovec, Biblica 64 p. 232) is, however, a later addition.   As Kilian explains: "Der Ausdruck כגר כאזרח (v. 16) stammt aus v. 22 bzw. gehört wie dieser Vers der gleichen Hand an" (Untersuchung p. 114), and: "Mit v. 22, der, wie bereits festgestellt, Rh angehört, hängt auch die Erweiterung v. 16b zusammen, die somit ebenfalls Rh zuzuweisen ist" (Untersuchung p. 118).   On the term עדה see Elliger, Leviticus p. 70.

54   Note that the law does not *require* that the גר offers sacrifices to Yahweh, but merely regulates for that eventuality.   Since the priestly laws do not limit the bringing of sacrifices to the Israelites, and the גר lives among them, the possibility is open for him: "Should he wish to bring a sacrifice, his offering must meet, then, all the usual requirements" (Joosten, People p. 68; 75-76).

for the growing needs of the community.[55]   The number of foreign people living "in Israel" in post-exilic times increased and the Jewish community faced problems for which there were not yet specific answers.   Such was the case of the law concerning blasphemy.[56]   In Ex 22,27 we have for instance, the following precept: "You shall not reveal God".   This law was not clear, however, with respect to the scope of the addressees and did not specify any punishment either.   This explains the origin of additional legislation like that of Lev 24,10-23 in which the גר is mentioned twice (V. 16.22).   The main concern of this text is with the punishment for blasphemy, especially in the case of a foreigner.   The mixed parentage of the offender would have raised the question as to whether the law of Ex 22,27 was applicable.[57]   The legislation of Lev 24,10-23 makes clear that in the new circumstances: blasphemy will be punished with the death penalty, the entire community will participate in the malefactor's execution, and that this law will be equally valid for the native and the גר.

Just as in the case of blasphemy, former legislation concerning murder (Ex 21,12) and slaughter of animals (Deut 12,15-16.20-28), was reconsidered in the Holiness Code in order to adapt it to the new circumstances of the Persian period.   Through the inclusion clause אזרח-גר these original measures were extended to include the גר, who also became subject to the same prescriptions as the native (Lev 17,1-16; 24,21b-22).

We find similar cases of new legislation in Num 9,6-14; 15,32-36; 27,1-11; 36,1-12.   All these texts follow the same basic pattern: a concrete situation raises a problem for which there is no precedent.   The case is adjourned until Moses makes a special inquiry within the sanctuary, where God speaks to him (Ex 25,22).[58]   When the decision is given, it stands as a guiding principle[59] for future cases[60]:

	A concrete situation raises a problem	The case is addressed to Moses	Moses consults God	The decision is given
Lev 24,10-23:	an alien cursed the name of God	v. 11b	v. 12	v 13-16
Num 9,6-14:	uncleanness through touching a corpse	v. 6b-7	v. 9	v. 10-14

---

55   Crüsemann, Tora p. 121-126 and de Vaulx, Nombres p. 14-20.
56   See for instance Kornfeld, Leviticus p. 96.
57   Van Houten, Alien p. 144.
58   See Deut 1,17b.
59   Num 15,29.   In Ex 12,49 is used the term תורה; in Lev 24,22: משפט; in Num 9,14; 15,15: חקה and in Num 15,15: תורה ומשפט.
60   Snaith, Leviticus p. 110. 136. 155.

Num 15,32-36:	violation of the Sabbath	v. 33b	v. 35a	v. 35b-36
Num 27,1-11:	inheritance of pro-perty by women	v. 1-4	v. 5	v. 6-11
Num 36,1-12:	inheritance of pro-perty by women	v. 1-4	v. 5a	v. 5b-9

This does not necessarily mean that such prescriptions were part of a global policy for the integration of the גר. These were rather ad-hoc measures created by the pressure of the circumstances, in a time in which the concern for cultic purity was particularly important.[61]   In Lev 24, for example, we are dealing with an offence which might endanger the security of the *whole community*, and in this particular case (not in every case[62]), the law must be made explicit. This was necessary because of the practice in certain legal systems of judging resident aliens by different laws.   Extra-territoriality was not endorsed by biblical law in the case of killing, bodily injury, nor in cases of blasphemy.[63] The legal provisions needed to prevent or minimise this potential danger were, therefore, imperative.

Let us turn our attention now to the content of the precepts. The גר-laws of the Book of the Covenant and Deuteronomy are given in order to guide the conduct of the Israelite towards the גר according to a principle of solidarity. This explains why, while the Israelites are addressed in the second person, the גר is referred to in the third person:

Ex 22,20a: *You* shall not wrong or oppress *a* גר
Deut 24,21:   When *you* gather the grapes of your vineyard,
              do not glean what is left, it shall be for *the* גר

In the Holiness Code we also find some laws given on behalf of the גר.   They *protect* (Lev 19,33) and *provide* for him (Lev 19,9-10).   These laws follow the same pattern as those of the book of the Covenant and Deuteronomy: they are addressed to the Israelite on behalf of the גר.

Lev 19,33:   When *a* גר resides with you ... *you* shall not oppress him.
Lev 19,34:   *You* shall love *the* גר as yourself.
Lev 19,9f.:   When *you* reap the harvest of your land

---

61   The land being holy, it must be preserved from the potential danger of contamination due to contact with foreign individuals, their customs and their gods. The גר must also be subjected under these prescriptions. See Kuhn, Proselyten, in: RECA Supp IX, col. 1256-1257 and Joosten, People p. 196-200.
62   The statement "You shall have one law for the alien and for the citizen" (Lev 24, 22; Ex 12,49; Num 9,14; 15,29), applies particularly to the laws which immediately precede this formula, not for all legislation in P.
63   Levine, Leviticus p. 168.

> you shall not glean the fallen grapes
> you shall leave them for the poor and *the* גר

Lev 23,22:   When *you* reap the harvest of your land
you shall not gather the gleanings of your harvest,
you shall leave them for the poor and *the* גר

3.1.4 The peculiarity of the גר laws in the Holiness Code

There is, however, a fundamental difference between the Book of the Covenant and the deuteronomic code, on the one hand, and the Holiness Code, on the other hand. Only in the late additions to the Holiness Code and P do we come across laws in which the גר is subject to the same precepts as the Israelite.[64] In Holiness Code/P the גר is expected to fulfill *some* specific requirements which are also expected of the Israelites:
"No person among you shall eat blood,
nor shall the גר who resides among you eat blood" (Lev 17,12)
The laws which come under this category are those in which the גר and the Israelite appear together:
• in the inclusion clause גר-אזרח.[65]
• in the constructions:
איש איש מבית ישראל ומן־הגר[66]
איש איש מבני ישראל ומן־הגר[67]
• and in the construction: כל־נפש מכם ... והגר[68]

The inclusion clause גר-אזרח appears four times in the Holiness Code, twice with the word order גר-אזרח[69] and twice with the word order גר-אזרח.[70] These four clauses are late[71] and add nothing particular to the content of the verses. This clause is commonly used to further specify the scope of those included in a law and used, therefore, after expressions such as: אתם (Lev 18,26); וכל־נפש אשר (Lev 17,15); והנפש אשר־תעשה (Num 15,30); וכל־אכל ... מעדת ישראל (Ex 12,19); וכל־ישראל (Jos 8,33). The

---

64   On the late additions to Holiness Code-P see Grelot, VT 6 p. 174-189 and Cazelles, Art. Pentateuque, in: DBS VII col. 844-855.
65   Lev 17,15; 18,26; 24,16.22.
66   Lev 17,8.10; 22,18.
67   Lev 17,13; 20,2.
68   Lev 17,12.
69   Lev 24,16.22. In P see also: Ex 12,19; Num 9,14; Jos 8,33.
70   Lev 17,15; 18,26. In P: Ex 12,49; Lev 16,29; Num 15,29.30; see also Num 15,15 (ולהגרים ... והיו לכם כאזרח); 15,16 (לכם ולנר); Ez 47,22 (ככם כנר לכם).
71   See Elliger, Leviticus p. 201; 218; 230; 243; 331; 332; Noth, Leviticus p. 108; 115; 16; 124; Kornfeld, Leviticus p. 69; 79; 96; 97.

inclusion clause is included, mostly, in prohibitive commands[72] (both in the Holiness Code and in P)[73] and it is used:

• to define the scope of those included in a law: "the גר as well as אזרח" Lev 24,16[74]. The noun אזרח functions here as a polar category to make explicit the universe of persons involved in the law.[75]

• to define expressions used for the community such as: כל־נפשׁ אשׁר[76], אתם[77] and in P: העדה[78] and כל־ישׂראל.[79]

• in those texts in which is made explicit that there is only one law for both the גר and the אזרח: Lev 24,22[80] (in P see also Ex 12,49).

Unlike the גר laws in the Book of the Covenant and the deuteronomic code, the laws of the Holiness Code which include both, the Israelite and the גר, have sanctions[81]:

	Prescription:	Sanction:
Lev 17,8:	the bringing of a sacrifice	כרת formula
Lev 17,10:	the slaughtering of animals	כרת formula
Lev 17,12:	the slaughtering of animals	כרת formula
Lev 17,13:	the slaughtering of animals	כרת formula
Lev 17,15:	eating נבלה	ונשׂא עונו formula
Lev 18,26:	sexual relations	כרת formula
Lev 20,2:	the Molech worship	מות יומת formula
Lev 24,16:	blasphemy	מות יומת formula
Lev 24,22:	murder	מות יומת formula

The fundamental common element to all these laws is their primary concern with the matter of holiness. It can be said, then, that in the Holiness Code the noun גר is mentioned in two kinds of laws: (1) laws given *to the Israelites for*

---

72   On prohibitive commands see p. 63.

73   On the prohibitive commandments in P see below note 117.

74   In P see Lev 16,29 "neither the אזרח nor the גר".

75   On the theme of merism see Krašovec, Biblica 64 p. 232. The noun אזרח appears sixteen times in the Old Testament: Ex 12,19.48.49; Lev 16,29; 17,15; 18,26; 19,34; 23,42; 24,16.22; Num 9,14; 15,13.29.30; Jos 8,33; Ez 47,22. In Ps 37,35 read ארז instead אזרח: KBL, DBHE, Luther, BK. In Ps 88,1 read האזרחי instead אזרח BHS. Lev 23,42 is strictly the only reference in the Old Testament in which the noun אזרח appears without any reference to the noun גר. The noun גר appears, however, in P and the Holiness Code independently from the term אזרח. This situation is similar to that of the גר and the pair "widow-orphan" in the book of Deuteronomy, where the pair "widow-orphan" appears only as part of the triad "גר-orphan-widow". The noun גר, however, appears independently from the triad.

76   Lev 17,15, see also Num 15,30.

77   Lev 18,26, see also לכם in Lev 16,29; 24,22 and Num 9,14.

78   Ex 12,19; Lev 24,16.

79   Jos 8,33.

80   See also Num 15,15 (ככם כגר) and 15,16 (לכם ולגר).

81   The only exception to this is Lev 22,18 (see p. 53 note 54). Note that the גר laws of the Pentateuch out of the Holiness Code and P have no sanctions.

the protection of the גר and (2) laws addressed equally to the Israelite and the
גר *for the preservation of holiness.*   The origin and aim of these two kinds of
law is different.

The laws concerned with *the protection of the* גר:

1) are reformulations of previous laws.[82]
2) are adressed only to the Israelite, the גר is mentioned simply as beneficiary.
3) aim at the amelioration of the material condition of the גר.
4) have no sanctions.
5) are followed by the formula: אני יהוה.[83]

The laws concerned with *the preservation of holiness:*

1) are exclusive of the Holiness Code and P: they are new prescriptions[84] and reformulations
of former laws which did not include the גר.[85]
2) include both the Israelite and the גר.
3) aim at the preservation of holiness in the community.
4) have sanctions.
5) include (a) the כרת formula[86], (b) the מות יומת formula[87] and (c) the ונשא עונו
formula.[88]

In other words: *when the laws deal with the matter of the preservation of
holiness, the* גר *is subject to the law just as the Israelite.*   Such is the case of
laws concerning:

• the slaughtering of animals:
Lev 17,10:   ואיש איש מבית ישראל ומן־הגר
Lev 17,12:   כל־נפש מכם ... והגר
Lev 17,13:   ואיש איש מבני ישראל ומן־הגר

• the presentation of a sacrifice:
Lev 17,8:   איש איש מבית ישראל ומן־הגר
Lev 22,18:   איש איש מבית ישראל ומן־הגר
• eating נבלה: Lev 17,15:   אזרח - גר
• sexual relations: Lev 18,26:   אזרח - גר
• Molech worship: Lev 20,2:   איש איש מבני ישראל ומן־הגר
• blasphemy: Lev 24,16:   גר - אזרח
• murder: Lev 24,22:   גר - אזרח

---

82   See p. 48.
83   אני יהוה אלהיכם (Lev 19,10.34; 23,22).
84   Lev 18,26; 20,2; 22,18.
85   In the case of blasphemy compare Ex 22,27 with Lev 24,16; in the case of murder:
     Ex 21,12 with Lev 24,21b-22; in the case of slaughter of animals: Deut 12,15-16.20-28
     with Lev 17,1-16.
86   Lev 17,8-9.10.13-14; 18,26-29. See Ex 12,19; Num 9,13-14.
87   Lev 20,2; 24,16.22.
88   Lev 17,15-16.

When the laws do not deal with the matter of holiness, they are addressed to the Israelite, the גר *(if mentioned), appears only as beneficiary of the law.* Such is the case of:
- laws concerned with the protection of the needy: Lev 19,10.33.34; 23,22.[89]
- laws concerned with the impoverished Israelite brother, such as those of Lev 25,35.47.47.47.[90]

This comparison shows that most of the references to the גר in the Holiness Code do not deal strictly with the גר but with the presevation of holiness, the גר is simply *mentioned* in these texts. In Lev 19,33.34, instead, the גר is the core of the prescription, not a tangential element.

It was mentioned above that *the laws concerned with the preservation of holiness* have sanctions. This is the case of the laws which use the כרת formula. In these cases, the definition of the audience and the transgression are described in the protasis, and the definition of the punishment in the apodosis:

	Protasis		Apodosis
	a Audience	b Transgression	Punishment
Lev 17,10:	If anyone of the house of Israel or the גר who reside among them ...	eats any blood	I will ... cut that person off from the people.
Lev 20,2:	Any of the people of Israel, or the גר who reside in Israel	who give any of their offspring to Molech	shall be put to death.
Lev 24,16:	The גר as well as citizens	when they blaspheme the Name of the Lord	shall be put to death.

The purpose of the laws concerned with the preservation of holiness, is not the integration of the גר*. The presence of the* גר *here is secondary.*

If we take into account that out of the eighteen references to the noun גר in the Holiness Code:
- four cases are reformulations of previous laws;
- in four cases the noun גר is used simply as a term of comparison[91],
- ten cases are laws concerned with the preservation of holiness and in which the role of the גר is clearly secondary, then, the contribution of the Holiness Code to the theme of the גר is rather modest. Strictly speaking, it does not say

---

89   In Lev 19,10 and 23,22 the גר is mentioned in relation to the עני.
90   In Lev 25,35.47 the גר is mentioned in relation to the תושב.
91   Lev 25,35.47.47.47.

anything new about the נר.[92] It simply includes him in some laws addressed
originally to the Israelites, and these were intended as preventive measure in
order to preserve the sanctity of the land.

3.2 The centrality of the notion of Holiness

A central feature of the Priestly world view is the belief that the world order
is a *created order* brought into being by Yahweh.[93]

"Order is brought about through divisions, separations, and distinctions between one element
and another (בדל). It is only as these lines of demarcation, or boundaries, are established
that order is realised".[94]

And F.C. Prussner states:

"Probably no major stream of tradition in the Old Testament is more theologically reflective
and integrated than the P-source. This material is organised and structured so as to present a
total world view and a structure of time, geography, cultural roles, weekly, seasonal, and
multiyear cycles, a view of the proper orders of life and how they interrelate, ritual and
routine for overcoming the disruptions in life and for the restoration of proper relationships
both between persons and between human and the divine".[95]

In the world of P there are, therefore, no loose elements, everything has a
place. The נר as one who lives in Israel has, consequently, a particular place
in the priestly society.[96] As we have already shown, in several laws of the
Holiness Code the נר is included only secondarily. He is referred to in some
prohibitive[97] or humanitarian[98] commandments. In some cases these texts are
reformulations of previous laws[99], or later additions.[100] These references to
the נר do not mean, therefore, that he is: "on the same footing as the native" in
relation to civil and religious matters.[101] These texts should be understood

---

92   Lev 19,34 depends on Deut 10,19, see p. 79 note 59.   Lev 25,23, a very important
      text, uses the noun נר metaphorically for the Israelites.
93   Schmid, Welt p. 31ff.
94   Gorman, Ideology p. 38. 41, quoted in Jenson, Holiness p. 215-216.
95   Hayes-Prussner, Theology p. 275. The division of history in epochs, together with a
      degree of chronological ordering, found in P, is considered by Hengel, a sign of a
      rational and systematic approach (Judaism p. 189).
96   See Joosten, People p. 54-73.
97   Lev 17,8.10.12.13.15; 18,26; 20,2; 22,18; 24,16.22.
98   Lev 19,10.33.34; 23,22.
99   See p. 48.
100 See p. 68-69.
101 See for instance Driver, Deuteronomy p. 165.

from the perspective of the encompassing notion of holiness which permeates the entire code.

3.2.1 The spatial dimension of Holiness

According to the priestly concept of *graded holiness*, there is a diminishing degree of holiness from the centre (the Holy of Holies, the Tabernacle, Israel) outwards. It is possible to detect different levels of this holiness spectrum. In the realm of the ritual, for instance, there is the dimension of the holy (קדוש), the clean (טהור) and the unclean (טמא). There are, accordingly, sacrificial animals, clean and unclean animals. But the *spatial* dimension of holiness is the clearest expression of this spectrum, both in its grading and its polarities.[102] The Tabernacle and the camp, for example, define a number of distinct zones or spheres, usually separated by clearly defined boundaries.[103] In this scheme, Israel stays at the centre, the non-Israelites in the periphery:

		Israel		Nations		
		Priesthood	=>	People	=>	Gentiles
God	=>					
		Temple	=>	Camp	=>	Wilderness
		Land		Earth [104]		

This *spatial* notion of holiness is important to understand the place of the גר in the Holiness Code: the same principle which explains the sequence outwards (Israel => the nations), explains inwards, the arrangement of the different social groups of the Israelite society. These groups may be ordered according to their *distance from the holy realm of the cult* :

---

102 Jenson, Holiness, p. 89.

103 Jenson, Holiness, p. 89-93. The narrative in P describes the camp with the tent of the meeting at the centre. Around the tent: the Levites, Aaron and his family, and in the outermost circle, the tribes. Beyond that, there is the wilderness, the realm of the profane, the Gentiles. Even specific narratives like the scene of the people at Sinai (Ex 19,10-25 24,1-18), are arranged according to this principle of the threefold degree of access to the holy. At Sinai, the *people* gather together near the altar at the foot of the mountain; the *priests* and elders take a closer approach. They go up to the Lord, worship and receive a vision. But only *Moses* goes further, enters the cloud and goes up the mountain and remains there. It is clear that there is a rough parallel between this narrative and those describing the material structure of the Tabernacle and the order of the camp. See Henton Davies, Art. Tabernacle, in: IDB, 4 p. 504.

104 Milgrom, Holiness p. 70.

the גר[105]

Priests => Levites => other tribes => unclean Israelites => non-Israel

the nations[106]

In a sacred society like that described in the priestly writings, it is the person's state of purity or impurity which determines his role in the society. In the chart above, the גר occupies an intermediate position between Israel and the nations.[107] According to this spatial notion of holiness, the nations which are closer to Israel are the ones which are more dangerous. The proximity of foreign elements may endanger Israel's security through the seduction of idolatry.[108] Due to this, the laws of the Holiness Code show a particular concern to govern the dealings of the Israelites with the Canaanites, and to adjust the conduct of the גר to the rules of cultic purity which preserve the holiness of land and people. In the parenetical framework of the legal code of Lev 18,6-23[109], the theme of the גר appears related to the presence of the surrounding nations, perceived as a threat for Israel.[110]

3.2.2 Holiness as common requirement

The residence of the גר "in Israel", directly affects the life of the community in matters which are decisive for the community. His residence must,

---

105 With a few exceptions (Lev 19,10.33.34; 23,22), the גר in the Holiness Code is a non-Israelite.

106 Jenson, Graded Holiness, p. 116.

107 See for example Milgrom, Leviticus p. 724-725.

108 Lev 18,1-5.24-30; 20,22-23.

109 Lev 18,3-5.24-30.

110 After the fall of Jerusalem the nations appear mainly as oppressors and plunderers. This idea permeates the writings of the Greek period (1 Macc 5,10.15; Esth 9,1-16; 11,2-12; Jud 8). The theme of the destruction of the Temple found in Mattathias's lamentation (1 Macc 2,6-14), is a permanent motif of this period. Note for instance the parallelism between *enemy* (ἐχθρῶν) and *alien* (ἀλλοτρίων) in 1 Macc 2,7 (cf. Bévenot, Makkabäerbücher p. 58). In 4Q Flor 1.1.3-5, this motif is adduced as rationale for the exclusion of strangers (בן נכר וגר) of "the Temple" (for the idea of the community as a Temple, see Dimant: 4Q Florilegium p. 165-189). The different theologies which took shape during and after the exile, share the common belief that the evil influence of the nations was a decisive factor for the disaster suffered by the nation, and that foreign nations represented a constant threat for Israel's future and security. This perception of the foreign nations explains the permanent fluctuation between the universalistic (Ruth and Jonah), and the particularistic tendencies (Joel, Ezra and Nehemiah) in the late writings of the Old Testament, see Horst, Art. Fremde, in: RGG[3] 2 col. 1126 and Altmann, Erwählungstheologie p. 1-29. The permanent struggle of Israel with other Palestinian states in post-exilic times, had a more persistent influence on its exilic and post-exilic history than the hurt inflicted on it by the great powers, see Müller, Phönikien p. 206.

therefore, be regulated. The holiness is not embodied in a limited group of persons (priests), animals (sacrifices), or in a space (sanctuary) but affects all: persons and animals, Israel and the גר.[111] The גר is included in some laws[112] because, just as the native Israelite, he draws his sustenance from the same sacral source (i.e. the common land).[113] *Both of them are, consequently, equally required to observe the code of holiness that this land entails.*[114] Just like every adult Israelite, the גר must also heed the prohibitive commandments, for their violation pollutes the land (Lev 18,26).[115]

Jewish scholars have drawn attention to the fact that the גר "is bound only by the prohibitive commandments not by the performative ones".[116] That is: "P imposes upon the גר only those obligations which affect the sanctity and purity of the congregation ... It does not require the גר to observe the regulations and ceremonies which are part of Israel's special religious heritage and which do not particularly involve ritual purity".[117] Among these prohibitive commandments we have:

• regulations concerning sacrificial procedures (Lev 17,8.10.12.13), in contrast to profane slaughter which is prohibited only to Israelites, Lev 17,2-7.[118]

• regulations concerning the impurity of incest, Lev 18,26; the impurity of נבלה, Lev 17,15 and the Molech worship, Lev 20,2.

• regulations concerning blasphemy, Lev 24,16.[119]

This explains why the references to the גר in the Holiness Code are (essentially[120]) prohibitions[121], or instructions followed by severe penalties in case of disobedience. The persons who do not obey the precepts:

---

111 Milgrom, Holiness p. 71.

112 Lev 17,8.10.12.13.

113 This is part of what Crüsemann calls "Heiligkeit als Rechtsprinzip" (Tora p. 355-360, espec. p. 359).

114 Weinfeld, DDS 229.

115 Milgrom, Art. Priestly Source, in: ABD, 5 p. 457.

116 Milgrom, Leviticus p. 1055.

117 See Weinfeld, DDS 231. Other obligations are: (1) the prohibition of eating leaven, whose presence was forbidden in Israelite territory during the Matzoth festival (Ex 12,19); (2) regulations concerning defilement by a corpse (Num 19,11); (3) the impurity of spilt blood (Num 35,15.34) and (4) the regulations concerning abstinence on the Day of Atonement (Lev 16,29).

118 See Milgrom, Leviticus p. 710-711.

119 Weinfeld, DDS p. 234.

120 Exceptions to this in the Holiness Code are: (1) the command to love the גר, Lev 19,34; (2) the reference to the plural form גרים in the motive clause of Lev 25,23; (3) the use of the noun גר as term of comparison in Lev 25,35 and (4) the reference to the Hebrew who is a slave of a גר in Lev 25,47. Exceptions to this in P are: the rules concerning animal sacrifices in Num 15,13-16 (see Noth, Numeri p. 101-102), and the references to the גר in the laws about the cities of refuge, Num 35,15; Jos 20,9.

121 Lev 17,12.13; 18,26; 22,18.

- shall be cut off from the congregation (כרת formula): Lev 17,8-9.10.13-14; 18,26-29.[122]
- shall be put to death (מות יומת formula): Lev 20,2; 24,16.22.
- or shall bear their own guilt: Lev 17,15.

Interestingly enough the גר is mentioned three times in the prescriptions about the *sin committed inadvertently*.[123] This fact witnesses the concern of the authors for the preservation of holiness and cultic purity in the land. There must be proper legislation to protect the community even in the eventuality of sin committed by a גר in ignorance! It must be noted that these punitive or preventive prescriptions of the Holiness Code are essentially different from those positive measures concerning the גר in the book of Deuteronomy.[124]

3.3 The גר in the Holiness Code: a proselyte?

In the late literature of the Old Testament there is a variety of *verbal* forms to designate those who join Israel:

1. Zech 2,15:   ונלוו גוים רבים
2. Is 56,3:   הנלוה בן־נכר
3. Is 56,6:   ובני הנכר הנלוים
4. Is 14,1:   ונלוה הגר
5. Esth 9,27:   כל־הנלוים
6. Esth 8,17:   ורבים ... מתיהדים[125]
7. Jdt 14,10:   ἐπίστευσεν ... περιετέμετο... προσετέθη
8. Tob 1,8 (א):   προσηλύτοις τοῖς προσκειμένοις[126]

This variety of expressions reflects the uncertainty of the authors in a transitional period. They were confronted with the reality of those who joined Israel, but had not yet found the commonly accepted, *nominal* technical term to

---

122 See Ex 12,19;   Num 9,13-14.

123 Num 15,26.29.30.

124 The גר in Deuteronomy is called to rejoice before the Lord during the pilgrimage festivals (16,11.14), and during the offering of the first fruits (26,11); to take part in the covenant ceremony (29,10), to learn to fear the Lord and to observe the law (31,12). These verbs (i.e. שמע; שמר; למד; ירא; קהל hi.: 31,12 and שמח: 16,11.14), have a particular theological weight within the language and theology of the book of Deuteronomy.

125 The participial form מתיהדים (Hith. den. from יהודי "to declare oneself Jew") is a reflexive denominative equivalent to the Greek verb ἰουδαΐζειν.

126 This Greek expression corresponds to the Hebrew הנלוים הגרים (similar to the construction ונלוה הגר in Is 14,1), Charles, APOT I p. 203; Kuhn, TWNT VI p. 735.

designate them.[127]   If the noun גר had in the Holiness Code a similar status to that of the later proselyte (as it is commonly assumed by several authors, see p. 49-50), it is difficult to see how some biblical authors hesitated about how to name those who joined Israel, if there already existed a standard word for this matter.   It is difficult to determine whether the references in Zech 2,15; Is 14,1 and 56,3.6 are later than the Holiness Code or not, but the references in Esth 9,27; Jdt 14,10 (and probably Tob 1,8) are, and in these texts as well, the same lack of consensus prevails about the term to designate them.   It seems clear, then, that at this stage the noun גר was not yet *the terminus technicus* for proselyte.   In fact, the idea of religious conversion in the Old Testament is in itself disputed.[128]   Furthermore, one could think that after the connection established in Is 14,1 between the terms גר and לוה niphal, the noun גר could become the standard designation for those who joined Israel in later references. But, as the references mentioned above show, this was not the case.   The relation between גר and לוה niphal in Is 14,1 brings the גר here *close* to the later proselyte.[129]   But this is not the case in the Holiness Code in which the verb לוה is not even attested.

Is 14,1 is no more than another attempt in the search for a definite nominal term for the person who joined Israel (see p. 74f.).   The later use of גר as *terminus technicus* for the proselyte (in the Mishna for instance[130]), could hardly have been established on the basis of this sole reference.   Is 14,1 is very unlikely *the* precedent upon which the equation גר = προσήλυτος was established.   This equation seems to have been exclusively an achievement of the LXX.

---

127   The term גלוים, as these examples make clear, was more frequently used than other terms.   Zeitlin's opinion that: "When conversion to Judaism was made possible, the term for it was מומר changer, i.e. one who changed his god for the God of Israel (Jer 2,11)" (Studies p. 410), does not seem to be correct.   The noun מומר was used, rather, as a derogatory term.   See for instance Levy / Fleischer / Goldschmidt, Wörterbuch III p. 51 on מומר.

128   Ohana, Biblica 55 p. 320-321;   Milgrom, JBL 101/102 p. 169-170;   Kaufmann, Religion p. 163-165;   300-301;   405.

129   In our opinion, texts like Ex 12,43;   Deut 31,12 and Ez 47,22 (גרים) cannot be considered references to religious "conversion".   Ex 12,19, the only other place in the Old Testament where we find the term γ(ε)ιώρας likewise does not seem to be an example of this.   Other late references to the גר are either: (1) extended uses of the term: Ps 39,13;   1 Chron 29,15;   Ps 119,19;   or (2) the plural form (גרים), which is used in connection with the anonymous masses of Canaanites, 1 Chron 22,2;   2 Chron 2,16. For the meaning of גר in Chronicles see Loewenstamm / Bláu, Thesaurus II p. 247 and Japhet, Ideology p. 334-351.

130   For the meaning of גר as "converted foreigner" in the Mishna see: mPeah 4,6;   mShebi 10,9;   mHal 3,6;   mPes 8,8;   mYeb 2,8;   11,2;   mKet 1,2.4;   3,1.2;   4,3;   9,9; mGit 2,6;   mKid 3,5;   mHul 10,4;   mBekh 8,1;   mNeg 7,1;   mZab 2,3.

As we have already mentioned, the noun גר often appears in the Holiness Code qualified by the verb גור.[131] This relationship with the verb גור gives to the noun גר a territorial or spatial dimension which is different from that of the גר used as a nominal technical term for religious convert. The noun גר is used in the Old Testament in general (and in the Holiness Code in particular[132]), mostly, in relation with a *territorial or spatial dimension* (i.e. the construction ב + גר)[133]:

a) in legal texts:

1. the גר in your cities: Ex 20,10
2. the גר in Egypt: Ex 22,20
3. the גר in Israel: Lev 22,18
4. the גר in your land: Lev 19,33
5. the גר in your camps: Deut 29,10

b) and in non-legal texts:

1. גר in the land: Jer 14,8
2. גר in the street: Job 31,32[134]

This means that one is גר *somewhere*.[135]   Even in Is 14,1 where the גר appears associated with the verb לוה niphal, this territorial aspect is still present: note the play between *Israel's land* (אדמתם, Is 14,1aγ) and *Yahwe's land* (אדמת יהוה, Is 14,2aγ).   This territorial or spatial dimension is overcome only when the noun גר is used in its full religious meaning, in the Mishna for instance.[136]

In the Qumran texts we can identify nine references to the noun גר: 4Q 464 3.2.3; 4Q Flor 1.1[4]; CD A col. VI, 21; 4Q Ord[a] 2[1]; 11QT 40[6]; CD A col.

---

131 The noun גר is qualified either by the participle הגר (Lev 17,10.12.13; 18,26; 19,34; 20,2) or by the imperfect יגור (Lev 17,8; 19,33).

132 Lev 17,8.10.12.13; 18,26; 19,33; 20,2; 22,18.

133 The combination הגר ב appears eight times in the Holiness Code: Lev 17,8.10.12.13; 18,26; 19,33; 20,2; 22,18: It appears seven times in P: Ex 12,49; Lev 16,29; Num 15,26.29; 19,10; 35,15; Jos 20,9; seven times in Deut: 5,12; 14,21.29; 16,14; 24,14; 26,12; 31,12; and one time in the Covenant code: Ex 20,10.

134 See also: הגירים ... בארץ ישראל (2 Chron 2,16).

135 For the use of the preposition ב for localisation in a place or territory, see Jenni, Präpositionen p. 173ff.

136 "From whom did they exact pledges? From Levites, Israelites, proselytes, freed slaves" (Shek 1,3); "And these are they that are liable to surcharge: Levites, Israelites, proselytes, freed slaves" (Shek 1,6); "They do not give a proselyte or a freed bondwoman to drink the waters of bitterness" (Eduy 5,6); "a gentile who became a proselyte" (Git 2,6); "The Ketubah of a female proselyte, captive or slave who was redeemed, proselytised or freed after the age of three years ..." (Ket 1,2.4); (translation from Danby, Mishna). In these references the "spatial dimension" is absent.

XIV 4.6; 4Q D[d] 11.2[10]; 4Q pNah 3.2[9]. From 4Q 464 3.2.[3] little has been preserved. In 4Q Flor 1.1[4]; CD A col. VI, 21; 4Q Ord[a] 2[1] and 11QT 40[6] גר has the meaning of "foreigner".[137] According to Mceleny proselytes formed a considerable segment of Diaspora communities.[138] In fact, while the גר is absent in the order of precedence of the community at Qumran[139], he is mentioned in the Damascus Document[140], which reflects a branch establishment with closer relationships with the surrounding community.[141] The similarity between the order given in the Damascus Document and that found in the Mishna (Shek 1,3.6)[142], where the noun גר is already used as a terminus technicus for proselyte, suggests that in CD A col. XIV 4.6 and 4Q D[d] 11.2[10] the noun גר was used with the sense of proselyte.[143] In 4Q pNah 3.2[9] the noun גר is used in association with the verb לוה niphal[144] as in Is 14,1 and Tob 1,8.[145] Here also the noun גר was probably used in the sense of proselyte.[146] The different renderings given to the noun גר in 4Q pNah 3.2[9] (as to several of the references listed above[147]) show, however, the lack of consensus existent among scholars about the exact meaning of this noun.[148]

---

137 In CD A col. VI,21 the noun גר is associated with אביון and עני; in 4Q Flor 1.1[4] with עמוני - מואבי - ממזר - בן נכר. On this important reference (i.e. 4Q Flor 1.1[4]) see Baumgarten, JJS 33 p. 215-225; idem, Studies p. 75-87; Blidstein, RQ 31/8 p. 431-435 and Brooke, Exegesis p. 101ff.

138 NTS 20 p. 325.

139 See for instance 1 QS 2,19-21: הכוהנים - והלויים - וכול העם; and in 1 QS 6,8: הכוהנים - והזקנים - וכול העם.

140 CD A col. XIV 4.6: הכהנים - והלוים - ובני ישראל - והגר.

141 See Deines, WUNT 70 p. 83 note 69.

142 "From whom did they exact pledges? From Levites, Israelites, proselytes, freed slaves" (Shek 1,3); "And these are they that are liable to surcharge: Levites, Israelites, proselytes, freed slaves" (Shek 1,6). These two references, which can be dated 70 before A.D., are probably the oldest instances from rabbinical Judaism; see Kuhn, TWNT, VI p. 736; Díez Macho, Targum p. 58-59.

143 Cf. Davies, JJS 46 p. 134-142. Maier thinks that taking into account the normal attitude of the Qumran community, is unlikely that גר in CD A col. XIV 4.6 can mean proselyte. He renders גר by *Fremdling* and explains that this term was added here due to the influence of the Old Testament laws (Texte II p. 60). On the attitude towards strangers in Qumran see Deines, WUNT 70 p. 58-91.

144 מלכים שרים כוהנים ועם עם גר נלום.

145 According to Kuhn, TWNT, VI p. 735; Charles, APOT 1 p. 203 and Díez Macho, Targum p. 58, behind the term προσκειμένοις in Tob 1,8 (א), we have the Hebrew הנלוים which is used here specifically for conversion to Judaism (Cf. Esth 9,27 כל-הנלוים).

146 See p. 103-104 and Japhet, Ideology p. 344ff.

147 Deines, WUNT 70 p. 82 note 67; p. 83 note 69; Baumgarten, RQ 8 p. 75 note; Davies, JJS 46 p. 136. Compare also texts like CD A col XIV 4.6 in the translation of Maier ("Fremdling", Texte 1 p. 64) García Martínez ("proselyte", Scrolls p. 573), Moraldi ("proselito", Manoscritti p. 260) and Dupont-Sommer ("prosélyte", Écrits p. 178); or 4Q Flor 1.1[4] in the translation of García Martínez ("prosélito", Textos p. 183)

3.4 Conclusion

The references of the Holiness Code in which the גֵר is referred to as the second wing of the Jewish community, can be understood as a legal accommodation to the *status quo* acquired by non-Jews, who joined Jewish communities during the Persian period. This new legislation expresses the concern of the Jewish authorities for the unification of the law to which the members of Jewish communities in the different provinces of the Persian empire were to be submitted.[149]

These laws attempted to prevent the defilement of the land in a time when concern for the sanctity and cultic purity of the congregation was particularly important, and their observance was a *condicio sine qua non* for the admission of the גֵר and his coexistence "in Israel".

This explains why late additions to the Holiness Code/P show a particular interest in defining, as clearly as possible, the conditions of membership in the community.   The priestly theology, based on practices, was particularly suitable for this purpose: it enabled anyone who followed these principles to become "as a native of the land".[150]   This explains the addition of the inclusion clause גֵּר-אֶזְרָח to several laws in the Holiness Code and P.   With the inclusion of this clause (which is a late addition[151]), old laws which did not include the גֵר were extended to subject him to the same prescriptions as the native.   In this way, the former legislation was adapted to the new circumstances of the Persian period.   This is, for instance, the case of the prescriptions about:

- blasphemy (Ex 22,27 => Lev 24,16)
- murder   (Ex 21,12 => Lev 24,21b-22)
- slaughter of animals (Deut 12,15-16.20-28 => Lev 17,1-16)

This interest of the Holiness Code and P in defining the conditions of membership in the community, explains also the addition of the

---

Moraldi ("forestiero", Manoscritti p. 573), Dupont-Sommer ("étranger", Écrits p. 409), Maier ("Fremdling", Texte 1 p. 185).

148 "Fremden" (Lohse, Texte p. 265; "proselytes" (García Martínez, Scrolls p. 339); "Stranieri" (Moraldi, Manoscritti p. 573; "prosélytes" (Dupont-Sommer, Écrits p. 363).

149 The phrase "in all your settlements" (בְּכָל־מוֹשְׁבֹתֵיכֶם), although referring originally to the land of Canaan (Ez 6,6.14), is used in relation to fundamental prescriptions which are to be kept in the Diaspora such as the unleavened bread, the Sabbath, the prohibition to eat fat or blood, and the day of atonement (Ex 12,20; Ex 35,3; Lev 23,3; Lev 3,17.26; Lev 23,31).   In these cases, the phrase refers to the Jewish Diaspora, see Grelot VT 6 p. 178f.

150 Ex 12,48; Num 9,14.

151 See Elliger, Leviticus p. 201; 218; 230; 243; 331; 332; Noth, Leviticus p. 108; 115-16; 124; Kornfeld, Leviticus p. 69; 79; 96-97.

excommunication formula (ונכרתה הנפש ההוא). A study of the historical development of this formula shows a tendency to restricted use:

- the person is first "cut off" from his *relatives:* מעמיו plural form,
- then, "cut off" from *Israel:* מעמה singular form,
- finally, "cut off" from the *religious community:* מעדת ישראל.[152]

In this connection, it is important to note that both the Holiness Code and P take the integration of persons of non-Jewish origin for granted. They do not question nor discuss the issue as was done in other circles (Is 56,3-6; Ez 44,6-9). Their approach is pragmatic, it answers the question: *what should be done if a* גר *living in Israel wants* ... to offer an offering, to celebrate Passover or if he blasphemes Yahweh's name?   The Holiness Code and P simply acknowledge the presence of the גר among the people, and attempt to define the rules which provide for the preservation of holiness in the land. If we think in the urgent need of a document which could unify and simplify the Jewish legislation in different parts of the Persian empire, it is easy to understand the pragmatic approach which guided the priestly editors, who were more interested in finding an acceptable internal consensus than in raising sensitive questions about problematic issues. They were simply interested in ruling a situation *de facto*.

Some authors explain the priestly legislation in function of a "Reichsautorisation".[153] It is assumed that the basic form of P, composed in Persian times, was written among other reasons, aiming at imperial recognition: the *Jewish authorities* were interested in getting the support of the Persian imperial organization to secure their cultural and religious identity; the *Persian authorities* were interested in unifying the legislation to which all the Jews in their empire were to be subject.[154]

It is true that the Persian authorities were interested in the region as well as in the compilation of local legislation. In the middle of the V century BC, after the revolts of Inaros (460) and Megabyzos (448) in Egypt, Persia had a particular interest in the pacification and stability of Palestine. Political conspirators and revolts in Egypt were one of the major concerns of the Persian

---

152 Hasel uses the terms: "*Sippen*gemeinschaft", "*Bundesvolks*gemeinschaft" and "*Kult*gemeinschaft" to speak about these different levels (TWAT, IV col. 362-364, italics is ours); see also Zimmerli, ZAW 66 p. 17-18.

153 See Blum, Studien p. 346ff; Crüsemann, Tora p. 381ff. On the "Reichsautorisation" see Frei, ZABR 1 p. 1-31 (with bibliography).

154 Speaking about the point of view of the Persian Administration, Grelot states: "Reconnaissant dans le judaïsme une communauté autonome régie par sa loi propre, elle ne pouvait que désirer voir cette loi fixer et les conditions d'appartenance au judaïsme se préciser rigoureusement. Ainsi tous les juifs bénéficieraient-ils d'une protection officielle pourvu que, se conformant au statut légal établi uniformément pour eux dans tout l'empire, ils pussent à bon droit se réclamer de la communauté d'Israël" (VT 6 p. 179).

authorities.[155]   This is the political background in which Ezra and Nehemiah's activities should be understood.[156]   Due to the diversity of peoples which conformed the empire, it was impossible to have one unified royal code for all. This explains the interest of the Persian authorities in the compilation of local codification.[157]   An example of this is the codification of the Egyptian laws by Darius[158], whose intention was "das altägyptische Recht als für die Satrapie Ägypten reichsrechtlich verbindlich darzustellen".[159]

On religious matters, it was policy of the Achemenids to cooperate with the authorities of religious communities as long as these were homogeneous, widespread religions.[160]   With the imperial ratification of ancient local laws, they intended to neutralize discontent and opposition and to win the loyalty of the local ruling class.   According to in der Smitten, Ezra was appointed with the purpose of strengthening the faction loyal to the empire.   His designation intended to change the political balance in Jerusalem and assure stability.[161] The royal administration, which aimed at the unification of the law to which all the Jews of the empire were submitted, expected its final codification as result of Ezra's activities in Jerusalem.[162]

The "Reichsautorisation", it is assumed, gave the Jewish communities of the empire a particular status to which specific rights were attached.[163]   This point might help to understand the growing presence of גרים among Jewish communities during the Persian empire, which can hardly be explained on the sole basis of religious motivations.   In such case, *this status must have been a sort of accommodation to the status quo of the new members of Jewish communities, which was later object of a religious development.*

---

155 Donner, Geschichte p. 451; 431-432; In der Smitten, Esra p. 113-114; 118.

156 Donner, Geschichte p. 451.   Two basic elements in relation with Ezra 7 are commonly accepted: that a basic form of the text refers in fact to a Persian document, and that the legal relationships presupposed in the text reflect a historical fact, see Blum, Studien p. 348-349 notes 55 and 59.

157 In der Smitten, Esra p. 117.   Blum speaks of "Anerkennung von Normen lokaler Körperschaften..." (Studien p. 346).

158 Porten, Archives p. 22 note 87.

159 In der Smitten, Esra p. 116-117.

160 Speaking about Darius' effect on religious matters, Porten explains that: "In *Asia Minor* he ordered the satrap Gadates to respect certain rights and privileges of the sacred gardeners of Apollo.   In *Judah* he ordered the pehah Tattenai to supply whatever material was necessary for the building of the Temple there and to provide sacrifices to be offered in the name of the royal family (Ez. 5:17-6:12).   In *Egypt* he restored the House of the goddess Neith at Sais, contributed to temples at Edfu and Abusir, and displayed his liberality toward other sanctuaries as well" (Archives p. 23, underlining is ours); that is, he returned to the religious authorities the state contributions for the cult that Cambyses had taken away.   The translation of the corespondent texts which illustrate these measures are given in Vincent, RJAE p. 258-263.

161 Smitten, Esra p. 114; 117.

162 Grelot, VT 5 p. 250-265.

163 Frei / Koch, Reichsidee p. 21-23.

According to Wiesehöfer, however, the measures mentioned by P. Frei (see footnote 163) were not part of Darius *religious* policies, but the religious implications of Darius's *administrative* policies. In his opinion, what P. Frei calls "Reichsautorisation" was no more than regional agreements in some administrative matters that were not so general and which did not include religious deals.[164] The suggestion of a Reichsautorisation is attractive. The problem of the interpretation of Darius's measures remains, however, open.

In sum, if we take into account that the Old Testament knows only verbal forms to name those who *joined* Israel, the explanation of the term גר by means of the later proselyte seems, therefore, inappropriate.[165] The fact that *the* גר, is presented as being subject to some of the same laws as the Israelite, does not necessarily means that he had a status similar to the one held by the later proselytes.[166] The religious duties required of the גר in the Holiness Code represent rather, the minimal request of the Israelite hosts to the גר in order to ensure the preservation of holiness in the land, which is a central motif of the Holiness Code.

---

164 ZABR 1 p. 36-46.

165 The noun גר is used in the Holiness Code only with a *territorial* dimension (i.e. verb
     גור + preposition ב), not with a religious one. It was only later, when the noun גר
     became properly a religious technical term (in the Mishna for example), that the noun
     גר was used without this territorial dimension.

166 Nödelke sees in the requirement of the circumcision the "Uebergang des politischen
     Begriffs 'Fremdling' in den religiösen 'Proselyt'" and states:"Es ist daher nicht zu
     verwundern, wenn das spätere Judenthum, von dem Irrthum ausgehend, daß die
     Bestimmungen des Pentateuchs von jeher wirkliche Gesetze gewesen, ja daß das
     israelitische Alterthum ganz im Licht der spätern Schulentwickelung zu betrachten sei,
     auch an vielen Stellen des A.T. Proselyten fand, wo wir einfache Schutzgenossen sehen"
     (Art. Fremde, in: BiL 2 p. 301).

4. The individual גר

As it was shown in the previous two chapters, the noun גר normally appears mentioned together with other characters. In the book of Deuteronomy, for instance, the גר is mentioned among the *personae miserae* ("גר-orphan-widow") or among some other members of the community ("sons, daughters, male/female servants, Levites"). In the priestly writings, the גר is mentioned as a polar category together with the אזרח and the בני ישראל. There are a few late references only in which the גר is mentioned by itself. In this chapter we analyze two of these references which have a particular theological weight.

4.1 Isaiah 14,1

The prose introduction to the poem in Is 14,4b-21 is the latest stage in the history of the formation of this chapter.[1] There is wide agreement about the late date of Is 14,1-4a[2] based on stylistic[3] and theological[4] grounds. The formation of this chapter can be described as follows:

• Is 13,2-22 (an oracle against Babylon) and Is 14,4b-21 (an ironical lament for the death of a world ruler), were originally independent. Is 14,1 was added as a conclusion to chapter 13.[5] This addition intended to show the implications

---

1   Fohrer sees three stages in the history of the formation of chapter 14: (1) the composition of the poem in V. 4b-21; (2) the reworking of V. 5 with the inclusion of Yahweh's name; (3) the inclusion of the frame V. 1-4a + 22-23 in prose, Jesaja I p. 190-193.

2   Duhm, Jesaja p. 92; Procksch, Jesaja p. 193.; Quell, FS F. Baumgärtel p. 136-145; Kaiser, Jesaja II p. 22; Wildberger, Jesaja p. 524-527; Barth, Jesaja-Worte p. 126; Vermeylen, Isaïe p. 294-296.

3   See for example: (1) the use of לוה niphal in v.1b, a typical post-exilic verb, Is 56,3.6; Esth 9,27; Dan 11,34; (2) the use of the expression בחר ב, which appears often in Deutero Is (41,24; 44,1.2), and in Trito Is (56,4; 66,3.4) and (3) the use of the term רחם in Is 49,10.13.15; 54,8.10; 55,7.

4   See for example: (1) the ambivalence between the conversion of individuals and the pilgrimage of the nations, a feature of the exilic and post-exilic prophecy; (2) the convergence of the image of the rule over the oppressors (Is 49,22-23; Is 60-62), that speaks about a late date (Dion, Universalismo p. 137-138); and (3) the idea of Babylon's destruction as sign of Yahweh's compassion, that -according to Duhm- is a typical late idea (Jesaja p. 92).

5   Erlandsson, CBOTS 4 p. 119; Feldmann, Isaias p. 176. According to Wildberger "V. 1 ist formal und gedanklich eine geschlossene Einheit" (Jesaja p. 524).

that the judgment against Babylon (13,2-22) had for Israel: the sufferings of the past and the present will culminate in a glorious future. God will bring an end to their sufferings.[6]

• A later author understood the ironical lament for the death of a world ruler (Is 14,4b-21), in the light of the preceding chapter (13,2-22) and added 14,3-4a and vv. 22-23. The name of Babylon was associated with the song in the two additions of 14,3-4a and 22-23[7], which provide the redactional framework for the lament. The verb היה (from the opening formula והיה ביום in v. 3aα) serves as a link between the song in 14,3-22. and the introduction in v. 1.[8]

• Is 14,2 is probably the latest addition.[9] An author who had a different idea about the relation between Israel and the nations added this verse later.[10]

There are interesting similarities between Is 14,1 and other prophetic texts:
• Is 14,1 and Zechariah 1-8:
– both use the expression "ובחר עוד ב": Zech 1,17; 2,16[11]
– both use the form לוה niphal: Zech 2,15[12]
– there is also a probable relation between Is 14,1aγ and Zech 2,26[13]
• Is 14,1 and Ez 47,22:
– both texts address the same themes of "גר" and "land".
– no requisite like circumcision or the keeping of the Sabbath is mentioned for the גר in any of these two texts.

Taking into account these elements, it can be concluded that Is 14,1 is a post-exilic text.[14] It is important to note that the noun גר is used here with nearly the same meaning which is used later.[15] As A. Geiger appropriately states: "Die Worte (Jes 14,1): ונלוה הגר עליהם, 'es schliesst der Ger sich (den Israeliten) an', sagen aus, dass der Ger als solcher noch nicht dem

---

6   See Schökel, Profetas p. 177 and Kilian, Jesaja II p. 101.

7   "the King of Babylon" (14,4a) and "Babylon" (14,22a).

8   See Erlandsson, CBOTS 4 p. 121 and GKC § 112 *y-z*.

9   Vermeylen, Isaïe p. 296.

10   Wildberger, THAT I col. 293.

11   See also Zech 3,2. For the meaning and discussion of the theological problems involved in the expression בחר עוד see Wildberger, TB 66 p. 322; idem, THAT I col. 292-293 and Seebaß, TWAT I col. 602; 606.

12   On לוה niphal see below notes 18 and 19.

13   See Duhm, Jesaja p. 92.

14   Procksch, Jesaja p. 193; Wildberger, Jesaja p. 538; Vermeylen, Isaïe p. 296; Clemens, Isaiah p. 138; Fohrer Jesajah I p. 192; Gray, Isaiah p. 233; Duhm, Jesaja p. 88. According to Vermeylen "il est probable cependant que le v. 1b constitue une nouvelle addition" (Isaïe p. 296); Duhm, Jesaja p. 92 states: "Der Zusammenhang hätte nicht darauf geführt, schon an גרים zu denken", and according to Kaiser, 14,1b interrupts the relation between 14,1a and 2a (Jesaja II, p. 23).

15   See HAL I p. 227; Marti, Jesaja p. 122; Dillmann / Kittel, Jesaja p. 131; Cheyne, Isaiah p. 73.75.313; Pope, Proselyte, in: IDB 3 p. 922; Procksch, Jesaja p. 193; Gray, Isaiah p. 246; Kaiser, Jesaja II p. 92; Feldmann, Isaias p. 177 and Bultmann, Der Fremde p. 190.

Judenthume angehört, aber es ist darin der Sprachgebrauch angebahnt von dem sich anschliessenden Ger, der dann absolut zu einem solchen wird".[16]

According to Is 14,1: "The גר will be joined (וְנִלְוָה) to Israel", that is, he is one of the נלוים.[17] After the Exile[18], the verb לוה niphal was used (almost as *terminus technicus*[19]) to designate the non-Israelites who joined Israel[20] and Yahweh.[21] Not only the גר (Is 14,1) and the בן נכר (Is 56,3.6), but *even* the גוים (Zech 2,15) joined the Lord and his people. The ambivalence found in some prophetic texts about the joining of *individuals* and the joining of *peoples* is a hint of the uncertainty which existed among biblical authors in relation to the nature and extension of the movement which was taking place at the time.[22]

• On the one hand, we have those texts which speak about the nations in the plural: "Many nations shall join themselves to the Lord on that day" (Zech 2,15); "at that time all the nations shall gather (in Jerusalem)" (Jer 3,17); "Many peoples and strong nations shall come to seek the Lord" (Zech 8,22).

• On the other hand, texts like Zech 8,23 juxtapose the nations with individual men who join the Jews: "in those days ten men.. shall take hold of a Jew and ... say 'Let us go with you, for we have heard that God is with you", see also Is 60.[23]

• There are also texts which deal with individual נלוים. Is 14,1 for example speaks about the גר and Is 56,3.6 about the בן נכר.[24]

What these prophets witnessed was probably no more than individual cases of persons who joined Israel (Is 44,5; 56,3.6; Zech 8,23), but their expectation never let go of the hope of seeing the entire world coming to Jerusalem (Jer 3,17; Zech 8,20-22; Is 49,22-23).[25]

It is interesting to note that Is 14,1 shares with other late texts like Deut 10,19, a very positive attitude towards the גר. Unlike the command to love the גר in Deut 10,19, which is based on *historical reasons* (Israel's forefathers

16   Geiger, Urschrift p. 352-353.

17   Is 56,3; Esth 9,27. See Donner, Aufsätze p. 81-95 and Bardtke, Esther p. 680-681.

18   In nine out of eleven total references, לוה is post-exilic: Num 18,2.4; Is 14,1; 56,3.6; Jer 50,5; Zech 2,15; Esth 9,27; Dan 11,34. Exceptions to this are probably Gen 29,34 and Ps 83,9. On Zech 2,15 see Petit-Jean, Oracles p. 92-93 and Hanhart, Sacharja p. 133.

19   "Anders als לוה in (Esther) 8[17] scheint נלוים einen geregelten Anschluß an die Juden zu bezeichnen. Ähnliche Spuren eines anfänglichen Proselytentums finden sich besonders in einigen meistens späten Prophetenstellen (Jes 14[1]; 56[3.6]; Sach 2[15]), wo das Ni. von לוה fast als ein technischer Terminus verwendet wird" (Gerleman, Esther p. 140).

20   Is 14,1; Esth 9,27. See also Dan 11,34.

21   Is 56,3.6; Zech 2,15. See also Jer 50,5.

22   See p. 64ff. and Dion, Universalismo p. 126-128.

23   If we understand Is 14,1-2 as a unit, as several authors do, it would belong here but we take Is 14,1 as an independent unit (see p. 72 note 5).

24   Esth 9,27 speaks about כל הנלוים.

25   See Dion, Universalismo p. 125-126.

were accepted and lived among the Egyptians, Deut 23,8; 26,5), the integration of the גֵּר in Is 14,1 is not based on historical but on *eschatological grounds*.[26] Is 14,1 like Ez 47,22-23 is oriented towards the future. It presents an eschatological view of Israel's future, which mirrors the great events of her past.[27]

- As Yahweh chose Israel (Ex 19,5) and brought her to Palestine (Ex 19,17) ... He will choose Israel again and will bring her back home, Is 14,1.
- As other peoples joined Israel before (Num 11,4) ... the גֵּר will join Israel too, Is 14,1.[28]
- As they were freed from their former slavery (Ex 1,14) ... they will be free from her present captivity, Is 14,1.[29]

It must also be noted that the motif of the *blessing to the nations* becomes fainter in the post-exilic times.[30] The motif of *nations bowing down* before Yahweh-Israel, on the contrary, becomes prominent in the exilic and post-exilic prophecies:

"The descendants of those who oppressed you
shall come bending low to you,
and all who despise you
shall bow down at your feet;
they shall call you the city of Yahweh
the Zion of the Holy One of Israel" (Is 60,14).[31]

---

26 The confusion of the Israelites after the fall of Jerusalem demanded an explanation. Israel had not been able to match Babylon's military power on an historical level, and salvation did not come as expected. Were the gods of the nations simply idols as the prophets used to say (Is 40,18-20; Jer 10,1-16)? How long should they wait to see Yahweh's punishment over the enemies (Lam 1,21-22; 3,64-66)? It was under these circumstances that eschatology grew. The prophets took these concrete events and transformed them into an universal event which involved all the nations (Is 41,1.5; 49,1), see Dion, Universalismo p. 87. As J. de Senarclens states: "Tout l'ancien Orient est ainsi bouleversé pour la seule raison que ce petit peuple (i.e. Israel) doit être vaincu ou reconduit dans son pays" (Le Mystère de l'histoire, Paris 1949 p. 163; 182, quoted in Martin-Achard, Israël p. 17).

27 See Fohrer, Jesajah I p. 193.

28 It is true that the integration of the גֵּר in Is 14,1 follows the pattern of the first exodus, but there is a significant difference between the "mixed crowd" of Ex 12,38 or "the rabble" of Num 11,4 and the גֵּר of Is 14,1. The reference to the גֵּר in Is 14,1 is no longer a marginal note but the description of the new Israel. A community in which there will be only one law for both of them (Ex 12,49; Lev 24,22; Num 9,14; 15,15.16.29).

29 According to Is 14,1-4a, at the end the nations will have two alternatives before Israel: either conversion or submission. Is 14,2a, for instance, mentions the slaves (עֲבָדִים - שְׁפָחוֹת) and the captives (שֹׁבִים); see also the use of the noun עֶבֶד in Is 60,10-12.

30 Zech 8,13; 9,9-10.

31 Is 25,6-8; 49,7.22-23; 60,3.10-12.14.16; 61,5; Zech 2,10-17; 14,16.

The question in relation to Is 14,1 is: if *the nations* are rejected and called into submission, how can the attitude towards *the individual* גר be so positive?[32]

The pilgrimage of the *nations* to Zion is a common image in post-exilic prophecy. It was a sign of Israel's vindication among the nations after the fall of Jerusalem, Is 60. The incorporation into the Jewish community is seen, however, in *individual* terms. B. Duhm commenting on Is 44,5 states: "Nicht als Völker wie c. 22 ff., sondern als Privatpersonen treten die Fremden zu Israel über".[33]   And this is understandable because individuals can more easily be assimilated: religiously, they are dependent on Israel's God; politically, they are not organized and, consequently, do not represent a threat for Israel's existence.   The גוים - עמים, on the contrary, meet Israel as political entities with their own religions; as nations who fight for their existence and rights on equal grounds with Israel. The difference between "individuals" joining Israel and עמים - גוים lies, therefore, not in their essential character but in the way Israel relates to them.[34]

From this perspective, *the incorporation of non-Jews was a sign of Israel's pre-eminence among the nations,* (Zech 8,20-23), in the words of Causse: "l'acte préliminaire de la restauration messianique".[35]   The גר is, then, part of that remnant among the nations who will be joined to Israel, Is 14,1.[36]   He will

---

32   In Is 14,1 the גר is already a non Israelite: "Die gerim sind hier (Jes 14,1) augenscheinlich nicht bloß Metöken, sondern Heiden, die zum Gott der Juden übertreten" (Duhm, Jesaja p. 92); and Kaiser states on the term גר in Is 14,1: " ... Es kann sich mindestens auch um die Nichtisraeliten handeln, die sich in der Diaspora zum Judentum hingezogen fühlten" (Jesaja II p. 23).

33   Duhm, Jesaja p. 303 on Is 44,5.   According to Westermann, Deutero-Isaiah: "erwartet nicht, daß die Israel umgebenden Völker dann mit einem Schlage und insgesamt sich dem Jahweglauben zuwenden. Vielmehr kündigt er an, daß es Einzelne sein werden, die sich dem Gott Israels und damit auch dem Gottesdienst Israels zuwenden werden. ... Für dieses neue Verständnis der Gottesgemeinde ist es nun besonders wichtig, wie der Prophet die Zugehörigkeitserklärung der von außerhalb Israels hinzukommenden beschreibt: 'der sagt ... der nennt sich ... der schreibt auf seine Hand ...' Mit all diesen Verben ist das Bekenntnis zu Israels Gott beschrieben, das auf persönlicher Entscheidung beruht" (Jesaja, p. 112).

34   "Es ist z.B. für das Dt kennzeichnend, dass ihm nicht eine Beschreibung des Wesens der Völker, sondern nur eine Darstellung der 'Völkergefahr' zu entnehmen ist .. Welche Gefahren liegen für Israel in der Existenz anderer Völker? Mit welchen Mitteln sind diese Gefahren abzuwehren?" (Bächli, Israel p. 13 note 12; see also p. 11; 44; 67-69).

35   Causse, EHPR 8 p. 62.   Kaiser considers: "daß das Verhältnis zwischen Israel und den Völkern (*gôjim*) in seiner Exclusivität und seiner darob nicht zu übersehenden Universalität durch die jüdische Erwählungsgewißheit bestimmt wurde" (JRP 14 p. 68).

36   Just as there is a rest among the Israelites (Is 46,3: שארית בית ישראל; Is 37,32: פליטה מהר ציון), there is also a rest among the nations (Is 45,20: פליטי הגוים).

also be taken along with the house of Jacob and be brought again into the land, Is 14,1; Ez 47,22-23.[37]

We have already mentioned the ambivalence between *individuals* and *peoples* mentioned as נלוים in post-exilic times.[38] It must be noted that in the case of the גר we are always dealing with single individuals and not with communities.[39] In Is 14,1 this tension between the individual and the peoples is clearly seen in the opposition between the terms גר and עמים: while the גר will *join* Israel (14,1bα), the עמים will *be possessed* by Israel (14,2a)! This tension is not something new. One can compare it:

• to the different attitudes found in the Book of the Covenant towards *individual* foreigners (Ex 23,9.12)[40] and foreign *peoples* (Ex 23,20-33)[41];

• to the sharp difference found in Deuteronomy between the גר mentioned in the laws on humanitarian behavior[42], and the עמים - גוים mentioned in relation to the חרם in the laws of warfare[43];

• to the difference between the גר and the גוים in the Holiness Code.[44] In the post-exilic period this attitude hardened: "Dieselbe Gemeinde, die dem 'Ger' ihre Arme öffnete, verschloß sich in um so strengerer Zurückhaltung den heidnischen Völkern rings umher".[45]

---

37 This attitude towards the גר should not be, however, immediately understood as pure universalism. It is true that in P we witness a growing tendency to his integration into the religious community, but as Bousset rightly states: "Dennoch kann man hier noch nicht von eigentlich universaler Tendenz reden. Vielmehr war die wirklich treibende Kraft bei dieser Entwicklung gerade der echt jüdische Partikularismus, das Bestreben, das heilige Land um den Tempel von allem heidnischen Unwesen zu reinigen und zu befreien. Dieselbe Gemeinde, die dem 'Ger' ihre Arme öffnete, verschloß sich in um so strengerer Zurückhaltung den heidnischen Völkern rings umher ... Im ganzen und großen deckten sich doch die Größen jüdisches Volkstum und jüdische Religion noch immer. Wirklich universalen Tendenzen begegnen wir sehr selten" (Bousset-Greßmann, Religion p. 77). See also Bertholet, Stellung p. 168 and Causse EHPR 8 p. 26.

38 See p. 74.

39 The consistent use of the noun גר in singular form is well illustrated by texts like Deut 29,10 in which, despite being quoted among plural forms, גר is used in singular form: טפכם נשיכם וגרך. Ez 47,22 is the *only* reference in the plural form in which the noun גר is used in a similar text to those found in the laws (P and Deut) and in Is 14,1.

40 On Ex 23,9-12 see Schwienhorst-Schönberger, Bundesbuch p. 378-393.

41 On Ex 23,20-33 see Schmitt, Frieden p. 13-24 and Crüsemann, Tora p. 209-213.

42 Deut 24,14.17.19-21. On the different protective measures taken in Deut on behalf of the גר see van Houten, Alien p. 83ff. 92ff.; Bultmann, Der Fremde p. 35ff. and Causse, RHPR 13 p. 289-323.

43 Deut 20,10-15: גוים; Deut 20,16-18: עמים. As Bächli states: "Wir stellen fest, dass die gôjim nach dem Dt grosse und schreckhafte Feinde sind, gekennzeichnet durch ihre רשעה, ihre תועבות und ihren falschen Gottesdienst. Zusätze zum ursprünglichen Bestand des Dts ziehen daraus die Konsequenzen: Wendet Jahve Israels Geschick, dann werden die gôjim arm, bedürftig und unterworfen sein", Bächli, Israel p. 34 and Rofé, Laws p. 33ff.

44 Lev 18,24-30; 25,35.44.

45 Bousset-Greßmann, Religion p. 77.

In sum, the pilgrimage of the nations to Jerusalem plays an important role in the eschatological oracles of the post-exilic prophets, Yahweh will finally vindicate Israel for the humiliation suffered under former enemies.   The גר mentioned in Is 14,1 belongs to this eschatological picture.   The presence of the גר among Yahweh's community in post-exilic times, is a sign of Israel's vindication.   The distinction between individuals and peoples is, however, sharp: while the attempt to integrate the individual is clear (Is 56,3ff.), the nations are still seen as a threat and rejected.[46]

4.2 Deut 10,19

Deut 10,19 is part of the parenetical section 10,12-11,32 which immediately precedes the deuteronomic Code.[47]   The combination "ועתה" in 10,12aα[48] introduces a shift in the argumentative approach and marks the transition from the *historical* survey (Deut 9,7-10,11) to the *moral-religious* implications to be drawn from it (Deut 10,12-11,7).[49]   Since the unit Deut 10,12-11,7 is a late addition, the connection between these two sections is secondary.[50]   The composition of the section 10,12-11,7 is complex.[51]   Two things are, however, clear:

1) This section has its setting in the realm of liturgy.[52]   Not only the language[53] but its affinities with Ps 146 suggest this:

---

46   See Stählin, TWNT V p. 11.

47   The name Israel (ישראל ועתה 10,12aα) appears in Deuteronomy in the parenetical sections: 4,1a; 5,1a; 6,3a.4a; 9,1a; 10,12a; 20,3a.   See Merendino, Gesetz p. 286.

48   The preposition ועתה "bildet immer den Wendepunkt der Erörterung" (Brongers, VT 15 p. 299); "mit ועתה kommt eine Erörterung oder Ansprache zu ihrer eigentlichen Aussage, zu dem Punkt, an dem aus dem Bisherigen gefolgert wird" (Seitz, Studien p. 83). See also Jos 24,14 and Ex 19,5.

49   See for example the interesting shift from a lyrical to a rhetorical tone in Is 5,1-5, where ועתה (vv. 3.5) separates the three stages of discussion (Schökel, Estudios p. 147).

50   Preuß, Deuteronomium p. 103 and Lohfink, Hauptgebot p. 229-230.

51   See Mayes, SBTS 3 p. 212-213; idem: Deuteronomy p. 207-209; Seitz, Studien p. 81ff.; Lohfink, Hauptgebot p. 219ff.; Nielsen, Deuteronomium, p. 120; von Rad, Deuteronomium p. 59-61.

52   Bultmann, in his analysis of Deut 10,19, points out the connection between Deut 10,14 and Ps 24,1 to explain "den Hintergrund, vor dem 10,17-19 erwachsen sind" (Der Fremde p. 125).   The connection between the themes of the creative power of Yahweh and that of Yahweh's justice and care on behalf of the defenseless is present rather in Ps 146.   The process of formation of 10,12-11,7 shows, besides, that vv. 17-19 have only a secondary relation to Deut 10,14.

53   Compare, for instance, the statement in Deut 10,17: Yahweh as "God of Gods" and "Lord of Lords", with Ps 136,2.3; and Deut 10,17: Yahweh as "the great, the mighty, the awesome", with Neh 9,32.

Psalm 146		Deut 10	
6aα:	Yahweh made heaven and earth	14a:	heaven ... and earth belong to Yahweh
6aβ:	... and all that is in them	14b:	and all that is in it
7aα:	who executes justice for the ...	18aα:	who executes justice for the ...
7aβ:	who gives bread to the ...	18aγ:	giving bread and clothing to the...
8b:	Yahweh loves the ...	18bα:	(Yahweh) loves the ...
9aα:	Yahweh watches over the נרים	18bα:	(Yahweh) loves the נר
9aβ:	he upholds	18a:	who executes justice
	the orphan and the widow.		for the orphan and the widow.

The relation of Ps 146,6-9 to Deut 10,14-18 is strengthened by the following facts:

• The terms "widow - orphan" are usually found in this particular word-order in the Old Testament. The word-order "orphan - widow" is found in those references in which this pair forms a triad with the term נר, which comes always in the first place: "1. נר => 2. orphan => 3. widow". Ps 146,9 and Deut 10,18 are the only two references in the entire Old Testament in which this *pair* (apart from the references to the triad), follows the order "1. orphan => 2. widow".

• In both cases we are dealing with hymnic participles in series: Ps 146: עשׂה (V. 6a; 7a); שׁמר (V. 6b; 9a); נתן (V. 7a); אהב (V. 8b); Deut 10: עשׂה (V. 18a); אהב (V. 18b).

• The pair "widow-orphan" is found in texts in which human beings are subjects of the action. Such verses are either accusations against the Israelites *who oppress* the widow and the orphan[54], or commands *not to oppress* them.[55] Ps 146,9 and Deut 10,18 are the *only* two texts in which Yahweh is the subject of the action. Only in these two texts the actions mentioned in relation with the orphan and widow, are something which is done *on behalf of* them and not *against* them.

2) Deut 10,17-19 is not a unit[56], the verse 19 is an addition.[57] While V. 17-18 combine material from other sources[58], V. 19a. is *unique* in the Old Testament.[59] This verse is part of the secondary material of the Deuteronomic

---

54 Is 1,23; Job 22,9; 24,3; Ps 10,2; 94,6; Ez 22,7; Mal 3,5.

55 Ex 22,21; Zech 7,10. See also Jer 7,6; 22,3.

56 As it is taken, for instance, by Bultmann, Der Fremde p. 121ff.

57 Braulik, Deuteronomium p. 84; Tigay, Deuteronomy p. 108; Mayes, Deuteronomy p. 211; Weinfeld, Deuteronomy p. 440; Cholewiński, Heiligkeitsgesetz p. 275.

58 See for instance the case of the following phrases: Yahweh as God of Gods and Lord of Lords (Deut 10,17): Ps 136,2.3; Yahweh as the great, the mighty, the awesome (Deut 10,17): Neh 9,32; Yahweh as one who does not show favour in judgement (Deut 10,17): Deut 1,16; Lev 19,15; Yahweh as one who does not take bribe (Deut 10,17): Deut 16,19; Yahweh as one who executes justice (Deut 10,18): 1 K 8,59; Ps 9,5; 140,13; Yahweh as one who gives bread and clothing (Deut 10,18): Deut 29,4-5.

59 The parallel reference of Lev 19,34 is later. This has been already well established: Jagersma, Leviticus 19 p. 66; Barbiero, L'asino p. 293; Kilian, Untersuchung p. 56f.; Elliger, Leviticus p. 250; Martin-Achard, THAT I col. 412 and Perlitt, FS G.

framework.[60]   The command in perfect in V. 19a does not fit with the hymnic style of V. 17-18.   The addition of V. 19a to V. 17-18 is due to its thematic association with the preceding verse, i.e. אהב in V. 19a. is due to אהב in V. 18b.[61]

Deut 10,19a is also an independent unit, thematically.   This verse interrupts the narrative[62], which shows how important for the author was the thought expressed here.[63]   Despite the reference to the *triad* in 10,18, verse 10,19a isolates the גֵר, leaves out the terms "bread and clothing", and concentrates on the theme of *love*.   What we have here is the result of an intentional *generalizing tendency*, i.e. the transition from specific measures given in order to ameliorate the condition of the גֵר[64], to an *unconditional principle* which is not bound to any particular (temporal or spatial) circumstance.   This categorical command pronounced in a liturgical context, differs clearly from other legal precepts on the גֵר.

Finally, we must bear in mind that the motive clause "because you were גרים in the land of Egypt", which follows Deut 10,19a, is used exclusively to found גֵר-commands.   The commands given on behalf of the *triad* use, instead, the "Egypt-עבד" motive clause (i.e. "Remember that you were a *slave* in the land of Egypt" Deut 24,18.22), not the "Egypt-גֵר" motive clause.[65]   In Ex 22,20a and Jer 22,3b, for instance, we have the same basic formulation[66]:

Ex 22,20a: You shall not wrong a גֵר *for you were* גרים *in Egyp*t.
Jer 22,3b: Do not wrong the   גֵר the orphan and the widow.

It is important to notice that from these two texts only Ex 22,20a, a command on behalf of the גֵר alone, is followed by the "Egypt-גֵר" motive clause.   The reason for this is that the "Egypt-גֵר" clause is found *only in relation with commands on behalf of the* גֵר[67], *never in relation with commands*

    Bornkamm p. 50 n. 75.   The synthetic character of Lev chapter 19 and that of Lev
    19,34 itself (as combination of Ex 22,20 and Deut 10,19), has been shown lately by
    Otto, FS H.Graf Reventlow p. 68-73.

60 Noth, ÜP p. 51.

61 Seitz, Studien p. 81 note 86; Cholewiński, Heiligkeitsgesetz p. 275. This is probably
    the reason for the statement: "Circumcise the foreskin of your hearts" in V. 16.   This
    idea is a spiritualised expression of late origin (Deut 30,6; Jer 4,4; Ez 44,9), which has
    no direct relation to the context, except for the mention of the election with the fathers
    in V. 15.   The circumcision, being the sign of the covenant (Gen 17,10), was included
    by way of thematic association.

62 Cholewiński, Heiligkeitsgesetz p. 275.   Cazelles in his notes to Deuteronomy in BJ,
    has this text in brackets.

63 Schökel, BP I p. 359.

64 Under such measures we have for instance the eating measures provided in Deuteronomy
    to assist the Levite, the גֵר, the orphan and the widow: 14,29; 26,12.13.

65 Schwienhorst-Schönberger, Bundesbuch p. 350.

66 That is: גֵר + negation's particle + verb ינה.

67 Ex 22,20; 23,9; Lev 19,34; Deut 10,19.

on behalf of the triad.[68]   This shows that in the command to love the גר in Deut 10,19a (followed by the "Egypt-גר" clause), we are dealing *only* with the גר, not with the triad.

4.3 The command to love the גר

It must be noted that this short command to love the גר, differs significantly in matters of form and content from other Old Testament references to the גר.

First of all, Deut 10,19a is the only reference in the Old Testament in which the גר is the exclusive object of a positive command.[69] This precept, in the form of a general principle and without direct relation to any specific problem or situation[70], is unique in the Old Testament.   The transition from V.18, which speaks about the *triad* and the theme of "food and clothing", to V. 19, which speaks exclusively about the individual גר and the theme of *love*, is striking.

Secondly, the precept "to love" in itself is unusual.[71] The two commands to love the גר found in the Old Testament[72] are matched only by the two commands to love Yahweh (!).[73] It must be noted that, unlike the Holiness Code[74], Deuteronomy does not have a correspondent commandment to love the brother or any other needy member of the society.   The command to love the גר is unique.

The statement that "Yahweh loves the גר" (10,18bα) is, on the other hand, also unusual.   The use of the verb אהב with Yahweh as subject, is circumscribed in the Old Testament to Israel.[75]   Yahweh loves, first of all,

---

68   See Schwienhorst-Schönberger, Bundesbuch p. 339.

69   A *negative* formulation of a command *on behalf of* the גר is found in Ex 22,20a; 23,9a; Lev 19,33.

70   In Deut the references to the גר are often related to eating measures (14,29; 16,11.14; 24,19.20.21; 26,12.13).   In P, on the other hand, גר references are often casuistic laws introduced by the formula: וכי־יגור אתך גר (Ex 12,48; Lev 19,34; Num 9,14; 15,14).

71   Besides Deut 10,19a (see also p. 79 note 59 on Lev 19,34), there is only *one* command similar to this in the Old Testament, the command to love the fellow Israelite (Lev 19,18).

72   Deut 10,19; Lev 19,34.

73   Deut 6,5; 11,1.

74   Lev 19,18.34.

75   There is only one exception to this: Is 48,14 in which the sufferings of Israel come to an end thanks to the intervention of a foreigner (Cyrus), whom Yahweh loves (אהבו). Compare this term with the designation of Abraham in Is 41,8 as אהבי. This designation of אהבו for a foreigner is most unusual. BHS proposes instead the reading הביאו. Duhm comments: "das folgende Wort (d.h. אהבו in 48,14) ist אהבי (c. 41,8) zu lesen. Es ist recht möglich, daß letzterer Ausdruck erst von späterer Hand verändert ist, weil man es anstößig fand, daß Cyrus ebenso "Freund Jahves" heißen sollte wie Abraham" (Jesaja p. 336).

Israel, the fathers, Abraham and Jacob.[76]   He also loves the righteous
(צדיקים), those who hate evil (שׂנאו רע) and those who pursue righteousness
(מרדף צדקה).[77]   Out of this realm of the human beings, he also loves justice
(משׁפט)[78], righteousness (צדקה)[79] and things which are holy (קדשׁ), the
Mount Zion and its gates.[80]   If we take into account that in Deut 10,19a the גר
is a foreigner[81], his mention here in relation to Yahweh's love is a significant
exception.

Since Deut 10,19a is originally independent from V. 17-18, and its
relationship with the motive clause 10,19b is also secondary[82], we can gain
some insight only indirectly about the circumstances behind this precept.   A
first look at the command in 10,19a allows us to make some basic observations:
• The transition from the *triad* "גר-orphan-widow" in 10,18 to the גר alone in
10,19a suggests that the circumstances behind this verse (i.e. 10,19a) are
related only to the גר, not to the triad.
• The fact that the author of 10,19a avoids any further reference to the "food
and clothing", and concentrates on the theme of love is not casual.   It suggests
that the central problem behind this text is not an issue concerning directly the
material condition of the triad "גר-orphan-widow", but the acceptance of the גר
within the community.[83]   The גר is not mentioned here as *pars pro toto*.   This
text should not be interpreted as another expression of Israel's concern for the
personae miserae .
• Since norms usually become explicit when they are being violated, the
command to love the גר suggests that in certain circles this love was *contra*

---

76   Israel: Deut 7,13; 10,15; 23,6; Is 43,4; Jer 31,3; Hos 11,1; 14,5; Mal 1,2; the
     fathers: Deut 4,37; Abraham: Is 41,8; 2 Chron 20,7 and Jacob: Mal 1,2; Ps 47,5.
77   צדיקים (Ps 146,8); מרדף צדקה (Prov 15,9); שׂנאו רע (Ps 97,10).   See also
     Prov 3,12a.
78   Is 61,8; Ps 37,28; 99,4; 33,5.
79   Ps 45,8;   Ps 11,7 (צדקות).   The two terms משׁפט and צדקה appear together in Ps
     33,5 ([יהוה] אהב צדקה ומשׁפט).
80   קדשׁ (Mal 2,11); the Mount Zion: Ps 78,68; Zion's gates: Ps 87,2.
81   Although the term גר does not always mean "foreigner", in Deut 10,19 and Lev 19,34
     the גר is, in fact, a foreigner, and should not be identified with the גר of the
     deuteronomic triad of *personae miserae.*
82   The כי type of motive clauses are usually late additions included for parenetical reasons.
     According to Gemser, the stipulations for the protection of the underprivileged in the
     Covenant Code as well as in Deut (in Deut 23,8 an Egyptian), are sanctioned by motive
     clauses (SVT 1, 63).   See also Mowinckel, AcOr (L) 1 p. 86.
83   Although the term love is not found in the prophets, they insist in love-oriented
     behaviour towards the needy ones, as the prophetic references to the triad show (Jer 7,6;
     22,3; Ez 22,7).

naturam.[84] The community was divided about this issue: in Deut 10,19 members of circles who were in favor of the integration of the רג, addressed members of other circles who, obviously, opposed this idea.

Some additional information about this precept allows us to see further.

Deut 10,19a is a post-exilic text.[85] *It was the new awareness of being themselves* גרים *(10,19b), which created a new sensitivity to the non-Jewish* רג. The connection of the motive clause in Deut 10,19b with the command in Deut 10,19a is secondary. The experience of the exile made Israel aware of "how it feels to be a רג" (Ex 23,9b). After the exile, the רג became a mirror of their own story. There was a part of their own identity in each רג. That is why the command to love the רג 10,19a makes reference to *Israel's own experience* (10,19b): it is an appeal to their collective memory. It was possible to identify with the רג because they had been גרים themselves.[86]

The fact that Deut 10,19a is a post-exilic text, means that this precept comes from a time in which Israel was no longer an *ethnic group* living in Palestine, but a *multicentered religious community* (Alexandria, Babylon, Antioch, Jerusalem).[87] The attitude of the Palestinian and the Diaspora Jews towards the Gentiles was different, and determined in each case by the particular circumstances of their social milieu.[88] Since the Diaspora Jews lived as a minority among Gentiles, permanent and positive relations with them were a *conditio sine qua non* for their survival.[89] The Diaspora community was, consequently, more universalistic in approach.[90] This explains why the first

---

84 "Si tratta di un amore che va contro l'inclinazione della natura, ed appunto per questo viene comandato" (Barbiero, L'asino p. 330). The statement refers specifically to the parallel text Lev 19,18. See also below p. 87-88 on Deut 23,8b.

85 See p. 79-80; Mayes, Deuteronomy 4, p. 213-214 (espec. p. 212 note 61) and Cholewiński, Heiligkeitsgesetz p. 275.

86 "On opère un renversement des situations. On peut se mettre à la place de l'autre, de l'immigré, pour avoir été jadis dans son cas" (Pons, EThR 63 p. 171). Kloppers and Barbiero emphasise the example of Yahweh as model to love the רג. Barbiero states: "l'amore per il ger imita l'amore di Jahweh per queste persone" (L'asino p. 202); and Kloppers comments: "The attitude towards the רג is determined by the Lord Himself who does justice to the גר משה עשה) and loves him (אהב). In the same way Israel as bearer of the image of the Lord, must do justice to the רג and love him" (Fax Theologica 6/2 p. 40).

87 For the notion of multicentrism in the exilic-post-exilic period see Talmon, Sektenbildung p. 247-249.

88 We do not speak here about a tension between the *Palestinian* and the *Diaspora* Judaism, but about different attitudes of the Palestinian and the Diaspora Jews towards Gentiles. The antithesis "Palestinian Judaism vs. Diaspora Judaism" has been shown to be incorrect. See Hengel, Judaism p. 60-61 252 and Schürer, History III.1 p. 140.

89 Pfeiffer, Introduction p. 181-189, espec. 185.

90 Schürer, History III.1 p. 162-64.

missionary efforts came from this community.[91]   The Judean Jews
experienced, instead, permanent confrontations and hostilities with the neighbor
states, whose political and economic influence had to be accepted due to the
impossibility of retaliation.[92]   Due partially to this, their contacts with
foreigners were less frequent.[93]

The distrust of some circles of the Palestinian community was probably not
restricted to non-Jews. The return of the exiles, in early post exilic times could
hardly have been taken with enthusiasm in Palestine.[94]   It is very likely,
therefore, that *Diaspora oriented* theologians, who had themselves experienced
frictions with local circles, formulated the programmatic precept: "You shall
love the גר", with the intention to challenge the nationalistic circles of the
Palestinian community, to accept *all* those who had newly joined the
community.[95]

4.4 Conclusion

The command to love the גר in Deut 10,19a is a late addition.   In Deut
10,19 command (19a) and motive clause (19b) had an independent origin, and
were combined only in post-exilic times.   The motive clause (19b), which is
based on the analogy of Israel as גר (Deut 23,8bβ), is originally a product of the
exile.   The majority of the גר references in the Old Testament appear in legal
texts which were written or edited during the exile.   The particular interest of
Israel for the theme of the גר from that moment, mirrors her own situation.
That is why the command to love the גר is founded in *Israel's own experience*.

The command to love the גר in Deut 10,19a is an appeal to integrate non-
Jewish individuals into the religious community. This is a programmatic text
issued by Gola-oriented circles to counter the exclusiveness of some Palestinian
circles in post-exilic times, and to be used in liturgical settings.

---

91   Bousset-Greßmann, Religion p. 56.60.77.83; Dalbert, Theologie p. 24-26; Bertholet,
     Stellung p. 207; 243; 124ff.; Leipoldt-Grundmann, Umwelt p. 310 note 84; Kuhn,
     Art. Proselyten, in: RECA Supp IX col. 1258-1259.

92   Albertz, Religionsgeschichte p. 378-379 and Müller, Phönikien p. 201-204.

93   See Tcherikover, 'Natives' and 'Foreigners' in Palestine, in: The Age of the Monarchies:
     Culture and Society (A. Malamat, ed.) 4, p. 87-95. See also Dion, Universalismo p.
     178.

94   "Palästina war während der Exilszeit ja keineswegs ein menschenleeres Brachland
     gewesen, das man ohne weiteres wieder in Besitz nehmen konnte. Alte und neue Rechte
     mußten gegeneinander abgewogen, alte und neue Ansprüche berücksichtigt werden"
     (Donner, Geschichte p. 444).

95   It is probable that at this time, the idea that only those who threw in their lot with Israel
     in exile and suffered with them as Jews should be considered as גרים, was already
     present. See Eisemann, Ezekiel p. 746-747 and Zimmerli, Ezechiel p. 1219.

Part 3

The noun גֵּר as *figura theologica*

"Dire l'autre enfin, c'est bien évidemment une façon de parler de *nous.*"
(F. Hartog, Le miroir d'Hérodote, Paris 1980, p. 370).

5. The Israelites as גרים

The references to the noun גר with which we have dealt in the second part of this study designate an individual[1], and appear mainly in association with the preposition ב. In these references the noun גר is used to designate a social type within Israelite society.[2] In addition to those references, the noun גר is also used to designate the Israelites. The analogy of Israel as גר, either "*in* the land of Egypt" or "*before* Yahweh", appears as a late motive clause introduced by the particle כי:

a) in legal texts:
1. Deut 23,8:   גר + ב   כי־גר   היית   בארצו
2. Deut 10,19b: גר + ב   כי־גרים הייתם בארץ מצרים
3. Lev 25,23:   גר + עמדי   כי־גרים ותושבים אתם עמדי

b) and non-legal texts:
1. Ps 39,13:   כי גר   אנכי עמך
2. 1 Chron 29,15: כי גרים אנחנו לפניך

It must be noted that in Deut 23,8 and 10,19 the noun גר, although referring to Israel as a community, is still used with the preposition ב and, therefore, with a territorial dimension.

5.1 The Israelites as גרים "in the land of Egypt"

5.1.1 Deut 23,8b

The relevance of this verse for our study lies in its new understanding of Israel's stay in Egypt. Deut 23,8 gives a positive idea of this period which does not correspond to the usual picture of Egypt in Deuteronomy as the "house of slavery".[3] Deut 23,2-9 consists of five negative commands (23,2; 3a; 4a; 8a; 8b), followed by the correspondent motive clauses (23,5a; 5b;

---

1   Ex 22,20; Deut 14,21; Lev 19,33-34.
2   The verb גור is also frequently used with the preposition ב, see for instance Gen 37,1: ויעקב גר בארץ־חם ;Ps 105,23: בארץ מגורי ... באָרץ כנען ;Ps 61,5: אגורה באהלך ;Ps 15,1: מי־יגור באהלך.
3   Deut 5,6; 6,12; 7,8; 8,14; 13,5.10. See p. 90.

6b; 8aβ; 8bβ).[4]   Deut 23,8b differs from the previous commands in the fact that it does not deal properly with acceptance into the assembly, but rather with a protective measure on behalf of the Egyptian immigrant.[5]

"You shall not abhor an Egyptian" (Deut 23,8bα).   The reason behind this command on behalf of individual Egyptians lies in the friendly relationships of Israel with Egypt at the time of its promulgation.   No agreement exists, however, concerning its possible date.   Suggestions have included the era of Solomon[6], the period of Hezekiah and Manasseh[7], the seventh century[8] and the last years of Zedekiah[9].

Since Egypt is the only country mentioned in Deut 23,2-9 which is not a direct neighbour of Israel, and the law is concerned with individual Egyptians and not with Egypt as a nation, the Egyptians referred to here were probably immigrants.[10]   Moreover, the privilege given to them was no more than an elementary form of protective right.[11]   The number of Egyptians living as immigrants at the time must have been significant, otherwise we would not have a law to regulate their mutual relations.   From the nature of the command ("not to abhor an Egyptian"[12]), it can be deduced that the Israelites, or at least a significant group of them, reacted negatively towards the presence of these

---

4   Kaiser, who considers Deut 23,2-9 as post-exilic, thinks that: "Was wir hier vor uns haben, ist ganz offenbar ein Gesetz, das dazu bestimmt ist, die Aufnahme von Proselyten in die Gemeinde Israels zu regeln" (JRP 14 p. 73).

5   As U. Kellermann states: "Das Gesetz von V. 8 zielt nun expressis verbis nicht auf den Eintritt von Fremden in den Qahal ... Es geht hier nicht um Kultpartnerschaft, sondern um den Schutz persona miserabilis im Wohngebiet Israels" (BN 2 p. 38-39. and 35). Hulst also agrees with this opinion: "Wie bei dem apodiktischen Satz über die Edomiter, ist aber auch hier zu bemerken, dass möglicherweise diese Bestimmung ursprünglich mit einem eventuellen Eintritt in die Gemeinde Jahwes nichts zu tun hat" (OTSt 9 p. 101).

6   U. Kellermann, BN 2 p. 42.

7   Mowinckel, AcOr (L) 1 p. 94; 102.

8   For Steuernagel it is difficult to understand this clause in relation to the *Urzeit:* "Das befriedigt aber nicht; denn wenn Israel an den einstigen Aufenthalt in Ägypten dachte, so erschien ihm Ägypten als das Sklavenhaus, aus dem es nur durch Jahwes machtvolles Eingreifen errettet wurde. Daß die Ägypter Israel bedrückten, kann aber kein Motiv dafür sein, daß man sie freundlich behandeln soll" (ZDPV, XXXV p. 99). He understands the clause כי גר היית בארצו as a reference to the establishment of Jewish colonies in Egypt during the seventh century BC., i.e. in the light of the friendly relationships between Jews and Egyptians based on the evidence of the Elephantine Papyri.   He states: "גר היית (statt des sonstigen עבד היית) weist schwerlich auf den vormosaischen ägyptischen Aufenthalt Israels, sondern eher auf die Entstehung jüdischer (Militär-) Kolonien in Ägypten während der letzten Vergangenheit" (Deuteronomium p. 136).   For a different view see Wijngaards, Deuteronomium p. 258.

9   Hempel, Schichten p. 233-234.

10   Galling, FS A. Bertholet p.184.

11   See Ex 22,20.

12   The commands in Deut 23,8bα (a negative formulation) and in Deut 10,19a (a positive formulation), show that the community was divided concerning the matter of the integration of foreigners.

immigrants within their territory. The reason for this rejection was probably related to traditions concerning Israel's former slavery in Egypt.[13]

Deut 23,8 consisted originally of two negative commands without the motive-clauses:[14]

8aα: You shall not abhor an Edomite.

8bα: You shall not abhor an Egyptian.

The negative commands לא do not necessarily require כי motive clauses.[15] In Deut 19-25, for instance, there are 12 cases of negative commands introduced by לא in 2 p. sing. (= Deut 23,8), without motive clauses.[16] The כי type of motive clauses are usually late additions included for parenetical reasons.[17] As S. Mowinckel suggests: "Man tut dabei am besten, von der Begründung der Gebote 'denn sie (die Edomiter) sind deine Brüder' und 'denn du bist selbst ger in Ägypten gewesen' abzusehen".[18]

We distinguish, therefore, between the main clause (Deut 23,8bα) and the motive clause (Deut 23,8bβ). The historical circumstances behind these sentences are different. While the positive attitude towards the Egyptians is probably pre-exilic, the analogy of Israel as רג is result of the Exile. Israel could hardly come to this conclusion before the Babylonian captivity.

In his study "Das Bundesbuch" Schwienhorst-Schönberger makes a comparison of the two formulae "Egypt-עבד" and "Egypt-גר" and concludes: "Die Ägypten-ger-Motivation kann deshalb nur eingesetzt werden zur

---

13 In this connection Hulst explains: "weil aber die Fremdlingschaft Israels in Ägypten als eine sehr harte Knechtschaft erfahren ist, lässt es sich leicht verstehen, dass man den *gerîm* ägyptischer Herkunft nicht immer freundlich gesinnt war und dass es für die Israeliten eine schwierige Aufgabe bedeutete, auch diese *gerîm* zu lieben" (OTSt 9 p. 101-102).

14 For apodictic sentences in prohibitive form in Deuteronomy see Boecker, Recht p. 177-179, and Gerstenberger, Wesen p. 31-37 espec. p. 36.

15 See Gerstenberger, Wesen p. 55-60.

16 Deut 19,14; 22,1.4.9.10.11; 23,16.20; 24,17a; 25,4.13.14; see Nielsen, Deuteronomium p. 194. In four cases the command has a motive clause: Deut 23,8a 8b; 23,19b; 24,17-18. Deut 23,8b is the only case of motive clause which includes the term רג.

17 See Rücker, ETS 30 p. 28-37. According to Gemser the stipulations for the protection of the underprivileged in the Covenant Code as well as in Deut (in Deut 23,8 an Egyptian), are sanctioned by motive clauses (SVT 1 p. 63). See also Doron, HAR 2 p. 62-64; 72-74.

18 According to Mowinckel: "es ist eine bekannte Sache, daß die Begründung sich nicht immer mit den tatsächlichen Motiven deckt; diese sind meistens nicht in irgendwelchen hübschen Gefühlen, sondern in realen, sozialen und politischen Zeitverhältnissen zu suchen" (AcOrL 1 p. 86). A similar opinion is expressed by Merendino: "Als sekundäre Erweiterungen sind die Begründungen vv.8aβ.bβ anzusehen, denn sie verwandeln das Gebot in ein Ermahnungswort und verlegen den Akzent mehr auf ihren Inhalt als auf die eigentliche Bestimmung v.9b" (Gesetz p. 279).

Begründung eines ger-Gebotes".[19] He gives as an example of this Deut 10,19. The references in Ex 22,20; 23,9 and Lev 19,34 also belong to this same pattern:

	First half	Second half
Dt 10,19:	You shall love the גר	because you were גרים in Egypt
Lv 19,34:	You shall love the גר	because you were גרים in Egypt
Ex 22,20:	You shall not ill-treat the גר	because you were גרים in Egypt
Ex 23, 9:	You shall not oppress the גר	because you were גרים in Egypt

Deut 23,8bβ (a Egypt-גר type of motive clause) does not belong, however, to this pattern. Unlike the references in Deut 10,19; Ex 22,20; 23,9 and Lev 19,34, the parallelism of the first half and the second half of Deut 23,8bβ is based not on the noun גר. The command "not to abhor" applies exclusively to Egyptians, not to every גר.[20] The reason for this difference lies in the fact that the command in Deut 10,19b represents a later development of the original command formulated for the first time in Deut 23,8bβ. This explains why, although the motive clauses are similar, the addressees of these laws are different. In Deut 23,8bα the measure includes only the *Egyptians*; in Deut 10,19 the measure includes persons of *any nationality*. This development is the result of a generalising tendency.

The difference between the Egypt-גר formula and the Egypt-עבד formula does not lie in their content (גר = positive / עבד = negative) but in their argumentation structure[21]:

• the Egypt-עבד motive clause enjoins the Israelite to keep the commands. The principle behind these commands is that of *gratitude*: the memory of the salvific acts of Yahweh in history, what Yahweh has done for Israel. That is why the עבד-formula is used to support commands on behalf of the needy in general, even when the term עבד does not appear in the main clause (Deut 24,18.22).

• the Egypt-גר motive clause, instead, supports the content of the command; the rationale of this motive clause is based on a principle of *reciprocity*, i.e.

---

19 Bundesbuch p. 350. The Egypt-עבד motive clause corresponds to the older strata of Deuteronomy and is introduced in each case with the verb זכרת. The "Egypt-גר" motive clause is introduced in each case by the particle כי. For the reference to זכרת in Deuteronomy without relation to the slavery in Egypt (i.e. 7,18; 8,2; 9,7; 24,9; 25,17), and Schottroff, Gedenken p. 117-126.

20 Buhl takes "Edomite-Egyptian" in Deut 23,8 as meaning "Die Fremden aus allen anderen Nationen" (Verhältnisse p. 49). No argument is given however, in support of this idea. He simply refers to Bertholet who states: "sicher gilt das Dt 23,9 den Edomitern und Ägyptern Zugesagte für alle Fremden, denen der Auschluss nicht von vorn herein abgeschlagen wird" (Stellung p. 173). The clause: "because you were גר in his land" is something that could be said (before the exile), restrictively of an Egyptian.

21 For what follows see Schwienhorst-Schönberger, Bundesbuch p. 346-353.

what others have done for Israel: "do to the גר among you as others did to you when you were גרים among them". As Spieckermann states:

"Israel versteht sich als ein Volk, das aus Fremde und Unterdrückung von Gott befreit worden ist und sich deshalb unter der bleibenden Verpflichtung weiß, in Dankbarkeit gegen die eigene Befreiung aus der Fremdlingschaft Fremdlingen *(gerîm)* in der eigenen Heimat zu begegnen. 'Denn ihr seid auch gerîm in Ägyptenland gewesen'".[22]

That is why the Egypt-גר formula is used to support גר-commands (Ex 22,20; 23,9; Lev 19,34; Deut 10,19).

5.1.2 The traditions of "slavery" and "sojourning"

As was mentioned before, Deut 23,8bβ gives a positive idea of Israel's sojourn in Egypt. This picture is most unusual and represents a variation of a well established tradition, (see p. 93f). Elsewhere in the Old Testament, writers look back to Egypt as a time in which the Israelites were *slaves*.[23] Egypt is portrayed in Deuteronomy as the "house of slaves"[24] and "the iron furnace".[25] Even laws given for the protection of the גר are founded in the book of Deuteronomy with the motive clause "Remember that you were a *slave* in Egypt".[26] Bertholet's commentary on Deut 23,8 illustrates a common opinion among scholars regarding the confusion created by this motive clause: "erst recht merkwürdig ist die Begründung für die Ägypterfreundschaft; sie wird sonst gebraucht, um zur milden Gesinnung gegen die Armen aufzufordern, gerade weil die Israeliten wissen müssen, wie schwer einem גר ums Herz ist; und diese Erinnerung soll sie plötzlich zur Dankbarkeit gegen Ägypten anspornen! So widerspricht sich doch kein Schriftsteller".[27]

In our opinion, part of this confusion comes from the fact that the clause "גר in Egypt" is sometimes wrongly equated with the clause "עבד in Egypt". J.G. Plöger, for instance, states that the clause: "remember that you were a *slave* in Egypt" (Deut 6,21; 16,12; 24,18), "findet sich in der kürzeren Form Deut 10,19b ki gerîm".[28] As result of this, it is assumed that the term גר in Deut 23,8bβ refers to Israel's bondage in Egypt. There is, however, no evidence to support the idea that גר in Deut 23,8bβ refers to Israel's bondage under Pharaoh.[29] The noun גר is used in relation to Egypt only twice besides Deut

22   Spieckermann, PTh 83 p. 56-57.
23   עברים (Lev 25,55; 26,13; Deut 6,21; Jer 34,13; Micah 6,4).
24   בית עברים (Deut 5,6; 6,12.21; 7,8; 8,14; 13,5.10. See also Ex 13,3.14; 20,2; Jos 24,17; Jud 6,8).
25   כור הברזל (Deut 4,20). See also 1 K 8,51; Jer 11,4.
26   Deut 16,11.12; 24,17-18.19-22.
27   Bertholet, Deuteronomium p. 72.
28   Plöger, Untersuchungen p. 113.
29   As it is assumed by Driver, Deuteronomy p. 262 and Thompson, Deuteronomy p. 240.

23,8 and 10,19: of Moses in Ex 2,22 (= 18,3) and of Abraham's offspring in
Gen 15,13.[30] Ex 2,22 is part of an etymological aetiology, its analysis is,
therefore, not relevant for our purpose here.[31]
In the (deuteronomistic?)[32] addition of Gen 15,13, the term גר is apparently
related to the Egyptian oppression. A closer view shows, however, that we
have here *two separate moments:*

1:	initial sojourn	Gen 15,13a	גר יהיה זרעך
2:	later oppression	Gen 15,13b	ועבדום וענו אתם

B. Jacob and S. Kreuzer confirm this important distinction. B. Jacob states:
"Die Knechtschaft begann erst lange Zeit nach der Einwanderung Jakobs und
seiner Familie und nach dem Tode Josephs und des ganzen Geschlechtes. Also
sind die Worte ועבדום וענו אתם als eine Parenthese zu verstehen".[33] And
S. Kreuzer states: "Israel als גר in Ägypten betont nicht die Knechtschaft,
sondern die Zuflucht, was den Genesiserzählungen und den ersten Versen des
Exodusbuches, vor dem Kommen eines neuen Pharao (Ex 1,8), entspricht".[34]
J. van Seters in his article "Confessional Reformulation in the Exilic
Period", has shown that "in the period of the exile, there was a conscious
confessional shift from Yahweh as the God of the exodus to Yahweh as the
God of the Patriarchs".[35] Gen 15 is, precisely, an example of this. The verse
7 of this chapter states:

---

30 In these two cases, as well as in Deut 23,8 the word גר appears together with the noun
    ארץ:נכריה ארץ (Ex 2,22); גר ... בארץ לא להם (Gen 15,13) and
    גר ... בארצו (Deut 23,8).
31 See Fichtner, VT 6 p. 378-380 and Siebert-Hommes, ACEBT 10 p. 16-20.
32 Although Gen 15,13-16. is widely accepted as a later addition, the origin of these verses
    remain disputed. According to Weimar: "Von dtr. Hand stammen 15,5aβ.ba.13 13-
    14a.b (ohne birkuš gadôl). 18bβ. 19-21" (Untersuchungen p. 52 note 153). According
    to Lohfink 15,13 represents "einen für diesen Zusammenhang geschaffenen Zusatz ohne
    Bezug zu einer bestimmten Quellenschrift" (Landverheissung p. 40); Wellhausen sees
    the verse as product of a later redaktor: "v. 13-16 und v. 7 verrät in Sprachgebrauch ...
    und Vorstellung ... Verwandschaft mit dem Vierbundesbuch" (Composition p. 22); see
    also Jepsen, FS A. Alt p. 152.
33 Jacob, Genesis p. 398.
34 Kreuzer, Exodustradition p. 97.
35 Van Seters, VT 22 p. 456. Albertz comments: "Angesichts der sich als brüchig
    erwiesenen Heilsgaben des Landes, des Tempels und des Königtums bot sich das
    Handeln Jahwes an den Vorvätern als die letzte nicht in Mitleidenschaft gezogene
    geschichtliche Basis an, auf die man weiter bauen konnte ... In ihr (Väterüberlieferung)
    wurden den israelitischen Familien der Exilszeit die Familien der Frühzeit gleich in
    mehrfacher Hinsicht als Identifikationsfiguren präsentiert .." (Religionsgeschichte p.
    419-420). According to the deuteronomistic Deuteronomy, the origins of Israel in
    Deuteronomy do not begin with the Exodus but with the Patriarchs.   Lohfink
    comments: "Andere Israel-Konzepte, etwa das des Jeremiah- oder des Ezechielbuches,
    kannten das deuteronomische Horeb-Israel, zogen aber für ihre Botschaft an ihre

And Yahweh said to Abraham:
"*I am Yahweh who brought you from* Ur of the Chaldeans,
to give you this land to possess" (Gen 15,7).

The form of the divine speech here is the "self-introduction formula
followed by a participial phrase. We find this same construction in the
introduction of the Decalogue which makes reference to the exodus event "*I am
Yahweh, your God, who brought you out of* the land of Egypt ..." Ex 20,2;
Deut 5,6; Lev 25,8:

Ex 20,2:   אנכי יהוה אלהיך אשר הוצאתיך <u>מארץ מצרים</u>
Gen 15,7:   אני יהוה   אשר הוצאתיך <u>מאור כשדים</u>

The form is basically the same except that in Gen 15,7 the phrase "Ur of the
Chaldeans" substitutes for "land of Egypt", which is the oldest form. The shift
from the *exodus* to *Abraham* as a point of departure of Israel's story, explains
why the author included this sojourning (גר) period in Gen 15,13: "The
Egyptian sojourn is now made an *interlude* between the promise to the
patriarchs and its fulfilment in the conquest (vv. 13-16)".[36]   H. Wildberger in
his study on the election in exilic times arrives at similar conclusions.[37]

In Deut 26,8, where the theme of the guidance out of Egypt is preceded by
the reference to Israel' stay in Egypt (Deut 26,5), we also find this scheme of
two separate moments:

Moment 1: initial sojourning Deut 26,5:   [38]ויגר שם .. ויהי־שם לגוי גדול
Moment 2: later oppression Deut 26,6a: וירעו אתנו המצרים ויענונו

The two periods of Israel's stay in Egypt are clearly separated: Deut 26,5 is
the time of the sojourn of the fathers in Egypt (ויגר), a time of well-being and
expansion. Here: "wird ganz im Sinn von Ex 1 zwischen der *Fremdlingschaft*
am Anfang und der *Knechtschaft* des zahlreich gewordenen Volkes
unterschieden; zudem wird das entsprechende Verbum גור verwendet".[39] The
period of oppression (עבדה קשה, Deut 26,6b), came only later. The motive
clause "because you were גר in his land" is a theological insight of the Exile,

Adressaten eine andere Perspektive vor -vielleicht auch allein schon deshalb, weil die
Verfasser der Grundtexte dieser Bücher, die Propheten Jeremiah und Ezechiel selbst,
immer vom Exodus ausgegangen waren" (Väter p. 110).

36   Van Seters, VT 22 p. 456, underlining is ours.

37   With respect to the sojourn in Egypt: "Man will die Erwählung tiefer in der Geschichte
verwurzeln. Hat Israel versagt, so bleibt doch Jahwes Liebe zu den Vätern unberührt und
bildet ein nicht zu erschütterndes Fundament für Hoffnung" (Wildberger, TB 66 p. 317).

38   According to Lohfink: "גור meint nicht einfach 'wohnen', sondern weist auf einen ganz
bestimmten Rechtszustand hin, der durch Dekret des Pharao geschaffen wurde und den die
Ägypter später brachen" (Credo p. 31, see also p. 38).

39   Kreuzer, Exodustradition p. 97-98, italics is ours.   See also Lohfink, Bearbeitung p.
54.

although the statement might not result *only* from this experience.[40]   Heaton thinks that Deut 23,8 is related to: "a lively tradition of an Egyptian sojourn before the conquest of Palestine ... a tradition which, although now artificially attached to the regular 'bondage-and-deliverance' scheme (Ex 1,8), is really independent".[41]

In sum: the significance of the motive clause in Deut 23,8bβ consists precisely in the fact that it introduces for the first time a differentiation in the understanding of Israel's past in Egypt.   The motive clauses Egypt-עבד and "Egypt-גר" do not represent, then, two different interpretations of the *same event* but refer to two different stages of Israel's past.   The Egypt-גר clause is not a *re-interpretation* of the former Egypt-עבד formula but the result of a *differentiation* in the understanding of Israel's past.[42]   The Egypt-גר formula (Deut 23,8bβ and 10,19b) refers to the initial sojourn of well-being under Joseph.   The Egypt - עבד formula is related exclusively to the theme of oppression under Pharaoh.

5.1.3 Deut 10, 19b

Just as in the case of Deut 23,8b, we distinguish here between the command (Deut 10,19a) and the parenetical motive clause (Deut 10,19b).[43]   The idea that the Israelites were "גרים in the land of Egypt" is a variation of a well established tradition, (see p. 90).   The opening statement of one of Israel's most important creeds, the Passover Haggadah, states:

"When, in time to come, your children ask you, 'What means the decrees, laws, and rules that the Lord our God has enjoined upon you?' you shall say to your children 'We were slaves to Pharaoh in Egypt and the Lord freed us with a mighty hand'" (Deut 6,20ff).

---

40 Blum assigns to the Joseph's story the function of a "Brücke zwischen den Vätern und dem Exodus" or a "konzeptionelle Verbindung von Väterzeit und Exodus" (Komposition p. 238).   He thinks, however, that this function does not imply the experience of the exile.   Galling concludes, "daß die auf die Mosezeit zurückblickende relativ günstige Beurteilung der Ägypter in Deut 23,8 ausgesprochen wurde, als die anti-ägyptische Akzentuierung der Auszugstradition noch nicht soweit verbindlich war, daß man ihr nicht mit der einfachen Feststellung: 'du bist ein ger in seinem Lande gewesen' begegnen konnte! Das weist uns in die Zeit vor der Staatenbildung" (FS A. Bertholet p. 185).   According to U. Kellermann Deut 23,8 "muß vor der Profilierung der Exodustradition mit dem Leitmotiv der Befreiung aus der Knechtschaft Ägyptens angesetzt werden" (BN 2 p. 37).

41 ET 58 p. 82; Daube sustains a similar opinion (Patterns p. 25).

42 Bultmann arrives to a similar conclusion: "Die Beschreibung des Status in Ägypten als *ger* konkurriert hier (i.e. Deut 23,8bβ) also nicht mit der als *'aebed*, vielmehr handelt es sich um zwei Verlaufsstadien der mythischen Volksgeschichte" (Der Fremde p. 116).

43 The command to love the גר in Deut 10,19a is discussed in p. 81 ff.

The idea that the Israelites were *slaves* in the land of Egypt is part of the fixed stock of narrative motifs which belong to the formula of the "Guidance out of Egypt"[44]; one of the oldest and most universal heritages of the Israelite tribes as a whole.[45]

The idea that the Israelites were "גרים in the land of Egypt" is, instead, a much more recent tradition. We know that the tradition of "*Israel* in Egypt" is in itself, already late. Whatever the "historical events" behind the exodus may have been, it was an event of a particular tribal group which only later, after being *generalized* and nationalized, came to be a *common* primary confession of *all Israel.*[46] A comparison of texts shows this clearly. The references to the גֵר in the deuteronomic code speak, for instance, about:

the גֵר	*in your*	gates:	Deut 14,29
the גֵר	*in your*	land:	Deut 24,14
the גֵר	*in your*	midst:	Deut 16,11

In all these cases the Israelite community is at the *center*. The גֵר is someone who comes from the *periphery*. In Deut 23,8 and 10,19 this pattern is inverted:

for you were   גֵר   *in his land (i.e. of the Egyptian):*   Deut 23,8bβ
for you were   גרים   *in the land of the Egyptians:*   Deut 10,19b

When we compare the sentence: "the גֵר *in your* gates" with the sentence: "for you were גרים *in the land of the Egyptians*", the difference is clear: the first sentence speaks about "*the* גֵר", the second speaks, instead, about "*being* גֵר". In these motive clauses, for the first time in the Old Testament, Israel is not at the center. Here, it is the land of Egypt which is at the *center*. This situation is the reversal of the first one (i.e. Deut 24,14): the Israelites now look for a place of refuge somewhere *outside of their land*. This perspective represents a dramatic change. Behind the גֵר in these texts (Deut 10,19b; 23,8bβ) is clearly the outlook of the exile.

5.1.4 The transition from Deut 23,8b to Deut 10,19b

This transition is based on the following analogy:
An Egyptian גֵר in the land of Israel ≈ Israel גֵר in the land of Egypt

---

44   The theme of the "Guidance out of Egypt" is found in Deuteronomy in two ways: with the formula בְּיָד חֲזָקָה (6,21; 7,8; 26,8) and with the formula מִבֵּית עֲבָדִים (5,6; 6,12; 8,14; 13,6.11; 24,18), see Lubsczyk, Auszug p. 79-111.

45   Noth, ÜP p. 47-51, with an extensive list of references of this old formula which occurs in widely different contexts. See also Plöger, Untersuchungen p. 107-114.

46   See Zobel, FS G. Sauer p. 109.

The analogy is based on the *gentilicium* "Egyptian":

Deut 23,8bα   Deut 23,8bβ

You shall not abhor an *Egyptian*   because you were גר in *his* land.

The meaning of the sentence would then be:

You shall not abhor an Egyptian (גר in your land)

because you were גר in his land.

What counts here is *the origin* of the person (i.e. to be an Egyptian). This is the requirement for admittance in the assembly (Deut 23,8-9). In this way:

if the person is an Egyptian, he will be accepted in the assembly.

if the person is an Edomite or a Moabite, he will not be accepted.

What we have in 10,19b, instead, is the analogy:

a גר in Israel   ≈≈   the Israelites as גרים in the land of Egypt.

This analogy seems to be the same as that of 23,8b. There is, however, an essential difference between them. The analogy of 10,19b is not based on the *origin* of the person (to be an "Egyptian" as in 23,8b) but, on the *condition* of the person, to be גרים:

Deut 10,19a   Deut 10,19b

You shall love the גר   because you were גרים in Egypt.

What counts here is *the condition* of being a גר.[47] The admittance in the assembly is based solely on this criterion. In this way:

if the person is a גר, he will be accepted in the assembly,

if the person is a נכרי, he will not be accepted.

In the transition from Deut 23,8b to Deut 10,19b the emphasis shifts from the term "Egyptian" to the term "גר". This substitution is the result of a *generalizing tendency* according to which an *exclusive* term like "Egyptian" is substituted by an *inclusive* term like גר, which includes not only Egyptians but persons of any origin. "Being גרים" in Deut 10,19b is no longer a *historical statement* (as in 23,8b) but a *theological one*. That means: a command like Deut 23,8bα ("You shall not abhor an Egyptian"), can be interpreted as an expression of gratitude towards the Egyptians for what they have done in the past for the Israelites (Gen 47,4). It must be noted that three of the five commands which we find in Deut 23,2-9 (23,4a.8a.8b) are based on a principle of reciprocity: Israel acts towards Ammonites, Moabites and Egyptians according to the way in which they have treated Israel in the past 23,5a.5b.8bβ. A command like Deut 10,19a, instead, cannot be explained on this basis, but on a new self-understanding on the part of Israel. The prepositional phrase בארץ מצרים in Deut 10,19b, has only a circumstantial value. The central issue of this command has very little to do with Egypt.[48]

---

47   A comparison of Deut 10,19b with a similar later text makes this point of the centrality of the term גר clear. In the negative command of Ex 23,9, just like in Deut 10,19, we have the noun גר both in the command and in the motive clause.

48   The phrase ואתם ידעתם את־נפש הגר in Ex 23,9bα makes clear that in the motive clause "because you were גרים in the land of Egypt" (Deut 10,19b; Lev 19,34b; Ex

According to Schwienhorst-Schönberger, the Egypt-גֵר formula is used only
to support גֵר commands, that is, commands in which the noun גֵר is found
both in the main and in the motive clauses.[49]   Although Deut 23,8b is also a גֵר
- type of motive clause, it does not follow this pattern.   The reason for this
exception lies in the fact that Deut 23,8b is the original form from which Deut
10,19b (and parallels) derive.

In sum, it can be said that Deut 10,19 is the result of a generalizing tendency
according to which an *exclusive* term like "Egyptian" is substituted by an
inclusive term like גֵר.   That is: a negative command given on behalf of
Egyptians (only), is substituted later by a positive command including persons
of any origin.   This transformation took place during the Babylonian exile[50], a
time in which different theological conceptions acquired a new dimension of
universality.[51]

5.1.5 The Babylonian exile and the Egypt-גֵר tradition

In his study "Israelites as gerîm", F. A. Spina asks: what experience in the
life of Israel after the settlement would have led to the invention of the גֵר -
tradition?   Although the only time apart from the Egyptian bondage in which
Israel, as a people, could be said to have been גֵרִים was the exile, there is only
one single reference to this.[52] He concludes: "Some explanation for the silence
of the sources on Israel being *gerîm* in Babylon is required".[53]   The request
for this explanation confronts us with the issue of the relationship between the
formula of the Israelites as "גֵרִים in the land of *Egypt* " and the Babylonian
exile.

We must bear in mind that between the first and the second deportation to
Babylon there was a dispute between those who remained in Jerusalem, and
those who were exiled in Babylon regarding the question: which of the two
communities was really the legitimate heir of the tradition (Jer 24; 29,16-20).[54]
After the fall of Jerusalem the political spectrum changed, and rivalry occurred

---

22,20b;   23,9b) is not the term "Egypt", as in Deut 23,8bβ, what it matters but the
term גֵר.

49   Schwienhorst-Schönberger, Bundesbuch p. 350.
50   See Causse, EHPR 19 p. 192-195; 236f.   In words of Barbiero "Nella considerazione dt
      per il *ger* inizia un processo che condurrà ad un superamento della concezione
      nazionalistica del popolo di Dio in direzione di una comunità religiosa" (L'asino p. 202;
      330; 294).
51   See for example Robertson Smith, Religion p. 78.
52   Ezra 1,4 (גֵר), see Spina, FS D.N. Freedman p. 329.   Spina has overlooked Ez 20,38
      (מגוריהם).
53   Ibid.
54   Baltzer, FS G. von Rad 1961 p. 33-43.

between the Egyptian and the Babylonian communities.[55]   The narrative sections of the book of Jeremiah (37,11 - 43,7) are widely understood as a narrative written from the perspective of the Babylonian community as a political weapon against the Egyptian Gola.[56] The origin of the Egyptian community is portrayed in this work as an open act of disobedience against Yahweh:

"Yahweh has said to you: O remnant of Judah do not go to Egypt ... and all the people did not obey the voice of Yahweh ... and came into the land of Egypt" (Jer 42,19; 43,4.7).

The request of the people to the prophet Jeremiah ("Pray for us to Yahweh our God, and whatever Yahweh our God says, tell us and we will do it" 42,20), is portrayed as a political maneuver.[57] Lohfink titles this section of Jeremiah's book "Die Erzählung vom verwerflichen Ursprung der ägyptischen Gola".[58] Under these circumstances, positive attitudes towards Egypt were opposed. In the deuteronomic law concerning the king (Deut 17,16) and in the declaration of curses (Deut 28,68), we have two related verses which are expressions of this "anti-Egyptian" feeling.[59]

"he shall not return (שוב) the people to Egypt in order to multiply horses, for Yahweh has said "You shall never return (שוב) that way again" (Deut 17,16).	"Yahweh will bring you back (שוב) to Egypt in boats, in the way of which I said 'You shall never again see it'" (Deut 28,68).[60]

The similarities between the oracles against Egypt in Ez 17; 29-32 with those found in Is 19 and Jer 46 suggest that the major prophets shared a common fund of themes with regard to Egypt.[61] The inclusion of Egypt among the "bad figs" in Jer 24,8 is a later reinterpretation which becomes fully intelligible

---

55 Lohfink, ZAW 90 p. 333-341; Gonçalves, Biblica 76 p. 294-296.

56 Lohfink, ZAW 90 p. 337. According to Gonçalves: "Le pays de Juda étant vide et la communauté d'Egypte illégitime, il ne reste que la communauté de Babylone; c'est elle la porteuse de la légitimité judéene. Les récits de Jr 37-43. sont un document de propagande de la communauté juive de Babylone" (Biblica 76 p. 295).

57 Stipp, Jeremia p. 255. Cf. Jer 42,21.

58 Lohfink asks: "ob die ägyptische Gruppe denn ein solches Potential darstellte, daß sie die babylonische durch ihre Existenz in eine Identitätskrise stürzen konnte" (ZAW 90 p. 333), and explains that the Egyptian community could argue on her behalf that not only the prophet Jeremiah, but also the princesses of the royal court were among them. This second argument had particular force due to the importance of the princesses of the royal court as a symbol of legitimacy in Orient, 2 Sam 16,15ff. (ZAW 90 p. 334).

59 For the relation between these two prohibitions see Reimer, Concerning Return p. 217-229; and Schley, VT 35 p. 369-372.

60 Note that while Jeremiah speaks of going (בא) to Egypt (42,15.17.22; 43,2; 44,8.12.14.28), Deut speaks of returning (שוב) to Egypt (28,68; 17,16). Abrego sees here an "anti-exodus" (Jeremías p. 202-206). See also Schökel, Profetas p. 604; idem, FS H. Cazelles p. 245-254.

61 Boadt, Oracles p. 174.

only in the light of the narrative of chapter 44.[62]   D.J. Reimer states that the pro-Babylonian and anti-Egyptian polemic brings the concern against going to Egypt to the fore. "In the charged political atmosphere surrounding the collapse of Judah, the words of Moses that Yahweh's people should never again see the Egyptians (Ex XIV 13) took on deeper significance, first as an evil to be avoided in the curses of Deut XXVIII 68, then as a prohibition in Deut XVII 16, where the avoidance of Egypt is fully legitimized as a command of Yahweh".[63]

Some authors think that there is a tradition of an *Egyptian sojourn* before the "conquest" of Palestine, *different from* the formula of the guidance out of Egypt (related to the theme of the *Israelites as slaves in Egypt*). This tradition, although now artificially attached to the regular "bondage-and-deliverance" scheme (Ex 1,8), is really independent from the tradition of Egypt as the "house of slaves".[64]   The Egyptian Gola, based on this tradition of the well-being of the forefathers in Egypt, introduces with the Egypt-גר formula a differentiation in the understanding of Israel's past in Egypt. This motive clause may be seen as an attempt of the Egyptian Gola to legitimize theologically its origins. The formula "because you were גרים in the land of *Egypt",* relates the experience of the Diaspora community to the period of the well-being of Jacob and his family under Joseph.[65]   It was this experience, rather than the later slavery under Pharaoh, which offered them an appropriate analogy to understand their new life in Egypt. The formula attempts, then, to counteract the image of Egypt as the former "house of slaves".

---

62   See McKane, Jeremiah p. 611;   Thiel, Redaktion p. 257;   261 and Nicholson, Preaching p. 110.
63   Reimer, Concerning Return p. 225.
64   See for instance: Heaton, ET 58 p. 82;   Galling, FS A. Bertholet p. 185;   U. Kellermann, BN 2 p. 37.
65   See the verb גור in Gen 12,10;   47,4;   Deut 26,5;   Is 52,4;   Ps 105,23.

6. The Israelites as גרים with Yahweh

The analogy of the Israelites as גרים with/before Yahweh is found three times in the Old Testament:

1.	גרים ... עמדי	Lev 25,23
2.	גר ... עמך	Ps 39,13
3.	גרים ... לפניך	1 Chron 29,15

This idea is attested for the first time in the legal realm (Lev 25,23b). Ps 39,13 and 1 Chron 29,15 depend on Lev 25,23b.[1] The noun גר is commonly used in the Old Testament with the preposition ב. These three motive clauses used, instead, the prepositions "עם" and "ל" (i.e. פנים + ל => לפניך).

6.1 Lev 25,23b

Lev 25,23b is a late text.[2] This conclusion is based on stylistic and theological grounds.

Stylistic grounds:
• The hendiadys גרים ותושבים (Lev 25,23b) is a typical formula of P's theology (see p. 101). The word תושב appears only in the priestly literature.[3]

---

1 See p. 102ff. and Cortese, Levitico p. 116.

2 According to von Rad: "Der Satz Lev 25,23 [...] ist uralt und der Grundsatz des alttestamentlichen Bodenrechtes" (TB 8 p.137, underlining is ours). Lev 25,23 includes the main clause (Lev 25,23aα) and the two motive clauses Lev 25,23aβ and 25,23b. It is true that the first motive clause "denn das Land ist mein" (Lev 25,23aβ), is a very old idea. The second motive clause "ihr seid Fremdlinge und Beisassen bei mir" (Lev 25,23b), however, can hardly be pre-exilic; cf. Kilian, Untersuchung p. 148; Noth, Leviticus p. 165; Graf Reventlow, Heiligkeitsgesetz p. 132-134. It must be noted that in a later article, von Rad modifies his first statement and says that "der Grundsatz, den Lev 25,23 ausspricht, sehr alt ist" (TB 8 p. 92, underlining is ours). The "Grundsatz" includes only Lev 25,23a, i.e. the main clause "Darum sollt ihr das Land nicht verkaufen für immer" (Lev 25,23aα), and the *first* motive clause "denn das Land ist mein" (Lev 25,23aβ), not the *second* motive clause ("ihr seid Fremdlinge und Beisassen bei mir" Lev 25,23b).

3 Ex 12,45; Lev 22,10; 25,6.40.45, for 1 K 17,1 see note in BHS. For the noun תושב in the hendiadys גר/ים ותושב/ים, see Gen 23,4; Lev 25,35.47a.47b; Num 35,15.

• The apodictic commandments of the Holiness Code use only one motive clause[4]; the use of a double motive clause in Lev 25,23b, is exceptional and is a sign of a later addition.

• While the main clause in Lev 25,23aα is in the second person singular וְהָאָרֶץ לֹא תִמָּכֵר לִצְמִתֻת, the second motive clause in Lev 25,23b is in the second person plural כִּי־גֵרִים וְתוֹשָׁבִים אַתֶּם עִמָּדִי. The combination of singular and plural forms in Lev 25 is not normally found within the same verse: in the prescriptions on the sabbatical year singular and plural forms are not combined (Lev 25,3-7 is in singular form, Lev 25,18-22 in plural form). The same is true in the case of the prescriptions about the year of jubilee (Lev 25,8.9a.15b.16 are in singular form, Lev 25,9b-13.23.24 in plural form).

Theological grounds:

• The analogy of *Israel as* גֵר has a late origin in the Old Testament, see p. 101.

• A characteristic feature of Lev 25,23-24 is what Elliger calls "das redende Ich Jahwes".[5]   We know that in the Holiness Code passages which were originally composed as sermons (and originally written in impersonal terms), were redrafted at a later date as utterances of God, mostly by making God speak in the first person in the introductory and concluding sentences.[6]   That is precisely what we have in the motive clause of Lev 25,23aβ.b "for the land is mine; with me you are but aliens and tenants".

• The rationale behind the law of the sabbatical year (Lev 25,1-7) was based on the fact that Yahweh was the real owner of the Land. *All* prescriptions found in the Pentateuch in relation to the harvest (the laws of the first fruits, the laws of the tithes and those of the gleaning in fields and vineyards), are based on this same premise.[7]   Although the idea of Yahweh as the sole owner of the Land is present in different ways throughout the Pentateuch, the idea found in V. 23b (that the Israelites were but גֵרִים וְתוֹשָׁבִים), has no pre-exilic parallel.[8]

---

4   Lev 17,14; 18,10.13; 19,20; 20,19.23; 21,6.7.12.14.15.23; 22,6.9.20.25; 23,28; 25,17; 25,34; 26,1.44.

5   Elliger, Leviticus p. 339.

6   Von Rad, Studien p. 18-19.

7   Some of these laws are old pre-Israelite agrarian customs which have been historicised. Now they are taken as an offering to Yahweh in the person of the poor ones, see Buis-Leclercq, Deutéronome p. 163.   As Pikaza explains: "Dios aparece aquí (i.e. in Lev 25,23) como el único dueño de la tierra. Los hombres la poseen tan sólo a nombre suyo y deben por ello pagar de esa tierra a Dios religiosamente un tributo. Como aquel que trabaja los campos de otro debe dar a su señor una parte de los frutos, también los que cultivan la tierra de Yavé deben ofrecer a su Dios lo mejor de sus cosechas" (Biblia p. 97-98).

8   Von Rad, TB 8 p. 93-94; 96.   The pre-exilic idea about the land was that it belonged to the family and was inalienable, see 1 K 21 and Gerstenberger, Leviticus p. 349-350. Behind Lev 25,23b is, instead, the conception that all persons are wholly dependent upon God, the owner of the land, and live on it more (גֵר) or less (תּוֹשָׁב) permanently; cf. Snaith, Leviticus p. 112.

The hendiadys גרים ותושבים (Lev 25,23b) is a typical formula of P's theology.[9] It appears in P according to different patterns:

1) as conjoint hendiadys (singular): גר ותושב: Gen 23,4; Lev 25,35.47a
2) as conjoint hendiadys (plural): גרים ותושבים: Lev 25,23
3) as juxtaposed hendiadys: גר תושב: Lev 25,47b
4) as conjunction + preposition: ולגר ולתושב: Num 35,15

It must be noticed that the people of Israel are said to have been גר only a few times in the Old Testament:

"גר היית in his land" (i.e. land of the Egyptian): Deut 23,8b[10]
"גר יהיה in a land which is not theirs" (i.e. Egypt): Gen 15,13[11]
"גרים הייתם in the land of Egypt": Deut 10,19b[12]

Apart from these three deuteronomistic references[13], Israel is said to have been גר in Lev 25,23b, and in 1 Chron 29,15 (Ps 39,13).

This shows that, while the formula "because you were גרים in the land of Egypt" (Deut 10,19b) is deuteronomistic, the pair גרים ותושבים, with reference to Israel, is a typical priestly statement. In other words, *while in the deuteronomistic history Israel was* גר *"in Egypt", in the priestly writings Israel is* גר *"before Yahweh".*

6.2 "גר *with Yahweh" as P formula*

Lev 25,23b modifies in two important ways the use of the noun גר. It introduces a new pattern in the relation between the גר and the *community* and between the גר and the *land.*

---

9   The combination of the terms תושב and גר is somehow strange. Cortese comments: "questo strano accoppiamento di parole (v. 23b) è escogitato per non ridurre gli Israeliti a semplici proseliti (gerîm) o a gente sprovvista di beni terrieri come i Leviti e, dal'altra parte, per non presentarli come padroni assoluti del loro appezzamento, come gli indigeni ('ezrâ)" (Levitico p. 116). The expression גר ותושב is used to refer either to non-Israelites (Lev 25,35.47a.47b) or to Israelites (Lev 25,23).
10   כי־גר היית בארצו (Deut 23,8b).
11   גר יהיה זרעך בארץ לא להם (Gen 15,13a).
12   כי־גרים הייתם בארץ מצרים (Deut 10,19b; Lev 19,34; Ex 22,20; 23,9). The deuteronomistic statement that Israel was a גר in Egypt (Deut 23,8; 10,19), was taken up later as motive clause in the Holiness Code (Lev 19,34) and in the book of the Covenant (Ex 22,20; 23,9).
13   On Gen 15,13 see Weimar, Untersuchungen p. 52 note 153; on Lev 19,34 see Martin-Achard, THAT I col. 412; on Ex 22,20 and 23,9 see Schwienhorst-Schönberger, Bundesbuch p. 338ff.; 346ff.

In the laws of the Pentateuch the גר is often distinguished from the *community* of Israelites. The Holiness Code distinguishes:
"between the House of Israel and the גר"[14] and
"between the sons of Israel and the גר"[15]

Lev 25,23b uses for the first time the noun גר to name Israel's assembly.
In this verse, the גרים *are the Israelites!* This is a fundamental change in the use of this noun. Until now the גר was a stranger or a foreigner living among the Israelites.[16] *Now the גרים are the Israelites themselves in relation to Yahweh*[17], the real owner of the land. It must be noted that in this case, as in the deuteronomistic references mentioned above, the designation of the Israelites as גרים is made directly by Yahweh.

In Lev 25,23b there is a new point of reference for the definition of the גר.
Although the term ארץ appears twice in Lev 25,23a, the use of the noun גר in V. 23b is defined not in relation to the *land* but in relation to *Yahweh* alone.[18]
This means that, while in the Old Testament the noun גר is used mostly with a social and territorial dimension[19], in Lev 25,23b גר is used with a *religious* dimension, i.e. to understand themselves in relation to Yahweh.

6.3 The status of the גר: a cultic origin?

Besides Lev 25,23b, the idea of being "גר with/before Yahweh" is found only in two other texts:

Ps 39,13:   For I am a גר with thee / a sojourner, like all my ancestors.[20]

כי גר אנכי עמך תושב ככל־אבותי

1 Chron 29,15: For we are גרים before thee and passing guests as all our fathers were

כי־גרים אנחנו לפניך ותושבים ככל־אבתינו

---

14   מבית ישראל ומן־הגר (Lev 17,8.10; 22,18).
15   מבני ישראל ומן־הגר (Lev 17,13; 20,2).
16   The suffix ך in the preposition עמך refers to the Israelite who is the native, i.e. the האזרח of Lev 25,47a.47b.
17   See עמדי in Lev 25,23b; עמדי is attested in the book of Leviticus only here, otherwise we find only the form עמי (Lev 26,21.23.27.40).
18   Note that even late references like Is 14,1 and Ez 47,22 still relate the גר to the theme of the land.
19   That is גר + ב, see p. 66 and 86.
20   Translation from Meek in AT.

H. Wildberger has suggested that Lev 25,23 has its origin in the cultic language of Psalm 15,1.[21]   Ps 15,1 and Lev 25,23b seem to speak, however, about different matters:

Ps 15,1:   speaks about: sojourning (גור)   *in*   (ב)   Yahweh's <u>tent.</u>
Lev 25,23: speaks about: being גר   *with* (עם)   <u>Yahweh.</u>

Ps 15,1 is related to the idea of religious asylum, a very ancient institution in the religions of the ancient Near East.[22]   Whoever enters within the limits of the sacred area becomes the host of the divinity.   Due to the extraterritorial character of the sanctuary, the human laws lose their validity within this space. As Ravasi states: "Chi entra nel tempio diventa ospite della divinità a cui compete ogni diritto d'intervento nei confronti dell'ospite".[23]   Moreover, besides its metaphorical use in Ps 39,13 and 119,19[24], the meaning of term גר in the book of Psalms is that of the *persona misera* [25], which is based on the pre-exilic deuteronomic triad.[26]

The idea behind Lev 25,23 is, instead, a typical post-exilic idea.   As Ehrlich's explains:

"Die Vorstellung aber, dass die Israeliten insgesamt ihr Land nicht zu eigen, sondern nur als Lehen von JHWH haben und als seine Schutzbefohlenen darin wohnen, drängte sich ihnen erst nach dem Exile auf, nachdem sie die Erfahrung gemacht hatten, dass die Zuziehung der Ungnade JHWHs sie daraus entfernen konnte".[27]

The use of the pair גר ותושב in other P texts shows that the idea of being just a stranger and an alien allowed to live among others, responds to P's theology, see Gen 23,4; Lev 25,35.47a.   The description of Canaan as the land in which the fathers lived as aliens is also typical of P.[28]   This idea, like the motif of Abraham[29], is exilic.

Finally, it is interesting to note that the introductory formula in Ps 39,13 כי גר אנכי עמך, has the same elements of Abraham's self presentation formula to the sons of Heth: גר ותושב אנכי עמכם (Gen 23,4).   Both texts introduce a petition: Ps 39 in the context of a prayer, Gen 23 in the context of a legal transaction.

---

21   Wildberger, EvTh 16 p. 418.
22   See p. 31 note 115.
23   Ravasi, Salmí I p. 276 note 5.
24   Ps 119,19 is clearly a late reference.   On the relationship between Ps 119 and Ps 39 see Croft, Identity p. 169; 176.
25   Ps 94,6; 146,9.
26   Deut 14,29; 16,11.14; 24,17.19.20.21; 26,12.13.
27   Ehrlich, Randglossen II p. 92.
28   Gen 17,8; 28,4; 36,7; 37,1; Ex 6,4 (all P).   See also Cortese, Terra p. 75-78.
29   Hardmeier, WuD 16 p. 27-47.   The preposition לפני (= 1 Chron 29,15 לפנך) is also used in the divine command given to Abraham in Gen 17,1: התהלך לפני.

Gen 23,4   גר ותושב אנכי עמכם

Ps 39,13   (כי) גר   אנכי עמך תושב

As usual in P, the pair גר ותושב in Gen 23,4 appears in hendiadys, while in
Ps 39,13 in parallelism. This explains the different position of the second noun
תושב. Although the function of the formula is in both cases the same (i.e. to
support a petition made in first person), Gen 23,4 is not a motive clause. This
element, and the fact that the idea of a pilgrim theology in the Psalms was
inspired by the priestly idea of the temporary sojourn of the forefathers in
Canaan[30], suggests that the motive clauses in Ps 39,13 and 1 Chron 29,15 are
dependent on the legal tradition and not vice versa.

In sum: Wildberger's idea, that Lev 25,23 has its origin in the cultic
language of Psalm 15,1, does not seem a convincing suggestion. Ps 15,1 and
Lev 25,23b deal respectively with different matters; while Ps 15,1 speaks about
the *uralt* institution of religious asylum for individuals, Lev 25,23b uses the
theological metaphor of the Israelites as גרים, which is a late religious concept
(גר עמדי). Lev 25,23b is an internal development of the priestly theology.
The statement about the land as Yahweh's property, leads logically to the
analogy of the Israelites as גרים: in Yahweh's land the Israelites can only be
גרים.[31] Furthermore, it must be noted that the basic construction גר + עם
(Lev 25,23b), is already found in Gen 23,4: גר ותושב אנכי עמכם (P).

6.3.1 Ps 39,13 and 1 Chron 29,15

When we see these two verses in the perspective of other references to the
גר in the Old Testament, we can distinguish two dimensions to the experience
of being גר: strangeness and dependency. These two dimensions are
illustrated by the metaphorical use of the noun גר. When the noun גר is used
of human beings the dimension of *dependency* is stressed. In Ps 39,13 the
Psalmist says "I am a גר with you ...". Here he sees himself as a *protégé* of
Yahweh, in a relationship which is based on a principle of mercy.

In Jer 14,8, on the contrary, the noun is used for Yahweh. Here the noun
גר has a different nuance:
"O thou who art the hope of Israel,
Its saviour in time of trouble,

---

30   See Hossfeld-Zenger, Psalmen p. 251.
31   On this theme see Joosten's insightful comments in People p. 196-200. Cholewiński
     sees in Lev 25,23 כי־לי הארץ כי־גרים ותושבים אתם עמדי a correction: "der in
     P vertretenen Auffassung, dass das Land unbedingtes Eigentum der Israeliten ist"
     (Heiligkeitsgesetz p. 334). He is probably thinking about Gen 17,8. Blum taken into
     account the expression ארץ אחזתכם in Lev 25,24 considers, however, that "die
     'Differenz' zwischen Gen 17 bzw. Lev 25 liegt in der jeweiligen Aussagerichtung"
     (Komposition p. 336).

Why shouldst thou be like a stranger in the land
Like a traveller who turns aside to lodge for a night?" (Jer 14,8)[32]
In this verse the dimension of dependency is impossible; the author stresses instead, the dimension of *strangeness*.
Why shouldst thou be (stranger)[33]
like a stranger in the land?

The term גר is used here in an elaborate appeal for help, similar to that of Ps 39,13.[34] An important development of this idea of dependency takes place outside of the Pentateuch: what appears in Lev 25,23 as a statement of Yahweh, turns into a *self-designation* in the prayer of the Psalmist (Ps 39,13) and the people (1 Chron 29,15). In both cases the motive clauses have a similar structure[35]:

Ps 39,13:   כי גר אנכי עמך תושב   ככל־אבותי
1 Chron 29,15: כי־גרים אנחנו לפניך ותושבים   ככל־אבתינו

The particle כי introduces in both cases a statement of self abasement in first person: אנכי (Ps 39,13); אנחנו (1 Chron 29,15). Reference to the fathers is made in both cases: אבותי (Ps 39,13) and אבתינו (1 Chron 29,15).[36]

The statements of Ps 39,13 and 1 Chron 29,15, function in both cases as an appeal which introduces a petition: since the person is no more than a guest and sojourner, he humbly entrusts himself to the protection and assistance of Yahweh as lord of the land. The transition of Israel's self understanding from former *patron* of the needy in the legal texts, to *protégé* in the prayers of Psalms and 1 Chronicles, represents a significant reversal of roles. The ones who used to help, now seek the help of Yahweh.

---

32   Translation: A.R. Gordon in AT.
33   According to Bourguet, this is the sense of the metaphor "Pourquoi es-tu étranger comme un étranger dans le pays?" (Métaphores p. 63).   Note that the LXX, which usually translates גר by προσήλυτος, has here πάροικος.
34   Jer 14,7-9 is a liturgy of penitence and petition. The people cry out to Yahweh for mercy and confess their utter dependence upon Him (= 1 Chron 29,15). In this text the גר (Yahweh) is not portrayed, however, as powerless. On the contrary, the complaint is addressed to him precisely because he is in the position to settle the problem, which seems to consist in Yahweh's apparent indifference. He acts as if he had no part nor commitment: "Why does he act as if he were simply passing through it (i.e. the land), making a digression in order to get a night's lodging *en route*" (McKane, Jeremiah p. 320). See also Duhm, Jeremia p. 128; Bright, Jeremiah p. 102 and Holladay, Jeremiah 1 p. 424.
35   There are also some differences: while Ps 39,13 is singular, 1 Chron 29,15 is plural; they use different prepositions: Ps 39,13 uses עמך; 1 Chron 29,15 uses לפניך and only in 1 Chron we have an appositive waw ותושבים.
36   According to Japhet, 1 Chron 29,15 is based on a quotation from Ps 39,13 (Ideology, p. 340).

The idea of self-abasement, which is present in 1 Chron 29,14-16, is not an exception. This element was common in the piety of post-exilic period.[37] The same motive is also present in Josaphat's and Ezra's prayers.[38] The confession and forgiveness of sins, which played only a subordinate role in earlier personal piety, became in post-exilic times the regular presupposition for the saving intervention of Yahweh on behalf of those commended to his protection.[39]

The sociological background of the metaphor of the Israelites as גֵּרִים, may be sought in the political situation of Palestine during the post-exilic period. Under the Persian rule Israel became גֵּר in its own land[40]: "Man kehrt nach 538 teilweise zurück ins alte Land, aber diese Rückkehr ist eine Rückkehr in eine Diaspora, ist eine Rückkehr in eine neue Fremde".[41] The self designation of גֵּרִים, brings the Israelites under the direct protection of Yahweh, and allow them to transfer the hopes, formerly pinned on the land, to Yahweh. This absolute dependence on God, empowered them to overcome the uncertainties and the sense of strangeness created by the possession of their land by foreigners, Neh 9,36-37.[42] As Schreiner states:

"Wer die Fremdlingschaft in seinem Dasein erlebt und verspürt, wird darauf hingewiesen, daß Jahwe sein mächtiger Schutzherr ist. Im Vertrauen auf ihn und im Anschluß an ihn ist das Fremdsein zu überwinden".[43]

---

37 In this connection O. Plöger states: "So wird man überhaupt zu erwägen haben, ob der Chronist mit seiner relativ häufigen Verwendung von Gebeten nicht einem Brauche folgt, wie er ebenfalls in der Gemeinde seiner Zeit üblich war und geschichtlich aus der Exilszeit herzuleiten ist, in der als Ersatz für das fehlende Opfer das Gebet eine besondere Rolle gespielt haben wird" (Spätzeit p. 61).   See also p. 60-66 espec. 64.

38 See 2 Cron 20,12 and Ezra 9,15.   The form-critical perspective of the prayer in Ezra 9 is unique, it comprises confession only, with no supplication: *general confession* (6-7); reflection on God's present mercies (8-9); *specific confession* (10-12); statement of future intent (13-14) and *general confession* (15).   This feature distinguishes this passage from the penitential psalms of lament or other passages such as Neh 1,5-11; 9,6-38; Dan 9,4-19; see Williamson, Ezra p.127ff.

39 Albertz, Religionsgeschichte p. 560.   After the exile, religion was no longer the national system of an ethnic group, the protection and favour of God was no longer seen as a *national right*, but as a matter of free grace: "the relation of the new worshippers to the god ... was constituted not by nature and inherited privilege, but by submission on the worshipper's side" (Robertson Smith, Religion p. 78).

40 Welten, FS R. Mayer 1987 p. 137.

41 Mosis, Exil p. 65-66.

42 See also Ezra 9,6-15, espec. verse 11;   Dan 9,4-19, espec. verses 16-18.

43 Schreiner, BiKi 42 p. 58.

6.3.2 "גרים like all our fathers"

In their prayers, the authors of Ps 39 and 1 Chron 29 distinguish two
historical moments, that of the forefathers and that of their generation before
Yahweh:

Ps 39,13:	All my fathers	<==>	I
1 Chron 29,15:	All our fathers[44]	<==>	We
	in the land		before Yahweh

Although their ancestors (both Patriarchs and subsequent generations[45]),
resided as גרים in the land of Canaan, the religious community of the post-
exilic times no longer takes the land as the point of reference to define
themselves, but rather Yahweh.

The statements of Ps 39,13aẞ and 39,13b both stress the aspect of
strangeness but, while the point of reference in the case of the ancestors is still
territorial (i.e. they were גרים *in the land)*[46], for the author's generation the
point of reference is *religious* (i.e. they are גרים *with Yahweh).* In this way,
what was said about the fathers in relation to the land of Canaan (past), is now
said about Israel in relation to Yahweh (present).[47]   In other words, the term
גר is not used in these prayers with the usual legal meaning but with a new
religious sense.

6.3.3 "גרים with you"

As was mentioned before, whereas in the legal context of Lev 25,23b it is
Yahweh himself who calls the Israelites גרים, in Ps 39,13 the noun גר is used,
instead, as a *self reference* : Ps 39,13: For I am a גר with thee ... (עמך).

---

44 Note that with the exception of Gen 23,4 the *nominal* form גר is never used for the
    fathers. The *verbal* forms are, however, common. See for instance גור (Gen 12,10;
    19,9; 26,3); ויגר (Gen 20,1; 21,34); גרתה (Gen 21,34); גרתי (Gen 32,5); גר
    (Gen 35,27; Ps 105,23); גרו (Ex 6,4).

45 These two prayers do not speak simply about "our fathers" but about "*all* our fathers"
    ככל־אבותי (Ps 39,13); ככל־אבתינו (1 Chron 29,15).   There are two possible
    groups referred to by ככל־אבתינו: (1) within the context of prayer, אבתינו is used
    with specific reference to Abraham, Isaac and Jacob, see for instance 1 Chron 29,18:
    אברהם יצחק וישראל אבתינו. See also ישראל אבינו in 1 Chron 29,10.   In
    this case, the relationship between the spiritual sojourning of the nation before Yahweh
    and the sojourning of the patriarchs is in view.   (2) The use of כל with אבתינו
    makes it more likely, however, that the reference is to the entire sweep of Israel's
    history, including both the patriarchs and their descendants (Estes, CBQ 53 p. 48).   The
    expression refers, then, not only to the Patriarchs but to all the previous generations, see
    Delitzsch, Psalmen p. 329; Schökel, Salmos p. 585.
46 Ps 105,12 = 1 Chron 16,19 (participle גרים).
47 Hermisson, Sprache p. 112-113.

The author of Ps 39,13 excludes the *human* עִמְּךָ (i.e. the עִמְּךָ in which ךָ =
the Israelite[48]), and stresses the *divine* עִמְּךָ of the Israelites before Yahweh
(i.e. the עִמְּךָ in which ךָ = Yahweh).   In this way, the transitory nature of
human existence is shown in its fragility before the divine presence.[49]

This metaphorical use of גֵּר in Ps 39,13 and 1 Chron 29,15 sheds light on
the nature of the גֵּר laws of the Pentateuch.   The noun גֵּר appears more than 70
% of the cases in legal texts, but below the surface of these legal texts lies a
principle of *mercy*.   In a patron - *protégé* relationship, the patron is not
necessarily compelled to act in the way expected by the person in need; but the
voluntary action on behalf of him who is weaker and needier than himself,
shows the nature of his ethical character.   That is why Job mentioned the
hospitality offered to the גֵּר as an argument on his own behalf in his trial
against God (31,32).[50]

---

48   In Lev 25,35.47.47 we have: גֵּר עִמָּךְ.   See also Lev 25,6: נֵרִים עִמָּךְ and Lev 25,39-
     40: עִמָּךְ ... תוֹשָׁב.
49   See Asensio, Gregorianum 34 p. 423.   See also Ps 73,25.28.
50   In the 125th chapter of the Egyptian Book of the Dead we find similar declarations of
     innocence in first-person prose. The dead person is portrayed as speaking in his own
     defense in the court of the afterlife. These two examples respond to the hierarchical
     ethos of the ancient Near East according to which the righteous man is primarily
     characterised by his treatment of the underprivileged. See Havice, Concern p. 292-295;
     45-51. According to the eudemonistic ethics of Deuteronomy, good actions on behalf
     of the needy are encouraged with the promise of reward. The laws of Deut 24,19 and
     14,28-29 are followed by the clause "so that the Lord your God will bless you in all
     your undertakings".   On the subject of the motives of charity see Bolkestein,
     Wohltätigkeit p. 45-53. This element can also be seen in the relation of the Psalmist
     to Yahweh. The fact of supporting his petition by introducing himself as a גֵּר (Ps
     39,13), illustrates one of the various ways in which he appeals to the *favour* of Yahweh.
     The attempt to move God on his behalf shows that His help was not something that
     was taken for granted.

Part 4

Alterity *and* identity, alterity *as* identity

7. The peculiar concern for the גֵּר in the Old Testament

In the first two parts of this study we have discussed the legal nature of the noun גֵּר and its usage for the individuum in the deuteronomic and in the Holiness codes. We have considered, next, its usage for Israel, especially its metaphorical use in a religious sense (third part). In these final chapters we want to point out some external connections of this subject, backwards and forward. That is, firstly to address the question: is there a point in which the use of the noun גֵּר in the Old Testament leaves behind the common elements shared with the surrounding cultures in relation to the matter of the stranger/foreigner and develops a new conception on its own? Secondly: what are the implications that this noun had in its later development beyond the limits of the Old Testament, i.e. the theme of the understanding of human existence as a *peregrinatio*.

7.1 The foreigner in the society of the ancient near East

Direct and indirect references to strangers and foreigners are common in the literature of the ancient near East. By indirect references we understand those based on an onomastic study.

Indirect references:

• The use of foreign *personal names*.[1]

• Names derived from foreign *toponyms*. In the archives of Ugarit we have names derived from foreign toponyms such as: "The Aradian", "the Tyrian", "the Giblite", "the Sareptian", "the man from Acco", "the man from Joppe", "the Yabnian".[2] In Ebla there are personal names which are identical to the name of a place (A-BA-GA, A-LU, BA-GA-MA), and sometimes the personal name corresponds to the place of origin of the person, such as DU-LU from DU-LU^KI.[3]

• The direct reference to the *place of origin* or nationality of the persons, such as the case of a Neobabylonian marriage contract between a Persian and the daughter of an Egyptian which mentions among the witnesses: Babylonians, an

---

1   For Ugarit see Gröndahl, Personennamen p. 10ff.; 203ff; 260ff; for Nuzi see Gelb / Purves / Mac Rae, Personal Names p. 193-197; for Egypt: Schneider, Personennamen p. 15ff.; for Amarna in particular see Hess, Personal Names p. 185-200.

2   Astour, RA 53 p. 71-72.

3   Krebernik, Personennamen p. 6.

Aramean, an Egyptian and two Persians.[4]   In the archives of Ugarit we have lists of personal names (sometimes nicknames), arranged according to the village, the city or the kingdom they belonged to, such as: "the man from the city of Mṣr.", "the man from the city of Snr", "the man from the city of 'rgz" or "the man from the city of Pdy".[5]

Direct references:

There are some other references to strangers and foreigners which can be called direct, that is: they use specific words to designate the stranger, such as the Akkadian adjectives "aḫû" (strange [person], foreigner, outsider)[6], "nakru" (foreign, strange and in substantival use: alien)[7], or the Sumerian ideogram "kur" (anderer, Feind).[8]

Although strangers and foreigners are mentioned in a wide range of documents (letters, administrative documents, royal inscriptions, confirmations by oath (i.e. Beschwörungen), incantations, reports of travels, omen texts and other kinds of literature)[9], no reference is made to them in legal codes[10], except in those cases in which they are mentioned in the sections dealing with:

• the sale and purchase of *slaves:* the code of Hammurapi for instance, mentions the "sons of another country" (see paragraphs § 280-281), but these are no more than slaves of foreign extraction.[11]   In the Middle Assyrian laws (Table L, paragraph 2, line 5), we have the words 'lū ubre' ("to a foreigner").[12]   But due to the fragmentary condition of the text, it is impossible to reconstruct the probable meaning of this reference.[13]   Even the Akkadian noun ubāru(m) ("Ortsfremder, Beisasse, Schutzbürger"[14]), compared by

---

4   Cardascia, RSJB 9 p. 115; other examples in Kohler, Rechtsleben p. 5-7.

5   Virolleaud, RA XXXVII p. 39-40.

6   See CAD A I/1 p. 210-211; AHw 1 p. 22.

7   See CAD N I/11 p. 189-192; AHw 2 p. 723.

8   "kur": anders sein, ein anderer, fremd, feind sein; see MSL II p. 130; SL III.1 p. 146; Delitzsch, SG p. 127 (with references).

9   See Reiner, ŠURPU p. 42 line 58; Meier, MAQLÛ p. 31 line 79; Leahy, Foreigners p. 225-234; Limet, ABAW N.F. 75 p. 130ff.; Cardascia, RSJB 9 p. 107ff.; Glassner, ZA 80 p. 60ff.; Loprieno, ÄA 48 p. 22ff.; Helck, Saeculum 15 p. 106ff.; Astour, RA 53 p.70ff.; Ebeling, Art. Flüchtling, in: RLA III p. 88-90; Leemans, Foreign p. 139-142; Stamm, Fremde p. 38ff.; Gelb, JNES 32 p. 79-80; and references to nakru (CAD N I/11 p. 190ff) and ubāru(m) (AHw 3 p. 1399).

10   As Cardascia has laconically stated: "On ne connaît aucun texte législatif réglant la condition de l'étranger" (RSJB 9 p. 105).   This result is confirmed after checking the list of references given in the AHw to terms such as "ubāru(m)" (3 p. 1399), "ubartu(m)" (3 p. 1399), "wabru(m), ubru(m)" (3 p. 1454)".

11   For the discussion of this text see Driver, Laws I, p. 482ff. and Koschaker, Studien p. 101-110.

12   Roth, Law p. 188; "uomo forastiero" (Saporetti, Leggi p. 138); "au bourgeois" (Cardascia, Lois p. 326).

13   See comments in Saporetti, Leggi p. 139.

14   AHw 3 p. 1399.

Stamm with the Hebrew noun גור[15], is used in proverbs[16], religious names[17], in instructions for the temple service[18], in the epic of Gilgamesh[19], in personal names[20], but not in legal texts.[21]

• the prescriptions to regulate the relationships of emigrants and *refugees*[22]: these laws distinguished between the *free emigrant*[23], i.e. that who leaves his original place for political or personal reasons (Eshnunna § 30; CH § 136; 30f.; Lipit Ishtar § 15f.), and the *slave* (Lipit Ishtar § 12-13; CH § 15-20; Hittite Laws § 22-24[24]). The flight of slaves of both sexes seems to have been quite common.[25]

7.2 The רג in Israel's legal tradition

A comparison of the role of the stranger in texts of the ancient near Eastern literature with that of the רג in the Old Testament, shows a significant contrast that is particularly clear because of the legal status of the רג in the laws of the Pentateuch.   As Limet explains in relation to the stranger in the Sumerian society: "Alors que son statut est souvent réglé juridiquement, en sa faveur ou contre lui, les codes de lois anciens, en Mésopotamie, n'y font pas allusion".[26] In the Old Testament, on the contrary, the noun רג is attested sixty three times in the Tora, fourteen times in the Nebiîm[27] and four times in the Ketubim.[28] Not only the number of these references but its distribution speaks by itself.   If we take into account that the Old Testament laws are part of the wider legal tradition of the ancient near East, and that even in the cases in which there is a different legal treatment, both address usually the same kind of problems[29], the

---

15   Stamm, Fremde p. 43; idem, Namengebung 264.   For the critic of this opinion see Levy, HUCA 27 p. 59.
16   Lambert, BWL 259.
17   Stamm, Namengebung 251.
18   Neu, Gewitterritual p. 77f.
19   Gilgamesh XII, 15 (ANET p. 97).
20   Faust, YOS VIII p. 24; Rouault, MUKANNIŠUM, 58,15 (= p. 81).
21   On ubāru(m) see Neu, Gewitterritual p. 76-79; Kühne, Korrespondenz p. 29; Cassin, RA 52 p. 27-28; Levy, HUCA 27 p. 59 and references given in AHw 3 p. 1399.
22   See Meissner, Babylonien p. 383f.
23   That is the case, for instance, of the maqtu: "fugitive" (CAD M/I p. 255); "Entlaufener" (AHw 2 p. 608); and the arbu: "fugitive" (CAD A/II.1 p. 239; "flüchtig, Ausreißer": AHw 1 p. 66); see Ebeling, Art. Flüchtling p. 88-89.
24   Imparati, Leggi p. 45-47.
25   Driver, Laws 1 p. 105f.
26   ABAW N.F. 75 p. 123.
27   Three times in Joshua; one time in 2 Samuel and ten times in the Prophets.
28   Three times in Psalms (two times with an extended meaning); one time in Job.
29   Westerbrook, CahRB 26 p.1.

difference between them in relation to the theme of the stranger/foreigner is, then, striking. This makes the theme of the resident alien a unique concern of the Old Testament with no parallel in the surrounding cultures.[30] Moreover, this interest of the Old Testament in the גר is a specific *legal* concern: it must be noted that, while we have sixty references to the גר in the laws[31], there is no single reference to him in the Proverbs![32] All the more significant when we consider that concern for the stranger outside of Israel, appears commonly in the wisdom literature.[33]

"Der Fremde ist rechtlos".[34] This laconic statement defines a basic difference between the status of the resident alien in Israel and in the surrounding cultures. The Old Testament, instead, speaks about the right of the גר (i.e. משפט גר).[35] The Israelite is commanded: "You shall not subvert *the rights of the* גר" (Deut 24,17)[36], and also: "Give the members of your community a fair hearing, and judge rightly (שפטתם צדק) between one person and another, whether citizen or גר" (Deut 1,16 NSRV). This means that the book of Deuteronomy protects the right of the גר to a fair trial *even*

---

30 This confirms Krapf's opinion in the sense that the legal protection of the resident alien (Fremdling) is "ein spezifisch israelitisches Anliegen" (VT 34 p. 88). Van der Toorn, making reference to the Akkadian term "kidinnu", states that "the notion of strangers living under a sacred protection was not unknown to the Mesopotamian" (Sin p. 16). The kidinnu was a person under *divine protection*, but this protection was not, however, identical to the *legal status* of the גר in Israel. See references to this term in CAD K p. 342-344 and AHw 1 p. 472-473.

31 See p. 18.

32 The Israelite law is specifically interested in the גר. This term appears sixty one times throughout *all legal codes* of the Old Testament. The noun נכרי, in an ethnical, political or geographical sense (see Humbert, Opuscules p. 111ff.), appears 29 times in the Old Testament: Ex 2,22; 18,3; Deut 14,21; 15,3; 17,15; 23,21; 29,21; Jud 19,12; Ruth 2,10; 2 Sam 15,19; 1 K 8,41.43; 11,1.8; 2 Chron 6,32.33; Ezra 10,2.10.11.14.17.18.44; Neh 13,26.27; Is 2,6; Lam 5,2; Zeph 1,8; Ob 11; but only four times in legal texts: Deut 14,21; 15,3; 17,15; 23,21; in Deut 14,21 together with גר. In these cases the reference to the נכרי is negative, see p. 30 footnote 107. No reference to the noun זר in an ethnical, political or geographical sense is attested in legal codes (2 K 19,24; Job 15,19; Is 1,7a; Jer 30,8; 51,51; Lam 5,2; Ez 7,21; 11,9; 28,7.10; 30,12; 31,12; Hos 7,9; 8,7; Joel 4,17; Ob 11). Ex 29,33 is used of an unauthorized person, i.e. a non priest (Ges[18] 2 p. 310); Deut 25,5 of someone foreign to the family or clan (DBHE p. 225).

33 See Bolkestein, Wohltätigkeit p. 7; 13.

34 Bertholet, Stellung p. 13.

35 On the meaning of משפט as "Rechtsanspruch" and the formula הטה משפט see Liedke, Gestalt p. 92-94 and idem., THAT II col. 1007. For the genitive construction see Joüon-Muraoka, Grammar § 129a.e.

36 This is the way in which the New JPS Translation (Tigay, Deuteronomy p. 228), renders the Hebrew sentence לא תטה משפט גר (Deut 24,17); G. von Rad translates: "Du sollst *das Recht des Fremdlings* nicht beugen !" (Deuteronomium, p. 109); Osty translates: "Tu ne feras pas dévier *le droit du résident*"; Bible de Jerusalem (Spanish Edition) translates: "No torcerás *el derecho del forastero*" (italics is ours).

against an Israelite on whom he depends [37], and confirms the idea that in Israel the protection of the גר was something beyond the mere conventionalities of traditional hospitality.[38] The legal protection of the גר, i.e. his *legal status* in Israel, is to be distinguished, on the one hand, from the traditional *divine protection*[39], and on the other hand, from the traditional *rules of hospitality* which belong to "the laws of good taste" in oriental societies.[40]

The absence of references to the stranger in the Mesopotamian laws is probably related to the feeling of superiority which was common in these cultures[41] and which led to the archaic counter position "us" versus "the others".[42] In Sumerian sources, for instance, the Amorites are described as "a ravaging people with canine instincts, like wolves"; and the individual Amorite as "the awkward man living in the mountains ... who has never known city(-life) ... who does not know (i.e. cultivate) grain ... who eats uncooked meat ... who on the day of his death will not be buried".[43] Relations outside of the community were commonly, official enterprises held with other kingdoms which provided indispensable building or defense materials such as stones, wood and minerals. In these cases formal delegations were exchanged and the persons involved were considered a special kind of strangers, such as diplomats and royal functionaries.[44] The contacts or relationships with other kinds of strangers besides pilgrims and mercenaries, were normally avoided. In the epic of Lugalbanda for instance, we have the following verse: "Ein unbekannter Hund ist schlimm, ein unbekannter Mensch ist schrecklich, auf dem unbekannten Weg am Rande des Berglandes, Utu, ist ein unbekannter Mensch ein noch schlimmerer Mensch".[45] Foreigners were, as a rule, treated

---

37   Tigay, Deuteronomy p. 13.   According to Buis-Leclercq, גרו in Deut 1,16, does not imply economical dependence but means simply: "l'étranger avec lui (i.e. the Israelite) est en procès" (Deutéronome p. 37).

38   See de Vries, Art. Gastfreundschaft, in: RGG³ II col. 1205;   Schreiner, Art. Gastfreundschaft, in: NBL 1 col. 730.

39   Such as the case of the kidinnu, see footnote 30.

40   Jacobsen, Tammuz p. 49.

41   On the position of Egypt and Babylon as centers of the world see: Helck, Saeculum 15 p. 109-110; idem, Verhältnis p. 311-312; Limet, ABAW N.F. 75 p. 126-127 and see the illustrations 8; 33; 34 and commentaries in Keel, Welt p. 31-33.

42   Liverani, Art. Nationality, in: ABD 4 p.1031-1032; van Houten thinks that the omission of the alien in the Mesopotamian laws: "can be explained by noting that these law codes are addressed to the citizens of a land in order to establish justice among them. The aliens as non-citizens are not part of the intended audience, although they may in fact be members of the society" (Alien p. 36).

43   Buccellati, Amorites p. 331-332.

44   Such is for instance the case in the report of Wen Amun (ANET p. 25-29).   This document shows, however, that even messengers-diplomats faced trials and tribulations, and were able to survive because of their native wit; see Liverani, International Relations p. 247-252; Oller, Messengers p. 1465-1473.

45   Wilcke, Lugalbandaepos p. 79 verses 158-160.

with hostility.[46]   The usual problems faced in occasional contacts with them were normally solved by customary law or by the rules of traditional wisdom.

7.3 Discontinuity of the Old Testament with its cultural environment

We must make a necessary distinction here: the significant number of references to the גר in the Old Testament should not be taken *per se*, as evidence that the perception of strangers in Israel was different from that of the surrounding cultures.   As Spieckermann states: "Israels Haltung zu den Fremden ist zunächst einmal die altorientalisch normale.   Hinter Fremden und Fremdem wird das Bedrohliche erkannt, das mit dem Unwesen von Feinden ineinsgesetzt werden kann ... Vor Fremden muß man sich hüten, nicht nur militärisch, sondern auch sittlich und religiös".[47]   The inclusion of the גר in the Old Testament laws was clearly determined, both in pre-exilic and in post-exilic times, by external circumstances: it is the wave of immigrants created by the fall of Samaria, which explains the emergence of the triad "גר, orphan widow" in the deuteronomic code; it is the concern for holiness prevailing in post-exilic times[48], which explains the inclusion of the גר under the same preventive laws compulsory for the אזרח in the priestly writings.

What we have in Israel is, then, not a *different* but a *differentiated* attitude towards strangers.   The Old Testament not only makes a distinction between the different kind of strangers (זר, נכרי and גר), but also shows a differentiated attitude towards each one of them.   This means that there are elements of continuity and discontinuity between Israel and the surrounding cultures in relation to their attitude towards strangers:
• continuity, because of the basic perception of foreigners as a threat (זרים), and the attitude of precaution and reserve in relation to some of them (נכרים).[49]

---

46   On this issue see the insightful explanation from Ihering (Geist des röm. Rechts auf den verschiedenen Stufen seiner Entwickelung. 1878, Band I p. 235), quoted in: Bertholet, Stellung p. 13.

47   Spieckermann makes specific reference to Is 1,17 (זרים), PTh 83 p. 53.

48   The difference established in this particular respect by the experience of the exile is described by H.-G. Link: "Während für das vorexilische Israel Kultus und Sündenvergebung keine wesentliche Rolle spielen, rückt beides für die exilische und nachexilische Jahwegemeinde in den Mittelpunkt ihrer Frömmigkeit" (Art. Versöhnung, in: TBNT p. 1305); see also Koch, EvTh 26, p. 217-239, especially p. 227.

49   According to Bertholet, the prophets play a key role in the shaping of this attitude towards strangers.   They (i.e. the prophets) represent "eine Reaktion gegen alles, was fremdländisch ist" (Stellung p. 79).   On this theme see the section "Die Reaktion gegen das Fremdländische bis zu ihrem Niederschlag im Deuteronomium" (Stellung p. 79-90), and Dion, Universalismo p. 85ff.; 173ff.

• discontinuity, because -unlike the surrounding cultures, *alterity* in Israel did not necessarily imply *hostility*.[50]   The Old Testament knows not only the *peregrinus/hostis* but also the *peregrinus/hospes*.[51]   The גֵּר was not considered a זָר (Deut 10,19).

What reasons might explain this element of discontinuity which is a *specificum* of the Old Testament?   When we look for the reasons behind this peculiar situation, Israel's own history seems to have played a decisive role. Not only the time in which their forefathers wandered in Canaan as in a land in which they were only aliens (אֶרֶץ מְגֻרֶיךָ), or the time in which "they" were גֵּרִים in the land of Egypt but, particularly, the time in which these traditions found their final form.   The majority of references to the גֵּר in the Old Testament appears in texts written or edited in exilic and post-exilic times.   The particular interest of Israel in the theme of the גֵּר from that moment on, mirrors its own situation.   *The attitude towards the גֵּר in the Old Testament reveals Israel's understanding of its own identity.*

---

50   We distinguish here between the guest who stayed for a short time and who was the object of traditional oriental hospitality (Jacobsen, Tammuz p. 49), and the stranger who sought to settle in the land: "Der Reisende wird geehrt, der fremde Ansiedler höchstens geduldet" (Nödelke, Art. Fremde, in: BiL 2 p. 300; on this distinction see p. 298ff.). Cf. also Schwienhorst-Schönberger, BuL 63 p. 108-109.   H. Bietenhard gives an interesting explanation about the relation between the ideas of strangeness and hospitality: "Der Fremde kommt von den Göttern her, ist deren 'Bote'. Aus Furcht vor den Göttern nimmt man sich des Fremden hilfreich an, nimmt ihn 'gastlich' in das Haus auf, und so wird der Fremde Schützling von Religion und Recht" (Art. Fremde/ξένος, in: TBNT p. 373).

51   Latin translations taken from Mandelkern, Concordantiae p. 259; 352.

8. The progressive theologisation of the notion of "foreignness"

As we have shown before, the use of the noun גר in the Old Testament alternates between its reference to the individuum and its reference to Israel. The majority of occurrences refer to the גר as individuum; the references to Israel are a minority. The correspondence between these two uses of the noun does not depend, however, on statistical but on theological grounds. They represent two important moments in Israel's history: the occurrences to the גר as individuum refer to the presence of strangers in Israel. In this case an Israelite community is portrayed as *host of the needy*.[1] The later occurrences to Israel as גר refer to Israel's presence before Yahweh.[2] In this case Israel is portrayed as *needy, in search of a Host*. The noun גר is, then, far more than a simple sociological term. Its use in the Old Testament acquires, progressively, a growing theological dimension. In the prayers of Ps 39 and 1 Chron 29 "being גר" is presented as *conditio humana*. These two uses of the noun גר have basic elements in common:

Firstly, the noun גר is seen in the Old Testament against the background of history. That is, the גר (either as social or as religious category), is seen as a particular example of a paradigmatical historical precedent:
- the status of the גר-individuum finds its *prototypos* in the former experience of the Israelites as גרים in Egypt: "You shall not ill-treat a גר, you know the soul of a גר, because you were גרים in the land of Egypt" (Ex 23,9). This primeval experience was seen not only as an essential part of their history, but also inculcated as "identitätsstiftende Schlüsselerfahrung" throughout the generations.[3]
- the status of Israel as גר (with Yahweh/on earth), finds its *prototypos* in the former experience of the patriarchs as גרים in the land.[4] The idea of a *peregrinatio*, used first to describe the life of the forefathers in Canaan[5], is used later to describe the life of the Psalmist/Israel on earth.[6]

Secondly, in both cases there is a progressive theologisation of the term:

---

1   "the גר in your cities ..." (Ex 20,10); "the גר in your midst" (Deut 16,11).
2   כי גר אנכי עמך (Ps 39,13); and כי גרים אנחנו לפניך (1 Chron 29,15).
3   Spieckermann, PTh 83 p. 52.
4   The idea of a pilgrim theology in the Psalms (Ps 105,12.23), was originally inspired by the priestly theology, see Hossfeld/Zenger, Psalmen p. 251.
5   ארץ מגריך (Gen 17,8; 28,4).
6   Note that, just as Abraham is enjoined to walk *before Yahweh* התהלך לפני (Gen 17,1bγ), Israel and the Psalmist (Ps 39,13; 119,54; 1 Chron 29,15), portray themselves also as גרים *before Yahweh* גרים אנחנו לפניך.

• the noun גֵּר, which originally designated a *person in the Judean territory* (the גֵּר within your gates[7]), designates in later texts a *person in the Jewish religious community*, Is 14,1. This means that: as the situation of the Israelites in the world changed, the condition and identity of the גֵּר in their midst also changed.[8]

• the use of the noun for Israel parallels this development. The noun גֵּר, used initially with a *spatial* dimension to name the forefathers as "גֵּרִים in the land of Egypt" (Deut 10,19: גֵּר + בְּ), was used in later texts with a *religious* dimension, the Israelites call themselves "גֵּרִים before Yahweh" (1 Chron 29,15: גֵּרִים + לְפָנֶיךָ).

8.1 The human life as pilgrimage

In the Old Testament the noun גֵּר acquires, together with its social dimension, a religious one. And it is this metaphorical use of the term, which plays a fundamental role in Israel's understanding of its past and present and also of its fundamental vocation: Israel did not only keep alive the memory of her forefathers as גֵּרִים but understood its own existence as a *peregrinatio*. The noun גֵּר accomplishes its final role in the Old Testament, as a religious category.[9]

In two of the major streams of theology in the Old Testament, Israel's own understanding is based on the category of the גֵּר, i.e. based in its understanding of life as a pilgrimage. It is not surprising, then, that the relationships of the Israelites to the resident alien in Deuteronomy as well as in the Holiness Code, are inspired by the same principle of love for the גֵּר.

1. Present: Israel self-understanding as גֵּר: Deut 10,19b   Lev 25,23
2. Future: the unique command to love the גֵּר: Deut 10,19a   Lev 19,34

8.2 Wirkungsgeschichte: the translation of the noun גֵּר in the Septuagint

The noun גֵּר made a lasting impact as result of its translation in the LXX. With the transition from the Hebrew Bible to its Greek translation, this term underwent a significant development in the Jewish and Christian communities. The noun גֵּר/גֵּרִים is translated in the LXX by four different terms:

---

7   Deut 16,11: גֵּר + בְּ. See p. 66 and 86.
8   Moore, Judaism p. 329.
9   K.L. Schmidt's study: "Israels Stellung zu den Fremden und Beisassen und Israels Wissen um seine Fremdling- und Beisassenschaft" (Judaica 1 p. 269-296), illustrates this well.

προσήλυτος   78 times[10]
πάροικος   11 times[11]
γ(ε)ιώρας   2 times[12]
ξένος   1 time[13]

Since γ(ε)ιώρας is the Greek form of the Aramaic גיורא[14], and ξένος appears only once[15], we will concentrate on the nouns προσήλυτος and πάροικος, and on the way in which these terms induced later developments in the Jewish and Christian communities.

8.2.1 Προσήλυτος: the Gentile as *Advena* in the Jewish community.

It is disputed whether the term προσήλυτος already had in the LXX a religious meaning[16], or was simply a synonym of πάροικος with the meaning of "one who has come near, immigrant"[17] and which was used later with an extended religious meaning: "one who has come over (from paganism to Judaism)".[18] These two alternatives both face difficulties:

1) If, on the one hand, προσήλυτος meant "proselyte":

---

10   Ex 12,48.49; 20,10; 22,20.20*; 23,9.9.9*.12; Lev 16,29; 17,8.10.12.13.15;
      18,26; 19,10.33.34.34*; 20,2; 22,18; 23,22; 24,16.22; 25,23*.35.47.47.47; Num
      9,14.14; 15,14.15.15.16.26.29.30; 19,10; 35,15; Deut 1,16; 5,14; 10,18.19.19*;
      14,29; 16,11.14; 24,14.17.19.20.21; 26,11.12.13; 27,19; 28,43; 29,10; 31,12;
      Jos 8,33.35; 20,9; Jer 7,6; 22,3; Ez 14,7; 22,7.29; 47,22*.23; Zech 7,10; Mal
      3,5; Ps 94,6; 146,9*; 1 Chron 22,2*; 2 Chron 2,16*; 30,25*.   References with an
      asterisc are those of the plural form גרים.
11   Gen 15,13; 23,4; Ex 2,22; 18,3; Deut 14,21; 23,8; 2 Sam 1,13; Jer 14,8; Ps
      39,13; 119,19; 1 Chron 29,15 (= גרים).
12   Ex 12,19 (γειώρας); Is 14,1 (γιώρας).   According to Geiger is γ(ε)ιώρας and not
      προσήλυτος the religious term in the LXX (Urschrift p. 353-355); see also Ohana,
      Biblica 55 p. 322.   Aquila's version of Lev 19,34 retains also γ(ε)ιώρας, the Greek
      transcription of the Aramaic form גיורא.
13   Job 31,32.
14   See Nestle, ZNW, 5 (1904) p. 263-264; Rosen, Juden p. 44.
15   For a discussion of this term see Spicq, Notes II p. 592-597.
16   προσήλυτος as "convert, proselyte", as it is taken by Kuhn, Proselyten, in: RECA Supp
      IX col. 1261; idem, TWNT, VI p. 732; Tov, RB 83 p. 537-538; C.W. Allen,
      Expositor 4/10 p. 265-266; 274-275; Becker, Gottesfürchtiger, in: TBNT p. 612-613;
      Le Deaut, LeDiv 19 p. 149; Simon, Prosélytisme p. 510-512; Hirsch, Proselyte, in:
      JewEnc, Vol X col. 220.
17   GELS II p. 402; Le Boulluec - Sandevoir, BA 2 p. 51-52; Harlé - Prolon, BA 3 p. 46-
      47 ("immigrant"); Dorival, BA 4 p. 274 ("immigrant"); idem, Bible Grecque p. 37;
      Lee, RB 87 p. 112-113; Geiger, Urschrift p. 353-355; Ohana, Biblica 55 p. 322;
      Lesètre, Étranger, in: DBV, X. 2° col. 758.
18   See Bauer, Wörterbuch col. 1431-1432; Kuli, EWNT III col. 411-412; Kuhn,
      Proselyten, in: RECA Supp IX col. 1249.

• some sort of conversion must be presupposed, but the idea of conversion within the Old Testament is in itself disputed[19];
• there seems to be no clear reason for the use of this term in texts like Ex 22,20; 23,9; Lev 19,34 and Deut 10,19, where it cannot mean "proselyte".

2) If, on the other hand, προσήλυτος is a synonym of πάροικος[20]:
• why is, then, the distribution of these terms so uneven (προσήλυτος: 78x; πάροικος: 11x)?
• how can we explain the fact that, while in P πάροικος is the ordinary translation of תושב[21], outside of P πάροικος is the ordinary translation of גר?[22] These are, certainly, not the only questions waiting for an answer in relation to this subject.[23]

We must recognise that there is no yet satisfactory explanation for the distribution of these two terms in the LXX. It is certain that, whatever the original meaning of προσήλυτος in the LXX may have been, this noun was later used of the Gentile converted to Judaism[24], and this is the sense in which the noun was used in Jewish inscriptions[25], in Philo[26] and in the New

---

19   Ohana, Biblica 55 p. 320-321; Milgrom, JBL 101/102 p. 169-170; Kaufmann, Religion p. 163-165; 300-301; 405.

20   Geiger, Urschrift p. 353-355; Ohana, Biblica 55 p. 322; Lee, RB 87 p. 112-113 and more recently the editors of the new French translation of the LXX "La Bible d'Alexandrie": Le Boulluec / Sandevoir, BA 2, p. 51-52; Harlé / Prolon, BA 3, p. 46-47; Dorival, BA 4, p. 274.

21   Ex 12,45; Lev 22,10; 25,6.23.35.40.45.47.47; Num 35,15.

22   Gen 15,13; Ex 2,22; 18,3; Deut 14,21; 23,8; 2 Sam 1,13; Jer 14,8; Ps 39,13; 119,19; 1 Chron 29,15. The only exception to this is Gen 23,4 where גר ותושב is translated by "πάροικος καὶ παρεπίδημος".

23   One could also ask: (1) if the noun προσήλυτος means in fact "proselyte", what is, then, the meaning of γ(ε)ιώρας?, a noun which is used in texts in which the meaning is closer to "proselyte" than any other reference in the Old Testament (Ex 12,19; Is 14,1); Ges[18] takes these two references as meaning "Proselyt" (p. 227), and so also does Geiger (Urschrift p. 353-355). It is certainly unsatisfactory to disregard them as "exceptional cases" (C.W. Allen, Expositor 4/10 p. 274); (2) An attempt is made by several authors to explain the uneven distribution of these two nouns by stating that in certain contexts, the plural form προσήλυτοι would not fit at all. C.W. Allen, for instance, explains that πάροικος is used in Deut 23,8 because in this case προσήλυτος "could not possibly mean proselyte" (Expositor 4/10 p. 274). But the noun προσήλυτοι is used in the parallel text of Deut 10,19 (!); (3) Even the existence of pre-biblical references of προσήλυτος is disputed, see Lee, RB 87 p. 112-113 and Kuhn, Proselyten, in: RECA Supp IX col. 1249.

24   See Kuhn, TWNT, VI p. 732-736 and idem, Proselyten, in: RECA Supp IX col. 1261-1272.

25   Frey, CII inscription N°. 21 (Vol. I p. 19-20); N°. 68 (Vol. I p. 40-41); N°. 202 (Vol. I p. 141); N°. 222 (Vol. I p. 158-159); N°. 256 (Vol. I p. 181-182); N°. 462 (Vol. I p. 340-341); N°. 523 (Vol. I p. 383-384); N°. 1385 (Vol. II p. 318).

26   Som., II.273; Spec. Leg., I.51; I.308.

Testament.[27]   This use of the noun προσήλυτος is the culmination of a long process.   A first step in this direction was already given in the Old Testament with the use of the noun גר in combination with לוה ni.[28], a verb used of those who joined or attached themselves to Israel and Yahweh.[29]

A comparison of the Masoretical text of Esth 8,17 with its rendering in the LXX, illustrates well this progressive theologisation of certain terms:

Esth 8,17 (TM):   many of the peoples of the country
                     professed to be Jews (מתיהדים).
Esth 8,17 (LXX):   many of the Gentiles
                     were circumcised and became Jews
                     (περιετέμοντο καὶ ιουδάιζον).

In this case, the meaning of the form מתיהדים (Hith. part. from יהד) in the MT, has clearly been amplified by the rendering περιετέμοντο καὶ ιουδάιζον. Since circumcision was the oldest and the decisive rite for the reception of proselytes, the addition of the form περιετέμοντο, witnesses the intention of the author to adapt this verse to the needs of his own circumstances.   The affiliation to the Jewish community in this particular case was due to the fact that "the fear of the Jews had fallen upon them" (Esth 8,17bβ).   Because of this several scholars do not take this verse as an example of a real conversion.[30] If we take into account that the verb התיהד did not become the usual term to refer to conversion (it is never used in this sense in the Mishna), it is probable that the participle מתיהדים in Esth 8,17 was not understood in the sense of a real conversion.[31]   This may explain why the Targum later changed the original reading מתיהדים to מתגירין (part. Hith. from גייר).[32] This is an example of the kind of amplifications of meaning that we commonly find in the Targum, where the Hebrew verb גור I (to sojourn) has been rendered by the Aramaic verb גייר "to convert someone to Judaism, to make a Proselyte of him"[33]:

27   Bauer, Wörterbuch col. 1431-1432; Kuli, EWNT III col. 411-412; Zorell, Lexicon
     Graecum col. 1140; Becker, Gottesfürchtiger, in: TBNT p. 612-613.
28   Cf. Is 14,1 and Tob 1,8. Behind the term προσκειμένοις in Tob 1,8 (א), we have the
     Hebrew form הנלוים (Díez Macho, Targum p. 58; Charles, APOT I p. 203; Kuhn,
     TWNT VI p. 735), which is used for conversion to Judaism (Cf. Esth 9,27). On Tob
     1,8 see Rabenau, Studien p. 164; 171-172; 188-190; Schwartz, RHPR 67 p. 293-297;
     Schürer, History III p. 243 and Jeremias, Jerusalem II Teil p. 50-52.
29   Is 56,3.6; Zech 2,15; Esth 9,27. For לוה in Qumrân see: CD-A IV, 3 and 1QS V,
     6.
30   Zeitlin translates מתיהדים in Esth 8,17 as "they *pretended* to be Judeans" (Studies p.
     409) and so does Holladay (יהד: "pretend to be a Jew", Lexicon p. 129). This is also
     the sense suggested by Gerleman's translation: "Und Viele ... bezeichneten sich als
     Juden" (Esther p. 126). Cf., however, Paton, Esther p. 297.
31   See Ohana, RB 55 p. 321.
32   See Haupt, AJSLL 24 p. 161.
33   Sokoloff, Dictionary p. 127; Kaufman-Sokoloff, Concordance p. 283.

Ex 12,49 (TM):   les immigrants qui résident
Ex 12,49 (PsJ):   les prosélytes qui se convertissent.[34]

Num 19,10 (TM):   the alien residing among them
Num 19,10 (PsJ):   the converts who convert among them.[35]

This marked interest in the theme of proselytism was also present in the
LXX. In Is 54,15 for instance, the LXX translates the root גּוּר II (to attack)
into προσέρχομαι, a verb used to translate the homonymous root גּוּר I (to
sojourn) in certain expressions such as וּכִי־יָגוּר אִתְּךָ גֵּר[36] and וְלָהָגֵר הַגֵּר (Ex
12,49). The root גּוּר I is also translated in the LXX by the verbs:
προσκείμενος, προσγενόμενος, προσπορευόμενος, προσγεγενημένων[37], which
convey the meaning of attaching oneself to, or uniting with, and were used later
to indicate the kind of action that a proselyte had to follow in identifying
himself with his new community.[38]   In this way, we have the following
variation:

Is 54,15a (TM):   הֵן גּוֹר יָגוּר אֶפֶס מֵאוֹתִי
                   If anyone stirs up strife, it is not from me.

Is 54,15a (LXX):   ἰδοὺ   προσήλυτοι   προσελεύσονταί   σοι
                   Behold, the proselytes will come to you (Jerusalem).

In relation to the interest of the LXX in the theme of proselytism can also be
mentioned that there are cases in the LXX, in which there is no corresponding
Hebrew word for the noun προσήλυτος.[39]   This may justify Momigliano's
opinion about the LXX: "La traduction doit avoir aussi favorisé le
prosélytisme, qui acquiert ainsi un tout autre développement dès que les Juifs

---

34 Le Déaut / Robert, Targum, p. 100-101.   Compare also Lev 17,8: "les étrangers qui
    s'établiront comme hôtes parmi vous" (TM) with: "les prosélytes qui se convertissent
    pour habiter" (Targum, italics is ours).   The translators of the Biblia Polyglotta
    Matritensia (Series IV, L. 3 Leviticus), add to their translation of Lev 17,8 the
    following note: "Traducimos gwr en sentido sociológico, lo mismo en vv. 10.12.13,
    pero podría traducirse 'prosélitos que se convierten para morar'" (Díez Macho, BPM, 3 p.
    115).
35 Levine, Versions p. 185.
36 Ex 12,48; Lev 19,33.
37 προσγενόμενος(Lev 18,26); προσπορευόμενος (Lev 19,34); προσγεγενημένων (Lev
    20,2); προσκείμενος (Lev 16,29; 17,10.12.13; Num 15,15.16.26.29; 19,10; Jos
    20,9).   In 2 Chron 15,9 the LXX renders the participial plural form גֵּרִים (usually
    translated by the verb παροικέω: Lev 25,6.45; 2 Sam 4,3; Ps 105,12; 1 Chron 16,19)
    by the construction: τοὺς   προσηλύτους   τοὺς   παροικοῦντας.
38 Meek, JBL 49 p. 178.
39 Lev 17,3; Deut 10,18 (where the LXX completes the triad by the addition of
    "προσηλύτῳ" to the pair "orphan, widow") and Deut 12,18.

eurent commencé à parler grec (...). Les livres sacrés étaient devenus accessibles à ceux qui s'intéressaient au judaïsme".[40]

In the course of time, then, the two terms involved in the equation גר = προσήλυτος, although originally meaning something else[41], became the nominal technical terms to designate the proselyte, both in the Greek-speaking world as well as in the Rabbinical literature.[42]   The influence of the LXX in this transformation was definite.

8.2.2 Πάροικος: the Christian as *peregrinus* in this world

R. Bainton describes the basic attitude of the ancient church in relation to the responsibilities in "this world" in terms which very closely resemble the language of 1 P 2,11: "All Christians placed their citizenship in heaven.   On earth they were all but pilgrims and strangers".[43]   The constancy of this idea in the Christian tradition can be illustrated by the title of Bunyan's major work "The Pilgrim's Progress from this World to That which is to Come" (1678), translated in more than two hundred languages[44] and called by Coleridge the "Summa Theologiae Evangelicae"[45]; by F.A. Lampe's famous Hymn (1719): "Mein Leben ist ein Pilgrimstand"; or by Francis of Assisi's Testament (see § 24).

The origin of this understanding of the Christian life can be traced to the noun πάροικος, one of the two basic renderings given by the LXX for the Hebrew noun גר.   The Alexandrian tradition (influenced by the Pythagorean idea of the metempsychosis[46], via Plato[47]), played a very important role in the shaping of this tradition.

The influence of Philo's ideas on the New Testament notion of πάροικος as sojourner on this earth (1 P 2,11), is evident.   Talking about the wise men, called by Philo *sojourners* (παροικοῦντες), he says:

"Their souls are never colonists leaving heaven for a new home.   Their way is to visit earthly nature as men who travel abroad to see and learn ... To them the heavenly region,

---

40   Sagesses p. 73. According to Cardellini: "Il grande evento della traduzione in greco dei testi sacri ha permesso lo sviluppo di un proselitismo un po'particolare rispetto a quello attuato nella madre patria" (RivBib 40 p. 162).

41   גר = "resident alien" and προσήλυτος = "one that has arrived at (a place)".

42   See Porton, Stranger p. 16ff.; 28ff.; 51ff.; 90ff.

43   Bainton, HTR 39 p. 203.   Bainton refers in a footnote to L. Salvatorelli (Bilychnis XVI (1920) p. 264-279; 333-352), for a list of passages in the patristic literature which illustrates this point.   See also Harnack, Mission p. 421; 268-270.

44   Rupp, Art. Bunyan, in: TRE 7 p. 418.

45   Ross, Art. Bunyan, in: ERE 2 p. 900-901.

46   Rhode, Psyche p. 158-170 espec. p. 161-166; Burkert, HWP, 9 col. 117-120.

47   Meno 81b-e; Phaedrus 245c-249c; 249b-c; Phaedo 72e; 80a-81e; Timaeus 41d-42e; 90a-d.

where their citizenship lies, is their native land; the earthly region in which they became sojourners is a foreign country".[48]   And in Agric 65 he adds: "For in reality a wise man's soul ever finds heaven to be his fatherland and earth a foreign country, and regards as his own the dwelling-place of wisdom, and that of the body as outlandish, and looks on himself as a stranger and sojourner in it".[49]

The understanding of Abraham as migrant and wanderer played a very important role in the Alexandrian tradition.   The translation offered by the LXX for the MT of Gen 14,13 is an example of this:

Gen 14,13 MT: One who had escaped came and told Abram the Hebrew. (העברי)
Gen 14,13 LXX: One who had escaped came and told Abram the migrant. (περάτη)

The LXX translates the Hebrew noun העברי with the neologism περάτη (wanderer, emigrant), used only here in the LXX.[50]   Philo and Origen give the same etymological explanation of this term.   According to Philo the name Hebrew means "Migrant".[51]   Origen accepts fully Philo's etymological explanation of this term[52], and in his XIX Homily to the book of Numbers he states that the word "Hebrews" means travellers (transeuntes).[53]

In his book "On the Migration of Abraham" ("Περί ἀποικίας"), Philo states that the first stage of the spiritual life is conversion.   He takes Abraham as model of this and describes his conversion as a triple migration.[54]   "Bien avant Bunyan (writes Monod), Philon a écrit un *Voyage du pèlerin de ce monde à celui qui doit venir* et suggéré que toute âme véritablement *hébraïque* ne possédait pas de cité permanente, mais cherchait celle qui est à venir".[55]   In this way, the life of Abraham turned into a pilgrimage and became the model for the future pilgrims who descended from him.[56]

---

48 Conf Ling 77-78 (Translation: F.H. Colson and G.H. Whitaker, in: LCL, IV p. 53).
49 Agric 65 (Translation: F.H. Colson and G.H. Whitaker, in: LCL, III p. 141).   Similar statements are found in his commentaries of biblical texts.   Commenting Gen 23,4 he asks: "does not every wise soul live like an immigrant and sojourner in this mortal body having (as its real) dwelling-place and country the most pure substance of heaven, from which (our) nature migrated to this (place) by a law of necessity?" (Quaest Gen IV. 74; translation: R. Marcus, in: LCL, Supp. I p. 352); and commenting the command given to Abraham to leave his land and relatives (Gen 12,1) he says: "he (Abraham) hastened eagerly to obey, not as though he were leaving home for a strange land but rather as returning from amid strangers to his home" (Abr 62; translation: F. Colson, in: LCL, VI p. 35).   On the notion of πάροικος in Philo see Bitter, Vreemdelingschap p. 16-31.
50 "περάτης: wanderer, migrant" (GELS II p. 366), see also Harl / Alexandre / Dogniez, BA 1 p. 158-159.
51 Migr 20 (LCL, IV p. 143).
52 Monod, RHPR 3/5, p. 388.
53 "Hebræi *transeuntes* interpretantur" (MPG 12 p. 725).
54 Migr 7-11 (LCL, IV p. 137).
55 Monod, RHPR 3/5 p. 389.
56 Lanne, Irenikon XLVII p. 170.

The LXX translates eleven times the noun גֵּר by the term πάροικος.[57]   These references deal:

• six times with *individuals:* common individuals (Deut 14,21; 2 Sam 1,13); special characters like Abraham and Moses (Gen 23,4;   Ex 2,22;   18,3); Yahweh (Jer 14,8).

• five times with *Israel:* in a literal sense, Israel as πάροικος in Egypt (Gen 15,13; Deut 23,8); in a metaphorical sense, Israel/the Psalmist as πάροικος with Yahweh (Ps 39,13; 1 Chron 29,15); and the Psalmist as πάροικος on earth (Ps 119,19).

The use of the noun πάροικος in the New Testament (as well as that of παροικέω and παροικία), depends on these Old Testament references. That is, this term evokes either concrete experiences of exile in the Old Testament (Israel in Egypt: Act 7,6 = Gen 15,13; Moses in Midian: Act 7,29 = Ex 2,15.22), or uses the Hebrew expression גֵּר וְתוֹשָׁב[58] in a metaphorical way (1 P 2,11; Eph 2,19).

The hendiadys גֵּר וְתוֹשָׁב appears eight times in the Old Testament. In five cases the LXX translates προσήλυτος καὶ πάροικος[59], in two cases πάροικος καὶ παρεπίδημος[60] and in 1 Chron 29,15 πάροικοί καὶ παροικοῦντες. In the New Testament this combination is used three times, in each case are used different terms: Eph 2,19 (ξένοι καὶ πάροικοι), Heb 11,13 (ξένοι καὶ παρεπίδημοι), and in 1 P 2,11 (παροίκους καὶ παρεπιδήμους).[61]   1 P 2,11 is the only reference in the New Testament in which πάροικος comes as first term of the binomium, which means that it translates גֵּר and not תוֹשָׁב, as is the case in Eph 2,19.[62] Note also that the use of πάροικος in 1 P 2,11 is based on the metaphorical use of גֵּר in the Old Testament, not on the legal reference.[63]   This sense of πάροικος corresponds to the sense that the Hebrew noun גֵּר already had in Ps 119,19.54.

Since some New Testament writers applied to the Christian Church, what was true of ancient Israel[64], the πάροικος-references of the LXX became paradigmatic for the Christian community, the new Israel[65]. In this way:

---

57   Gen 15,13; 23,4; Ex 2,22; 18,3; Deut 14,21; 23,8; 2 Sam 1,13; Jer 14,8; Ps 39,13; 119,19; 1 Chron 29,15. The noun πάροικος translates תוֹשָׁב ten times: Ex 12,45; Lev 22,10; 25,6.23.35.40.45.47.47; Num 35,15.

58   Gen 23,4; Ps 39,13; 1 Chron 29,15.

59   Lev 25,23.35.47.47; Num 35,15.

60   Gen 23,4; Ps 38 (39),13.

61   The difference in the translation is probably due to the fact that προσήλυτος in the New Testament has a definite technical meaning (i.e. proselyte), which was not yet established definitively in the LXX.

62   The noun πάροικος is absent only from the reference in Heb 11,13. On the reason for this see Grässer, Hebräer p. 138 note 33.

63   Although Gen 23,4 is not a prayer, it has in common several important aspects in relation to Ps 39,13 and 1 Chron 29,15: it is used in first person; it introduces a petition and it functions as the ground for the appeal.

64   Schmidt, TWNT V p. 850.

65   On this expression see Grelot, Israël p. 578-579.

• As Israel was πάροικος in the land of Egypt[66], so the Christian Church becomes πάροικος in a foreign land, i.e. on earth[67]. The term παροικία, used in Act 13,17 of the stay of the Israelites in Egypt, became during the first century a terminus technicus for the Church (1 P 1,17).[68]   As shown above, Philo's influence on this notion is evident.

• As the Psalmist was πάροικος on earth (Ps 119,19), so also becomes the Christian, πάροικος in this world (1 P 2,11).

In Ps 119,19 the Psalmist presents himself with the statement: גר אנכי בארץ. The translation of the term בארץ is disputed. The term, commonly translated by "earth"[69], is translated by "land" in a few cases.[70]   The noun גר is used in combination with the expression בארץ fourteen times in the Old Testament.   In these cases the noun ארץ appears, as a rule, qualified: (a) by geographical terms: "the land of Egypt"[71], "the land of Israel"[72];   (b) by possessive pronouns: "in his land"[73], "גר in your land"[74];   (c) by adjectives: "גר in a foreign land"[75];   or in the phrase "גר in a land that is not theirs".[76] The only two exceptions to this pattern are Jer 14,8 and Ps 119,19.   The parallelism of גר with the participial form ארח (wanderer) in Jer 14,8, makes clear that in Jer 14,8 ארץ means land.   But such parallelism does not exist in the case of Ps 119,19; on the contrary, in 1 Chron 29,15b (where the noun גר is used in a similar way), this noun is followed by the sentence: "our days on earth (על־הארץ) are like a shadow"[77], which suggests that the meaning of ארץ in Ps 119,19 is in fact "earth".

It must be noted, however, that the metaphorical use of the noun πάροικος in the New Testament, differs from its metaphorical use in the LXX.   In Ps

---

66   Gen 15,13; Deut 23,8.
67   ἐπὶ τῆς γῆς (Heb 11,13).
68   Harnack, Mission p. 421 note 4.   From this term derives the designation for the local church in some Europeans languages: parroquia, parrocchia, paróquia, parohie, paroisse, parish, Parochie, Pfarrei.
69   This is the way in which is rendered by BJ, Osty, TOB, Luther, BP, NEngB and several commentaries: Schökel, Salmos p. 1435; Deißler, Psalm p. 111; Gunkel, Psalmen p. 518; Kraus, Psalmen p. 987; Weiser, Psalmen p. 486; Ravasi, Salmi 3: 434.463; Baethgen, Psalmen p. 360; L.C. Allen, Psalms p. 127. See also Spieckermann, PTh 83 p. 66; Bertholet, Stellung p. 168 and Muntingh, Concepts p. 51.
70   D. Kellermann, TWAT I col. 991; Kautzsch / Bertholet, HSAT(K) II p. 251; Ehrlich, Psalmen p. 303; NSRV and AT.
71   גרים בארץ מצרים ... (Ex 22,20; 23,9; Lev 19,34; Deut 10,19).
72   גרים בארץ ישראל ... (1 Chron 22,2; 2 Chron 2,16).
73   גר ... בארצו (Deut 23,8).
74   Singular: גרך ... בארצך (Deut 24,14) and plural: גר ... בארצכם (Lev 19,33).
75   גר ... בארץ נכריה (Ex 2,22; 18,3).
76   גר ... בארץ לא להם (Gen 15,13).
77   The use of the same term (i.e. ארץ) to refer to the land, Canaan and the earth in general creates an interesting ambiguity.   If in 1 Chron 29,15 על־הארץ is rendered *upon the land*: "David would be recognizing that even the promised land of Canaan was not a permanent home for the worshipper" (Estes, CBQ 53 p. 48).

39,13, the Psalmist declares himself πάροικος in relation to Yahweh.[78] This statement has a positive sense: it is used as a self-designation in prayer and emphasises dependency upon Yahweh's mercy and longing for intimacy and *nearness* with Yahweh. In 1 P 2,11 the noun πάροικος has, instead, a negative sense[79]: because of their special election (1,1), Christians are a select community whose distinct way of life provokes a fundamental *distance* with the society in which they live in exile (1,17). The use of πάροικος in 1 Peter shows the determination of the author to renounce this world in which they, because of their faith, were stigmatised and discriminated.[80] The author looks forward, therefore, at a new home beyond the realm of their present circumstances. The Christians as pilgrims live on this earth "dans un climat de guerre froide".[81]

In this context, the recourse to the image of election in 1 P 1,1 (ἐκλεκτοῖς), borrowed also from the Old Testament tradition[82], can be understood as an attempt of the author to assimilate the discrimination and hostility which the Christian community as a minority, experienced at the time. The noun πάροικος acquires in this way, an elitist tone: the awareness of belonging to this select community, comforts them and strengthens them to overcome the adversities of the present time. Being πάροικος in this world means, then, not only to be confronted with the isolation and hostility of this society; but more importantly, being part of those elected whose unique sense of hope enables them to overcome the troubles of *this world*.[83]

Out of the three terms used in the New Testament to translate the hendiadys גר ותושב (πάροικος, παρεπίδημος and ξένος), it was πάροικος which became usual to convey the idea of the Christians as sojourners in this world[84]:

"They dwell in their own countries, but simply as sojourners. As citizens, they share in all things with others, and yet endure all things as if foreigners. Every foreign land is to them as their native country, and every land of their birth as a land of strangers ... To sum up all in one word -what the soul is in the body, that are Christians in the world" (Diog. V.5).[85]

---

78   Compare the difference between a text like Lev 25,23 "προσήλυτοι καὶ πάροικοι ὑμεῖς ἐστε ἐναντίον μου", in which the point of reference is *Yahweh*, with a text like 1 P 2,11, in which the point of reference is *the world*.

79   For what follows see Stegemann, Sozialgeschichte p. 272; 287f; Brox, Petrusbrief p. 56f.; 111f.; Grässer, Hebräer 138f. and Feldmeier, Metapher p. 99ff.

80   This idea is also inspired in the experience of Israel: it is because Israel as God's גר keeps His Law that becomes a foreign body in the world (Stählin, TWNT V p. 27). See in this connection two very important references: Wis 2,15 and Esth 3,13e.

81   Spicq, Épitres p. 97.

82   According to Is 43,16-21, the Lord will give waters in the wilderness, to give drink to his chosen people ("τὸ γένος μου τὸ ἐκλεκτόν" Is 43,20).

83   For the elitist sense of πάροικος see Feldmeier, Metapher p. 99f and Brox, Petrusbrief p. 112-113.

84   *Diog* 5,5; Ast. Am. *hom.* 2 (PGM 40: 181b); Cosm. Ind. *top.* 2 (PGM 88: 72c).

85   Translation: Roberts-Donaldson, ANF 1, p. 26-27.

The noun παροικία, used first as a metaphor for earthly life as a temporary abode[86], became established as part of the administrative language of the church in the third and fourth centuries.[87] And the verb παροικέω was used to refer to the person's temporary sojourn in this life.[88] Terms like πάροικος, παροικία, and παροικέω contributed, then, to consolidate the idea of the Christian life as a *peregrinatio* in this world.   Clement of Alexandria for instance, states:

"'I am a stranger in the earth, and a sojourner with you', it is said[89] ... the elect man dwells as a sojourner, knowing all things to be possessed and disposed of ... The body, too, as one sent on a distant pilgrimage, uses inns and dwellings by the way, having care of the things of the world, of the places where he halts; but leaving his dwelling-place and property without excessive emotion; readily following him that leads him away from life; by no means and on no occasion turning back; giving thanks for his sojourn, and blessing (God) for his departure, embracing the mansion that is in heaven" (Strom IV.165,2-4).[90]

Like the Alexandrians, Saint John Chrysostom portrays the present life of the Christians as a sojourn in a foreign country (παροικία).[91] In his *Homilia de capto Eutropio* he states:

"Weißt du denn nicht, daß unser gegenwärtiges Leben eine Fremde ist? Bist du denn ein Bürger? Ein Wanderer bist du! Verstehst du, was ich sage? Du bist kein Bürger, sondern ein Wanderer und ein Reisender. Sage nicht: ich habe diese oder jene Stadt. Keiner hat eine Stadt. Die Stadt ist oben. Die Gegenwart ist ein Weg".[92]

---

86   *2 Clem* 5,1; Clem. *str.* 4.26 (164,3; PGM 8.1376A-B); Bas. *hom. in Ps.* 32 (I.136E; PGM 29.336C); Bas. *Is.* 27 (I.401B; PGM 30.172C); Gr. Naz. *or.* 14.21 (PGM 35.884C); Cyr. *glaph. Gen.* 5 (I.174B); Proc. G. *Is.* 16,6-14 (PGM 87.2117B).

87   Labriolle, RScR XVIII p. 65-66. The use of the term "Parroco" is officially adopted in the Council of Arles (314 A.D.), see Damizia, EC IX p. 859.

88   *Diog* 6.8; Pion. *v. Polyc* 6; Cyr. *Zach.* 92 (3.780C); Bas. *ep.* 223 (3.337E; PGM 32.824C); Cyr. *Ps.* 14,1 (PGM 69.805B); Thdt. *Ps.* 38.14 (I.855) and 54.16 (966).

89   Gen xxiii,4; Ps xxxix,12. (MT 39,13).

90   Translation: Roberts-Donaldson, ANF 2, p. 440; and in VII.77,3 he adds: "He (i.e. the Gnostic) attracted by his own hope, tastes not the good things that are in the world, entertaining a noble contempt for all things here ... having a clear conscience with reference to his departure, and being always ready, as 'a stranger and pilgrim' with regard to the inheritances here; mindful only of those that are his own, and regarding all things here as not his own ... despising all the gold on earth and under the earth, and dominion from shore to shore of ocean, so that he may cling to the sole service of the Lord" (Translation: Roberts-Donaldson, ANF 2 p. 545).

91   See Roldanus, Sacris Erudiris XXX p. 234ff.

92   Homilia de capto Eutropio et de divitiarum vanitate, MPG 52 p. 401; translation: K. Niederwimmer, in Zobel, FS G. Sauer p. 130.

Irenaeus of Lyon, takes Abraham's pilgrimage as a model for Christian asceticism.[93] The condition of being a stranger, that appears frequently in the context of exhortations in the patristic literature of the first three centuries[94], intended to inspire an attitude of detachment and *non-établissement* in relation to "this world"[95]:

"Ferner sagt Cassianus: 'Die Untertanen dieser weltlichen Herrscher zeugen und werden erzeugt; unser Wandel aber ist im Himmel, woher wir auch den Heiland erwarten'. Daß auch dies richtig gesagt ist, wissen wir; denn wir sollen als 'Fremdlinge und Gäste' wandeln, die Heiratenden, als ob sie nicht heirateten, die Erwerbenden, als ob sie nicht erwürben, die da Kinder zeugen als solche, die Sterbliche zeugen, das heißt als solche, die bereit sind, ihren Besitz zurückzulassen, als solche, die, wenn es nötig ist, auch ohne Gattin leben würden, als Leute, die die Schöpfung nicht mit leidenschaftlichem Verlangen genießen, sondern mit aller Dankbarkeit und mit dem Gefühl, innerlich darüber erhaben zu sein" (Strom III.95,3).[96]

---

93   Lanne, Irenikon XLVII, p. 187.   This idea played also a decisive role in the development of the early monasticism, see Solignac, Art. Pèlerinages, in: DS 12/1, col. 887-894 and Le Déaut / Lécuyer, Art. Exode, in: DS 4/2, col. 1972-1990.   The relationship between Irenaeus of Lyon and Philo has been long recognized, see Orbe, Antropología p. 32 ff.; 59 ff.; 340.

94   See Roldanus, CBP 1 p. 27-52.

95   Roldanus, CBP 1 p. 31-33.   The concrete modalities of such detachment are explained differently by the different authors according with their particular circumstances.

96   Translation: O. Stählin, BKV XVII p. 315.

Conclusion

The use of the noun גֵּר in the Old Testament alternates between the reference to the *individuum* and the reference to *Israel*.

1. The גֵּר in Israel

1. The noun גֵּר is a specialised development of the root גור I, which emerges as a generic term in legal codes and whose meaning is not identical to the participial form גָּר. In situations of need and misfortune, both Israelites and non-Israelites looked for a place of refuge out of their home towns, but while the verb גור was mostly used for those Israelites who went to dwell temporarily abroad, the noun גֵּר came to designate the *legal status* granted to those strangers who, living in an Israelite community, were ruled by its internal regulations.

2. The reference to the individual גֵּר in the laws of the Pentateuch can be divided into two groups: (1) laws addressed to the Israelites for the protection of the גֵּר, and (2) laws compulsory for both Israelite and גֵּר, in order to preserve the holiness of the community.

In the first group we have laws given in order to guide the conduct of the Israelite towards the גֵּר according to a principle of solidarity. The laws are concerned with the duty of the Israelite in relation with the גֵּר (*protégé*). The Israelites, consequently, are addressed in these laws in the second person, the גֵּר is referred to in the third person. The use of the noun גֵּר implies here a *relationship* between two persons. These laws, found in the Covenant code, the deuteronomic code and in the older strata of the Holiness code, can be divided into two groups: (1) laws given for the *protection* of the גֵּר: this is the oldest type of legal references to the גֵּר in the Old Testament, Ex 22,20; and (2) laws given for the material *provision* of the needy, among whom the גֵּר is included. These laws have no sanctions, Deut 14,28-29.

In the second group we have laws concerned with the duties of "the Israelite and the גֵּר" for the preservation of holiness in the community. In these late priestly laws the use of the noun גֵּר implies *membership*. The object of these laws is not the גֵּר, but the community. The גֵּר is mentioned only as one of the subjects for whom such preventive laws are compulsory. These later laws deal with prohibitive commands and are found exclusively in the priestly writings. The Israelite community in these laws is described as being composed of two factions, defined by the inclusion clause גֵּר - אזרח, or constructions such as: "the house of Israel - the גר" or "the sons of Israel - the גר".

3. The combination of the noun גר with the pair "widow-orphan" in the laws given on behalf of the triad "גר - orphan - widow", is a novelty of Deuteronomy which brought together persons who were in a similar situation of need. The inclusion of the widow and the orphan in these laws can be explained in relation to the increasing urbanisation which took place in Israel during the VIII century BC. Formerly the provision for the needs of widows and orphans was a family matter, there was no need for legal measures to provide for them. Such measures became necessary only when the old forms of solidarity were substituted by individualism and orphans and widows lost the natural support of their families. The emergence of the noun גר as a legal term is related to the need for a generic nominal term to designate in the laws, the status of immigrants settled in Israel after the fall of Samaria in 721 BC. This term attempts to preserve Israel's identity in situations of political turmoil, in which immigrants were to be accepted as having similar rights and duties as those of the native citizens. This noun functioned, on the one hand, as an internal boundary between the native members of the Israelite community and those newly accepted and, on the other hand, as a sort of external boundary of the community in relation to other immigrants, whose religious practices were commonly perceived as a threat to their own material security and religious purity.

4. The laws addressed to the pair "Israelite - גר" in the Holiness Code, attempt to prevent the defilement of the land in a time when the concern for the sanctity of the community was particularly strong. At this stage the גר was not yet a proselyte. The obligations required of him are only those which affect the cultic purity of the congregation. Other regulations and ceremonies that do not particularly involve ritual purity were not required of him. The observance of these prohibitive measures was a condition for the admission of the גר and his coexistence "in Israel". These priestly laws can be interpreted as a legal accommodation to the *status quo* acquired by non-Jews, who became members of Jewish communities during the Persian period. This new legislation expresses the concern of the Jewish authorities for the unification of the law, to which members of Jewish communities in the different provinces of the Persian empire were to be submitted.

In sum, we can say that:

a) when the laws of the Pentateuch deal with the *protection of the needy,* they are addressed exclusively to the Israelite, the גר (if mentioned), appears as *protégé* of the law. When the laws deal with the matter of *preservation of holiness,* the גר is subject to the law just as the Israelite.

b) there is an important element of discontinuity between Israel and the surrounding cultures in relation to their attitude towards strangers: unlike the surrounding cultures, *alterity* in Israel did not necessarily imply *hostility.* The

Old Testament knows not only the *peregrinus/hostis,* but also the *peregrinus/hospes.* This element of discontinuity, which is a *specificum* of the Old Testament, is explained by Israel's own history.   The majority of references to the גר in the Old Testament are late, the experience of the exile made Israel aware of "how it feels to be a גר" (Ex 23,9).   After the exile the גר became a mirror of their own story.   The attitude towards the גר in the Old Testament reveals, therefore, Israel's understanding of its own identity.   That is why the command to love the גר is founded in *Israel's own experience* (Deut 10,19).

2. Israel as גר

In the course of time the noun גר acquires, together with its social dimension, a religious one.   This metaphorical use of the term played a fundamental role in Israel's understanding of its fundamental vocation.   The Israelites did not only keep alive the memory of their forefathers as גרים, but understood their own existence as a *peregrinatio.*   The noun גר accomplishes its final role in the Old Testament, as a religious term.

Out of the concrete experience with the גר, emerges the use of this noun for Israel.   The noun appears exclusively in motive clauses and it is used: (1) to justify laws given to Israel on behalf of the גר with the motive clause "because you were גרים in the land of Egypt"; (2) to ground Israel's own petitions "as גר" in prayers (i.e. the metaphor of the Israelites as גרים before Yahweh).   In the first case the Israelites are portrayed as benefactors, in the second case they are portrayed as beneficiaries.

Unlike the forefathers who were גרים in the land (noun גר used in a *territorial* sense), the point of reference in the prayers of Ps 39 and 1 Chron 29 is *religious*: they are גרים before/with Yahweh.   What appears in Lev 25,23 as Yahweh's statement   (with me *you are* גרים),   turns in the prayer of the community into a self-designation: "because *we are* גרים and transients before you" (1 Chron 29,15).   The sociological background of the metaphor of the Israelites as גרים, may be sought in the political situation of Palestine during the post-exilic period.   We have in the Old Testament testimony of the frustration generated by this situation, Neh 9,36-37.   The self designation of גרים, bring them under the direct protection of Yahweh, and allowed them to transfer the hopes, formerly pinned on the land, to Yahweh. This absolute dependence on God, empowered them to overcome the uncertainties and the sense of strangeness created by the possession of their land by foreigners.

These two uses of the noun גר (i.e. גר as individuum and Israel as גר), are both seen against the background of history: the status of the גר-individuum finds its *prototypos* in the former experience of the Israelites as גרים in Egypt; the status of Israel as גר finds its *prototypos* in the former experience of the patriarchs as גרים in the land of Canaan. Both uses of this noun are also the object of a progressive theologisation: the noun גר (-individuum), which originally designated a *person in the Judean territory,* designates later a *person in the Jewish religious community* ; the noun גר (-Israel), used initially with a *spatial* dimension of the forefathers in the land of Canaan, is used later with a *religious* dimension; the Israelites call themselves "גרים before Yahweh".

3. Later developments

With the transition from the Hebrew Bible to its Greek translation, this term underwent a significant development. In the course of time, the two terms involved in the equation גר = προσήλυτος, although meaning originally something else, became the nominal technical terms to designate the proselyte, both in the Greek speaking Jewish communities and in the Rabbinical literature. What was initially an *Advena* in Judean *territory,* later became an *Advena* in the Jewish *religion.* The influence of the LXX in this transformation was definite.

The noun πάροικος played also a significant role in the early Christian theology. With the adoption of the πάροικος-identity, the early Christian communities attempted to overcome discrimination by taking distance and inscribing themselves into a definite reality which was transcendent. This new identity allowed them to experience the problems of "this world" as something transient and relative. The condition of being stranger in this world was used later, in exhortations to promote an ethics of detachment and *non-établissement.*

Appendix

1. Egyptian literature

Text 1: "I announced the needs of the humble,
the widows and the fatherless likewise".[1]

Text 2: "Ich war einer, der das Leiden vertrieb
und die Bedürftigkeit fernhielt,
der die Ehrwürdigen begrub und für die Alten sorgte,
der die Not des Nichts-Habenden vertrieb;
ein Schatten des Waisen, Helfer der Witwe;
der ein Amt einem übertrug, der noch in den Windeln war".[2]

Text 3: "Because thou art the father of the fatherless,
the husband of the widow, the brother of the divorcee,
and the apron of him that is motherless".[3]

Text 4: "Servant of the poor,
father of the fatherless
--- of the orphan.
Mother of the fearful,
‹dungeon› of the turbulent,
protector of the weak
advocate of him who has been deprived
of his possessions by one stronger than he,
husband of the widow
Shelter of the orphan".[4]

---

1   Mentuhotep, 11th Dynasty, in: Janssen, Autobiografie, p. 100; quoted in Havice, Concern p. 30.

2   "Inschrift 17 von den Statuen des Harwa, des Majordomus des thebanischen Gottesweibes Amenerdais; N° VI und II, rechte Seite", in: E. Otto, Inschriften, p. 152.

3   The eloquent peasant to the Chief Steward N° 60; translation: J.A. Wilson, ANET p. 408.

4   Stela of Intef the Herald (18th Dynasty), in: Breasted: ARE, vol. 2 (N° 768,17-18), p. 299.

Text 5:   "Les veuves ne disent-elles pas:[1] C'est toi notre époux!
          Et les petits enfants: C'est notre père et notre mère!
          Les riches se glorifient de ta bonté
          [2]et les pauvres (honorent) ta face.
          Le prisonnier se tourne vers toi,
          et celui qui est sous l'empire de la maladie crie".[5]

Text 6:   "[9]I was rich in grain. When the land was in need.
          I maintained the city with kha and with heket.
          I allowed [10]the citizen to carry away for himself the grain,
          and his wife, the widow and her son".[6]

Text 7:   "I did justice, more stiff (or penetrating?)
          than the beard of barley.
          I saved the poor from the rich.
          I listened (?) to the cry (of her who was) bereft of her husband.
          I brought up the orphan".[7]

Text 8:   "[9]Mon coeur (désire) te voir,
          mon coeur est dans la joie, Amon,
          [10]protecteur du pauvre!
          Tu es le père de celui qui n'a pas [11]de mère
          l'époux de la veuve".[8]

2. Mesopotamian literature

Text 1:   ".. (finally) Urukagina made a covenant with Ningirsu
          that a man of power must not commit an (injustice)
          against an orphan or widow".[9]

Text 2:   "The orphan (naked man?) and the widow,
          the mighty man shall not oppress ..
          The orphan was not delivered up to the wealthy man;
          the widow was not delivered up to the mighty man;
          the man of one shekel was not delivered up

---

5   Hym to Amon # 76, Papyrus Chester Beatty IV (N° VIII 1-2), in: HPEA p. 241.
6   Inscription of Kheti II (9/10th Dynasty), in: Breasted: ARE, vol. I (N° III 408, 9-10), p. 189.
7   Selected Inscriptions from Het-Nub (N° 3) relating to the Wazîr and Nomarch Kay; Graffito VIII, 6, in: Griffith, El Bersheh. Part II (Special Publication of the EEF), p. 52.
8   Hym to Amon # 71 ("Prière d'un aveugle à Amon"), VIII 1-3, in: HPEA p. 204-205.
9   Votive inscription from the cones of Urukagina of Lagash, in: Kramer, Sumerians p. 319.

to the man of one mina".[10]

Text 3: "In my bosom I carried the peoples
of the land of Sumer and Akkad;
they prospered under my protection;
I always governed them in peace;
I sheltered them in wisdom,
in order that the strong might not oppress the weak,
that justice might be dealt the orphan (and) the widow,
in Babylon...".[11]

Text 4: "Schamasch wenn du aufgehst, / werden die Weltufer erhellt!
Die Waise, die Witwe, / ... (und) die Freundin
erwärmen sich bei deinem Aufgang /
(wie) alle Menschen!".[12]

Text 5: "Du bist der Herr, bist, wie die Menschen sagen,
gleich Vater und Mutter;
du erleuchtest hell ihr Dunkel wie Schamasch.
Dem Entrechteten und Mißhandelten /
schaffst du täglich (wahrhafte) Gerechtigkeit,
verhilfst der Weise und der Witwe zu dem Ihren, / ...".[13]

Text 6: "Ohne dich werden sie aus Not und Unglück / nicht herausgeführt;
ohne dich werden Weise (und) Witwe / nicht betreut.
Es rufen dich an, Herr, / die Weise (und) die Witwe;
den entbehrenden Witwer / beschenkst du mit einer Gattin".[14]

Text 7: "Who knows the orphan, who knows the widow.
Knows the oppression of man over man, is the orphan's mother,
Nanshe, who cares for the widow,
Who seeks out (?) justice (?) for the poorest (?).
The queen brings the refugee to her lap,
Finds shelter for the weak.
[*Nanshe's social conscience is further revealed in lines which read*]
"To comfort the orphan,
to make disappear the widow ..

---

10   Code of Ur Nammu § 162-168, translation: J.J. Finkelstein, in: ANET p. 524.
11   Code of Hammurabi, epilogue, reverse, § XXIV: 50-60; translation: T.J. Meek in:
     ANET p.178.
12   Hymn to Shamash # 57, in: SAHG p. 323.
13   Hymn to Marduk # 46, in: SAHG p. 303-304.
14   Hymn to Marduk # 47, in: SAHG p. 308.

to turn over the mighty to the weak ...
Nanshe searches the hearth of the people".[15]

Text 8:   "Das Re(cht Nansches und) Nin(girsus) hatte er be(achtet):
          Dem Armen tat (der Reiche) nichts (zu Leide),
          der Wi(twe tat) der Mä(chtige) nichts (zu Leide),
          in einem Hause, das keinen Erb(sohn hatte),
          ließ er (des Hauses) Toch(ter beim),
          'Schaf(fett-Verbrennen 'einstehen)".[16]

3. Ugaritic literature[17]

Text 1:   "He (i.e. Daniel) judged the cause of the widow,
          tried the case of the orphan".[18]

Text 2:   "Je me tenais assis à la porte sous un grand arbre,
          sur l'aire, jugeant la cause de la veuve,
          tranchant le cas de l'orphelin".[19]

Text 3:   "You do not judge the cause of the widow
          You do not try the case of the importunate[20]
          You do not banish the extortioners of the poor.
          You do not feed the orphan before your face
          (nor) the widow behind your back".[21]

---

15   Description of the Lagashite goddess Nanshe in a hymn, in: Kramer, Sumerians p. 124-125.
16   "Lieder auf Tempel (N° 32): Tempelbau-Hymne Gudeas von Lagash, Zylinder A, XVIII", in: SAHG p. 180.
17   In the Ugaritic literature we find also several references to underprivileged persons, for instance: the "oppressed" qsr nps (Keret 16,VI,33); the "sick man" zbl (Keret 14,2,99); the "blind" 'wr (Keret 14,2,100): the "poor" dl (Keret 16,VI,46). See del Olmo Olete, Mitos p. 536; 544; 592; 599; and Whitaker, Concordance p. 19-20; among them, references to the pair 'widow-orphan'.
18   Aqhat 17,ii,v,8; see also Aqhat 19, col. 1,24 "(he) judged (the case of the widow), (tried) the case (of the orphan)", in: Gibson, Myths p. 107; 114.
19   Epsztein, Justice p. 178; Aqhat A,v, 6-8. See also Caquot, TO p. 443 and Vesco RThom 6 p. 252.
20   Gibson translates 'qsr nps' by "importunate" (Myths p. 102), Olmo Olete by "oprimido" (Mitos p. 620).
21   Keret 16,VI,46-50, in: Gibson, Myths p. 102.

Abbreviations

ÄA	Ägyptologische Abhandlungen, Wiesbaden
AASOR	The Annual of the American Schools of Oriental Research
AB	Actualidad Bíblica
ABAW	Abhandlungen der (K.) Bayerischen Akademie der Wissenschaften
ABD	The Anchor Bible Dictionary
ACEBT	Amsterdamse Cahiers voor Exegese en Bijbelse Theologie
AcOr (L)	Acta Orientalia, Leiden
AES	Archives Européenes de Sociologie
AfO	Archiv für Orientforschung
AHw	Akkadisches Handwörterbuch, W. von Soden, 1959-1981
AJSLL	American Journal of Semitical Languages and Literature
AnBib	Analecta Biblica
AncB	The Anchor Bible
ANET	Ancient Near Eastern Texts related to the Old Testament, J.B. Pritchard (ed.), 2° Ed. 1969
ANF	The Ante-Nicene Fathers. Translated by A. Roberts and J. Donaldson, reprint 1962
AnOr	Analecta Orientalia
AOAT	Alter Orient und Altes Testament
APOT	Apocrypha and Pseudepigrapha of the Old Testament, R.H. Charles, 1913
ARE	Ancient Records of Egypt. Historical Documents, J.H. Breasted, Rev. Ed. Chicago 1962
ARM	Archives Royales de Mari
AT	The Complete Bible. An American Translation, J.M. Powis Smith / T. Meek (ed.), 1939
ATANT	Abhandlungen zur Theologie des Alten und Neuen Testaments
ATD	Das Alte Testament Deutsch
BA	La Bible d'Alexandrie
BBB	Bonner Biblische Beiträge
BDB	Brown-Driver-Briggs, A Hebrew and English Lexicon of the Old Testament, Seventh printing 1980
BEThL	Bibliotheca Ephemeridum Theologicarum Lovaniensium
BHK	Biblia Hebraica, ed. R. Kittel, 7. Aufl. 1951
BHS	Biblia Hebraica Stuttgartensia, ed. K. Elliger / W. Rudolph, 1967/77
BiKi	Bibel und Kirche
BiL	Bibel-Lexikon, D. Schenkel, (Hrsg.), Bd. 1-5, 1869-1875
BiOr	Bibliotheca Orientalis

BJ	La Bible de Jérusalem
BK	Biblischer Kommentar
BKV	Bibliothek der Kirchenväter, Kemptener Ausgabe, 1911ff
BL	Bibel-Lexikon, Hrsg. v. H. Haag 1951-1956
BN	Biblische Notizen
BOT	De Boeken van het Oude Testament
BP	Biblia del Peregrino, L.A. Schökel (ed.), Edición de Estudio, I/III, 1996-1997
BPM	Biblia Polyglotta Matritensia, edited by A. Díez Macho 1980
BS	Bibliotheca Sacra
BuL	Bibel und Liturgie
BWL	Babylonian Wisdom Literature, W.G. Lambert, 1960
BZAW	Beihefte zur Zeitschrift für die alttestamentliche Wissenschaft
CAD	The Assyrian Dictionary of the Oriental Institute of the University of Chicago, 1956ff.
CahRB	Cahiers de la Revue Biblique
CBOTS	Coniectanea Biblica. Old Testament Series
CBP	Cahiers de Biblia Patristica
CBQ	The Catholic Biblical Quarterly
CII	Corpvs Inscriptionvm Ivdaicarvm I-II, J.-B. Frey, 1936-1952
CSIC	Consejo Superior de Investigaciones Científicas
CTB	Calwer Taschenbibliothek
DBHE	Diccionario de la Biblia Hebreo Español, edited by L.A Schökel, 1994
DBS	Supplément au Dictionnaire de la Bible, 1928ff.
DBV	Dictionnaire de la Bible. Vigouroux, 1912ff.
DCH	The Dictionary of Classical Hebrew, edited by D.J.A. Clines, 1993ff.
DDS	Deuteronomy and the Deuteronomic School, M. Weinfeld, 1972
DS	Dictionnaire de Spiritualité. Fondé par M. Viller et al., 1984ff.
EB	Études Bibliques
EC	Enciclopedia Cattolica (Città del Vaticano)
EdF	Erträge der Forschung
EEF	Egypt Exploration Fund
EH	Exegetisches Handbuch zum Alten Testament, Münster
EHPR	Études d'Histoire et de Philosophie Religieuses
EKK	Evangelisch-Katholischer Kommentar zum Neuen Testament
EncB	Encyclopædia Biblica, ed. T.K. Cheyne and J. Black, 1899-1903
ERE	Encyclopaedia of Religion and Ethics, 1908-1926
ET	The Expository Times
EThR	Études Théologiques et Religieuses
EThSt	Erfurter theologische Studien, Leipzig
EvTh	Evangelische Theologie
EWNT	Exegetisches Wörterbuch zum Neuen Testament,
FJFr	Forschungen zur Judenfrage
FRLANT	Forschungen zur Religion und Literatur des Alten und Neuen Testaments

GELS	A Greek - English Lexicon of the Septuagint, J. Lust / E. Eynikel / K. Hauspie, 1992-1996
GKC	Gesenius's Hebrew Grammar, W. Gesenius / E. Kautzsch, Tr. A.E. Cowley, 2. Aufl. 1910
HAL	Hebräisches und Aramäisches Lexikon zum Alten Testament, Hrsg. von L. Köhler, W. Baumgartner and J.J. Stamm
HAR	Hebrew Annual Review
HAT	Handbuch zum Alten Testament
HK	Handkommentar zum Alten Testament
HNT	Handbuch zum Neuen Testament
HPDBA	Hymnes et prières aux dieux de Babylonie et d'Assyrie, M.-J. Seux
HPEA	Hymnes et prières de L'Égypte Ancienne, A. Barucq - F. Daumas, 1976
HSAT(K)	Die Heilige Schrift des Alten Testaments, Kautsch, E. et al., 4. Auf. 1922-1923
HTR	Harvard Theological Review
HUCA	Hebrew Union College Annual
HWP	Historisches Wörterbuch der Philosophie
IAT	Les institutions de L'Ancien Testament, I/II, R. de Vaux, 1958-1960
ICC	The International Critical Commentary
IDB	The Interpreter's Dictionary of the Bible
IEJ	Israel Exploration Journal
ISBE	The International Standard Bible Encyclopaedia
JBL	Journal of Biblical Literature
JewEnc	The Jewish Enciclopedia, 1901-1906
JJS	Journal of Jewish Studies
JNES	Journal of Near Eastern Studies
JPS	The Jewish Publication Society
JRP	Jahrbuch der Religionspädagogik
JSOT	Journal for the Study of the Old Testament
JSOTSS	Journal for the Study of the Old Testament Supplementary Series
KAT¹	Kommentar zum Alten Testament, Leipzig
KAT²	Kommentar zum Alten Testament, Gütersloh
KBL	Lexicon in Veteris Testamenti Libros, Hrsg. von L. Köhler, W. Baumgartner, 1958
KeH	Kurzgefaßtes exegetisches Handbuch zum Alten Testament, Leipzig
KHC	Kurzer Hand-Commentar zum Alten Testament
LÄ	Lexikon der Ägyptologie
LeDiv	Lectio Divina
Luther	Die Bibel nach der Übersetzung Martins Luthers neu bearbeitet, Stuttgart 1984
MAB	Manuel d'Archéologie Biblique, I-II, A.G. Barrois, 1939-1953
MLS	Materialien zum Sumerischen Lexikon, B. Landberger
MPG	Patrologiae cursus completus, series Graeca, J.P. Migne
MT	The Massoretic Text

MTZ	Münchener Theologische Zeitung
NBL	Neues Bibel Lexikon, hg. v. M. Görg, / B. Lang, 1991ff.
NCBC	The New Century Bible Commentary
NEASB	Near Eastern Archeology Society Bulletin
NEngB	The New English Bible
NEB	Die Neue Echter Bibel
NGTT	Nederduitse Gereformeerde Teologiese Tydskrif
NRSV	The New Revised Standard Version
NTS	New Testament Studies
OBO	Orbis Biblicus et Orientalis
OH	Osnabrücker Hochschulschriften, Schriftenreihe des FB
Osty	La Bible. Traduction française par É. Osty et J. Trinquet
OTS	Oudtestamentische Studiën
OTSt	Old Testament Studies
PIOL	Publication de l'Institute Orientaliste de Louvain
PTh	Pastoral Theologie, Göttingen
RA	Revue d'Assyriologie et d'Archéologie Orientale
RB	Revue Biblique
RE	Real-Enzyklopädie für Protestantiche Theologie und Kirche, 3. Aufl. 1896-1913
RECA	Real-Encyclopädie der classischen Altertumswissenchaft, A. Pawly / G. Wissowa Hrsg., NB 1984ff.
REJ	Révue des études juives
RGG	Die Religion in Geschichte und Gegenwart, 2. Aufl. 1927-1932, 3. Aufl. 1957-1965
RHPR	Revue d'Histoire et de Philosophie Religieuses
RHR	Revue de l'Histoire des Religions
RivBib	Rivista Biblica
RJAE	La Religion des Judéo-Araméens d'Éléphantine, A. Vincent, 1937
RLA	Reallexikon der Assyriologie, hg. von E. Ebeling und B. Meissner
RQ	Revue de Qumran
RScR	Recherches de Science Religieuse
RSJB	Recueils de la Société Jean Bodin
RSLR	Rivista di storia e letteratura religiosa
RThom	Revue Thomiste
SAHG	Sumerische und akkadische Hymnen und Gebete, hg. von A. Falkenstein und W. von Soden
SB (T)	La Sacra Bibbia, Turin
SBi	Sources Bibliques, Paris
SBTS	Sources for Biblical and Theological Study
SC	Sources Chrétiennes. Collection dirigée par H. Lubac et J. Daniélou, 1943ff
SG	Sumerisches Glossar, F. Delitzsch, 1914
SKAB	Schriften der Katholischen Akademie in Bayern

SKG.G	Schriften der Königsberger Gelehrten Gesellschaft -Geisteswissenschaftliche Klasse
SL	Sumerisches Lexicon, A. Deimel Rom 1925-1937
SRB	Supplementi alla Rivista Biblica, Brescia
SSN	Studia Semitica Neerlandica
SSNT.MS	Society for the Study of the New Testament Monographical Series
SVT	Supplements to Vetus Testamentum
TB	Theologische Bücherei
TBNT	Theologisches Begriffslexikon zum Neuen Testaments, 1971
TGI	Textbuch zur Geschichte Israels, K. Galling Hrsg., 1950
THAT	Theologisches Handwörterbuch zum Alten Testament, 1971
ThPh	Theologie und Philosophie
ThW	Theologische Wissenschaft, Stuttgart
TLZ	Theologische Literaturzeitung
TO	Textes Ougaritiques I, Mythes et Légendes, A. Caquot, 1974
TOB	La Bible. Traduction Œcuménique
TOTC	Tyndale Old Testament Commentaries
TRE	Theologische Realenzyklopädie
TS	Theological Studies
TThZ	Trierer Theologische Zeitschrift
TWAT	Theologisches Wörterbuch zum Alten Testament
TWNT	Theologisches Wörterbuch zum Neuen Testament
ÜP	Überlieferungsgeschichte des Pentateuchs, M. Noth, 2. Aufl. 1960
UT	Ugaritic Textbook, C.H. Gordon, Rom 1965
VT	Vetus Testamentum
WBC	Word Biblical Commentary
WMANT	Wissenschaftliche Monographien zum AT und NT
WuD	Wort und Dienst
WUNT	Wissenschaftliche Untersuchungen zum Neuen Testament
YOS	Yale Oriental Series
ZABR	Zeitschrift für Altorientalische und Biblische Rechtsgeschichte
ZAW	Zeitschrift für die alttestamentliche Wissenschaft
ZB	Zürcher Bibelkommentare
ZDPV	Zeitschrift des Deutschen Palästinavereins
ZNW	Zeitschrift für die neutestamentliche Wissenschaft und die Kunde der älteren Kirche
ZThK	Zeitschrift für Theologie und Kirche

Bibliography

Abba, R., Priests and Levites in Deuteronomy, *VT* XXVII (1977) p. 257-267

Abrego, J.M., *Jeremías y el final del reino. Lectura sincrónica de Jer 36-45*, Estudios del Antiguo Testamento 3, Valencia 1983

Albertz, R., *Religionsgeschichte Israels in alttestamentlicher Zeit 1/2*, ATD 8/1-2, Göttingen 1992

——, "Ihr seid Fremdlinge in Ägypten gewesen" -Fremde im Alten Testament, in: *Der Mensch als Hüter seiner Welt. Alttestamentliche Bibelarbeiten zu den Themen des konziliaren Prozesses*, CTB 16, 1990, 61-72

Allen, C.W., On the meaning of προσήλυτος in the Septuagint. *The Expositor* 10 (1884) p. 264-275

Allen, L.C., *Psalms 101-150*, WBC 21, Waco 1983

Allenbach, J. et al, *Biblia Patristica. Index des citations et allusions bibliques dans la littérature patristique.* Le troisième siècle (Origène excepté), Paris 1977

Alt, A., Das Großreich Davids, in: *Kleine Schriften II*, 3. Aufl., München 1964 p. 66-75

——, Die Ursprünge des israelitischen Rechts, in: *Kleine Schriften I*, München 1959 p. 278-332

Altmann, P., *Erwählungstheologie und Universalismus im Alten Testament*, BZAW 92, 1964

Amusin, J.A., Die Gerim in der sozialen Lesgislatur des Alten Testaments, *KLIO* 63/1 (1981) p. 15-23

Asensio, F., Sugerencias del salmista peregrino y extranjero: Ps 39,13, *Gregrorianum* 34 (1953) p. 421-426

Astour, M. C., The Merchant Class of Ugarit, in: *Gesellschaftsklassen im Alten Zweistromland und in den angrenzenden Gebieten*, ABAW NF Heft 75, 1972, p. 11-26

——, Les Étrangers a Ugarit et le statut-juridique des Habiru. *RA* 53 (1959) p. 70-76

Auffarth, C., Protecting Strangers: establishing a fundamental value in the religion of the Ancient Near East and Ancient Greece, *Numen* Vol. XXXIX/2 p. 193-214

Bächli, O., *Israel und die Völker*, Zürich 1962

Baentsch, B., *Exodus-Leviticus*, HK I.2.1., Göttingen 1903

Baethgen, F., *Die Psalmen übersetzt und erklärt*, HAT II.2., 3. Aufl., Göttingen 1904

Bainton, R., The Early Church and War, *HTR* 39 (1946) p. 189-212

Baltzer, K., Das Ende des Staates Juda und die Messiasfrage, in: R. Rendtorff / K. Koch (Hrsg.), *Studien zur Theologie der alttestamentlichen Überlieferungen*. Festschrift G. v. Rad zum 60. Geburtstag, Duisburg-Ruhrort 1961 p. 33-43

Bamberger, B.J., *Proselytism in the Talmudic Period*, Cincinnati 1939

Barbiero, G., *L'asino del nemico. Rinuncia alla vendetta e amore del nemico nella legislazione dell'Antico Testamento*, AnBib 128, Roma 1991

Bardtke, H., *Das Buch Esther*, KAT XVII,5, Gütersloh 1963

Barr, J., Semantics and Biblical Theology - a contribution to the discussion, in: *Congress Volume. Uppsala*, SVT 22, Leiden-New York-Köln, 1972 p. 11-19

―― , "Semitic Philology and the Interpretation of the Old Testament", in: G.W. Anderson (Ed.), *Tradition and Interpretation*, Oxford 1979 p. 31-64

―― , *The Semantics of Biblical Language*. 2. Ed., Oxford 1962

Barrois, A.G., *Manuel d'Archéologie Biblique*, Tome II, Paris 1953

Barth, H., *Die Jesaja-Worte in der Josiazeit*, WMANT 48, Neukirchen-Vluyn 1977

Barucq, A. / Daumas, F., *Hymnes et prières de L'Égypte ancienne*, Paris 1980

Bauer, W., *Griechisch-Deutsches Wörterbuch zu den Schriften des Neuen Testaments und der übrigen urchristlichen Literatur*, 6. Aufl., Berlin 1988

Bauer, H. / Leander, P., *Historische Grammatik der hebräischen Sprache des Alten Testamentes*. Erster Band, Halle a. S. 1922

Baumgarten, J.M., Exclusions from the Temple: Proselytes and Aggripa I. *JJS* 33 (1982) p. 215-225

―― , "The Exclusion of Netinim and Proselytes in 4Q Florilegium", in: idem, *Studies in Qumran Law*. Leiden 1977 p. 75-87

Becker, U., Art. Gottesfürchtiger, Proselyt/προσήλυτος", in: *TBNT*, 9. Aufl., Budapest 1993 p. 612-614

Beer, G., Das Stehenlassen der Pe'ah Lev 19,9, *ZAW* 31 (1911) p. 152

Bennett, W.H., Art. Stranger and Sojourner, in: *EncB*, IV, London 1903 col. 4814-4818

Benzinger, I., *Hebräische Archäologie*, 3. Aufl., Leipzig 1927

Benzinger, P., Art. Fremdlinge bei den Hebräern, in: *RE*, VI, Leipzig 1899 p. 262-265

Bertholet, A., *Deuteronomium*, KHC V, Tübingen 1899

―― , *Die Stellung der Israeliten und der Juden zu den Fremden*, Freiburg - Basel 1896

―― , Art. Fremde, in: *RGG* 2. Aufl., II, Tübingen 1928 col. 774-776

Bettenzoli, G., I Leviti e la riforma deuteronomica, *RSLR* 22 (1986) p. 3-25

Bévenot, H., *Die beiden Makkabäerbücher übersetzt und erklärt*, HSAT IV.4, Bonn 1931

Bietenhard, H., Art. Fremde/ξένος, in: *TBNT*, 9. Aufl., Budapest 1993 p. 373-375

Bitter, R.A., *Vreemdelingschap bij Philo van Alexandrie: een onderzoek naar de betekenis van paroikos.* Utrecht Diss., 1982

Blidstein, G., 4Q Florilegium and Rabbinic Sources on Bastard and Proselyte, *RQ* 31/8 (1974) p. 431-435

Block, D.I., Art. Sojourner, in: *ISBE*, IV, Michigan 1989 p. 561- 564

Blum, E., *Die Komposition der Vätergeschichte*, WMANT 57, Neukirchen-Vluyn 1984

—— , *Studien zur Komposition des Pentateuch.* BZAW 189, Berlin 1990

Boadt, L., *Ezekiel's Oracles against Egypt. A Literary and Philological Study of Ez 29-32*, BiOr 37, 1980

Boecker, H.J., *Recht und Gesetz im Alten Testament und im Alten Orient*, Neukirchen-Vluyn 1984

Bolkestein, H., *Wohltätigkeit und Armenpflege im vorchristlichen Altertum*, Utrecht 1939

Boman, Th., Review of *The Semantics of Biblical Language*, by J. Barr, TLZ 87 (1962) p. 262-265

Born, A. van den, Art. Fremde, in: *BL* (H. Haag, Hrsg.), 2. Aufl., Einsiedeln 1968 col. 494

Boulluec A. le - P. Sandevoir, *La Bible d'Alexandrie. LXX*, II, L'Exode, Paris 1989

Bourguet, D., *Des Métaphores de Jérémie.* EB 9, Paris 1987

Bousset, W. / Greßmann, H., *Die Religion des Judentums im späthellenistischen Zeitalter*, HNT 21, 4. Aufl., Tübingen 1966

Braulik, G., *Deuteronomium I/II*, NEB, Stuttgart 1986-1992

Breasted, J.H., *Ancient Records of Egypt. Historical Documents*, 2 Vol., Rev. Ed., Chicago 1962

Bright, J., *Jeremiah*, AncB 21, New York 1965

Brongers, G.A., Bemerkungen zum Gebrauch des adverbiellen $w^{ec}attah$ im Alten Testament, *VT* 15 (1965) p. 289-299

Brooke, G.J., *Exegesis at Qumran. 4Q Florilegium in its Jewish Context.* JSOTSS 29, Sheffield 1985

Broshi, B., La population de l'ancienne Jérusalem, *RB* 82 (1975) p. 5-14

—— , The Expansion of Jerusalem in the reigns of Hezekiah and Manasseh, *IEJ* 24 (1974) p. 21-26

Brown, F. / Driver, S.R. / Briggs, C.A., *A Hebrew and English Lexicon of the Old Testament*, Seventh printing, Oxford 1980

Brox, N., *Der erste Petrusbrief*, EKK XXI, Zürich-Einsiedeln-Köln 1979

Buccellati, G., *The Amorites of the UR III Period*, Naples 1966

Buhl, F., *Die sozialen Verhältnisse der Israeliten*, Berlin 1899

Buis, P. / Leclercq, J., *Le Deutéronome*, SB, Paris 1963

Bultmann, C., *Der Fremde im antiken Juda*, FRLANT 153, Göttingen 1992

Burkert, W., Art. Seelenwanderung, in: *HWP*, 9, Basel 1995 col. 117-121

Caquot, A., *Textes Ougaritiques, I., Mythes et Légendes*, Paris 1974

Cardascia, G., Le statut de l'Étranger dans la Mésopotamie Ancienne, in:
    L'Étranger, *RSJB* 9 (1958) p. 105-117

—— , *Les Lois Assyriennes*, Paris 1969

Cardellini, I., Stranieri ed "emigrati-residenti" in una sintesi di teologia
    storico-biblica, *RivBib* 40 (1992) p. 129-181

Cassin, E., Quelques Remarques à propos des Archives Administratives de
    Nuzi, *RA* 52 (1958) p. 16-28

Causse, A., Israël et la vision de l'humanité, *EHPR* 8 (1924) p. 5-149

—— , L'idéal politique et social du Deutéronome. La fraternité d'Israël,
    RHPR 13 (1933) p. 289-323

—— , La crise de la solidarité de la famille et de clan dans l'Ancien Israël, in:
    RHPR 10 (1930) p. 24-60

—— , Les dispersés d'Israël, *EHPR* 19, 1929

Cazelles, H., Art. Pentateuque (Textes Sacerdotaux), in: *DBS*, VII, Paris
    1966 col. 822-858

—— , La mission d'Esdras, *VT* 4 (1954) p. 113-140

Charles, R.H. (Ed.), *Apocrypha and Pseudepigrapha of the Old Testament I*,
    New York 1913

Cheyne, T.K., *Introduction to the Book of Isaiah*, London 1895

Cholewiński, A., *Heiligkeitsgesetz und Deuteronomium. Eine vergleichende
    Studie*, AnBib 66, Roma 1976

Clemens, R.E., *Isaiah 1-39*, NCBC, London 1980

Clines, D.J.A. (ed.), *The Dictionary of Classical Hebrew,* II: א - ב,
    Sheffield 1995

Cohen,M., Le "ger" biblique et son statut socio-religieux, *RHR* 207 (1990)
    p. 131-158

Cortese, E., L'anno giubilare: Profezia della Restaurazione? (Studio su Lev
    25), *Riv Bib* 18 (1970) p. 395-400

—— , L'Esegesi di H (Lev. 17-26), *Riv Bib* 29 (1981) p. 129-146

—— , *La Terra di Canaan nella storia sacerdotale del pentateuco*. Sup Riv
    Bib 5, Roma 1972

—— , *Levitico*, La Sacra Bibbia, Casale Monferrato 1982

Croft, S.J.L., *The Identity of the Individual in the Psalms*, JSOTSS 44,
    Sheffield 1987

Crüsemann, F., Das Bundesbuch - Historischer Ort und institutioneller
    Hintergrund, in: J.A. Emerton (Ed.), *Congress Volume Jerusalem 1986*
    SVT 40 Leiden-New York-Köln 1988 p. 27-41

—— , *Die Tora*, München 1992

—— , Fremdenliebe und Identitässicherung. Zum Verständnis der
    "Fremden"-Gesetze im Alten Testament, *WuD* 19 (1987) p. 11-24

—— , "Ihr kennt die Seele des Fremden." (Ex 23,9), *Concilium* 29 (1993) p. 339-347

Dalbert, P., *Die Theologie der jüdisch-hellenistischen Missionsliteratur unter Ausschluß von Philo und Josephus*, Hamburg 1954

Dalman, G.H., *Aramäisch-Neuhebräisches Handwörterbuch zu Targum, Talmud und Midrasch*, Hildesheim 1967

Damizia, G., Art. Parroco, in: *EC*, IX, Città del Vaticano 1952

Danby, H., *The Mishna*. Reimpression, London 1954

Daube, D., *The Exodus Pattern in the Bible*, Cambridge 1963

Davies, P.R., Who Can Join the 'Damascus Covenant'?, *JJS* 46 (1995) p. 134-142

Deimel, P.A., *Sumerisches Lexikon*. Teil III Band 1, Roma 1934

Deines, R., Die Abwehr der Fremden in den Texten aus Qumran, in: R. Feldmeier und U. Heckel, Hrsg.: *Die Heiden: Juden, Christen und das Problem des Fremden*, WUNT 70, Tübingen 1994 p. 58-91

Deißler, A., *Psalm 119 und seine Theologie*, München 1955

Delitzsch, F., *Sumerisches Glossar*, Leipzig 1914

Diez Macho, A. (Ed.), *Introducción General a los Apócrifos del Antiguo Testamento*. Tomo 1, Madrid 1984

—— , (Ed.), *Biblia Polyglotta Matritensia. Targum Palaestinense in Pentateuchum*. Additur Targum Pseudojonatan ejusque hispania versio, L. 1. Genesis, Madrid 1988

—— , et al., *Biblia Polyglotta Matritensia. Sumptibus. CSIC Series IV L. 3 Leviticus*, Madrid 1980

—— , *El Targum. Introducción a las traducciones aramaicas de la Biblia*, Madrid 1979

Dillmann, A., *Die Genesis*, KeH 11, 3. Aufl., Leipzig 1875

—— , *Die Bücher Exodus und Leviticus* (hg. v. V. Ryssel), KeH 12, 3. Aufl., Leipzig 1897

—— , / Kittel, R., *Der Prophet Jesaja*, KeH, 6. Aufl., Leipzig 1898

Dimant, D., 4Q Florilegium and the Idea of the Community as Temple, in A. Caquot / M. Hadas / J. Riaud (Ed.), Hellenica et Judaica, Leuven-Paris 1986 pp. 165-189

Dion, P.E., Israël et l'Étranger dans le Deutéronome, in: *L'Altérité. Vivre ensemble différents. Approches Pluridisciplinaires*, Montreal - Paris 1986 p. 211-233

—— , *Universalismo religioso en Israel. Desde los orígenes a la crisis macabea*, Spanish Translation, Navarra 1976

Donner, H., Jesaja LVI 1-7: Ein Abrogationsfall innerhalb des Kanons-Implikationen und Konsequenzen, in: *Aufsätze zum Alten Testament*, BZAW 224, Berlin 1994 p. 165-179

—— , *Geschichte des Volkes Israel und seiner Nachbarn in Grundzügen*, ATD Ergänzungsreihe 8/1-2, Göttingen 1984-1986

Dorival, G., *La Bible d'Alexandrie. LXX IV, Les Nombres*, Paris 1994
Doron, P., Motive Clauses in the Laws of Deuteronomy: Their Forms,
   Functions and Contents, *HAR* 2 (1978) p. 61-77
Driver, G.R. / Miles, J.C., *The Babylonian Laws*. Vol I, Oxford 1952
Driver, S.R., *Deuteronomy*, ICC, 3. Ed., Edinburgh 1902
―― , *The Book of Leviticus. A new English translation* (Polychrome
   Edition), Leipzig 1904
Duhm, B., *Das Buch Jesaja*, HK III/1, 3. Aufl., Göttingen 1914
Dupont-Sommer, A. / M. Philonenko, *La Bible. Écrits intertestamentaires*,
   Paris 1987

Ebeling, E., Art. Flüchtling, in: *RLA*, III, Berlin 1957 p. 88-90
Ehrlich, A.B., *Randglossen zur Hebräischen Bibel. Textkritisches,
   Sprachliches und Sachliches*, I-IV, Leipzig 1908-1912
Eisemann, M., *The Book of Ezekiel. A new translation with a commentary
   anthologised from Talmudic, Midrashic and Rabbinic Sources*, New York
   1988
Elliger, K., *Leviticus*, HAT I/4, Tübingen 1966
Epsztein, L., *La justice sociale dans le Proche-Orient Ancien et le peuple de
   la Bible*, Paris 1983
Erlandsson, S., *The burden of Babylon. A study of Isaiah 13,2-14,23*,
   CBOTS 4, Lund 1970
Estes, D.J., Metaphorical Sojourning in 1 Chronicles 29:15. *CBQ* 53 (1991)
   p. 45-49

Faley, R.J., Leviticus, in: R.E. Brown / J.A. Fitzmyer / R.E. Murphy (Ed.),
   The Jerome Biblical Commentary, Englewood Cliffs 1968 p. 67-85
Falkenstein, A. / Soden, W. von, *Sumerische und akkadische Hymnen und
   Gebete*, Zürich - Stuttgart 1953
Faust, D.E., *Contracts from Larsa. Dated in the Reign of Rîm-Sin*, YOS
   VIII, 1941
Feldmann, F., *Das Buch Isaias 1-39*, EH 14, Münster 1925
Fensham, F.C., Widow, Orphan and the Poor in Ancient Near Eastern
   Legal and Wisdom Literature, *JNES* XXI (1962) p. 129-139
Fichtner, J., Die etymologische Ätiologie in der Namengebung der
   geschichtlichen Bücher des Alten Testaments, *VT* 6 (1956) p. 372-396
Fohrer, G., *Jesaja. 1. Band Kapitel 1-23*, 2. Aufl., ZB, Zürich - Stuttgart
   1966
Frei, P., Die persische Reichsautorisation. Ein Überblick, in: *ZABR* 1
   p. 1- 35
―― , / Koch, K., *Reichsidee und Reichsorganisation im Perserreich*. OBO
   55, 1984

Frey, J.-B., *Corpvs Inscriptionvm Ivdaicarvm. Recueil des inscriptions Juives qui vont du IIIe siècle avant Jésus-Christ au IVe siècle de notre ère*. Vol. I-II, Città del Vaticano 1936-1952

Friedrich, G., Semasiologie und Lexikologie, *TLZ* 94 (1969) p. 801-816

—— , Zum Problem der Semantik, *KuD* 16 (1970) p. 41-57

Gall, Frhr. v., Die Entstehung der humanitären Forderungen des Gesetzes, *ZAW* 30 (1910) p. 91-98

Galling, K., Das Gemeindegesetz in Deuteronomium 23, in: W. Baumgarten / O. Eißfeldt / K. Elliger / L. Rost (Hrsg.), *Festschrift Alfred Bertholet zum 80. Geburtstag*, Tübingen 1950 p. 176-191

—— , Hrsg., *Textbuch zur Geschichte Israels*, 3. Aufl., Tübingen 1950

García Martínez, F., *Textos de Qumrán*, Tercera edición, Madrid 1993

—— , / Tigchelaar, E.J.C., *The Dead See Scrolls. Volume One 1Q1-4Q273. Study Edition*. Leiden-New York-Cologne 1997

Geiger. A., *Urschrift und Uebersetzungen der Bibel*, Breslau 1857

Gelb, I.J. / Purves, P.M. / Mac Rae, A.A., *Nuzi Personal Names*, Chicago 1963

—— , Prisoners of War in Early Mesopotamia *JNES* 32 (1973), p. 70-98

Gemser, B., The Importance of the Motive Clause in Old Testament Law, in: G.W. Anderson et al. (Ed.), *Congress Volume. Copenhagen 1953*, SVT 1, Leiden 1953 p. 50-66

Gerleman, G., *Esther*, BK XXI, Neukirchen-Vluyn 1973

Gerstenberger, E., *Das 3. Buch Mose. Leviticus*, ATD 6, 6. Aufl., Göttingen 1993

—— , *Wesen und Herkunft des 'apodiktischen Rechts'*, WMANT 20, Neukirchen-Vluyn 1965

Gese, H., *Alttestamentlische Studien*, Tübingen 1991

Gesenius, W., *Hebräisches und chaldäisches Handwörterbuch über das Alte Testament*, 2. Aufl., Leipzig 1823

—— , *Hebräisches und chaldäisches Handwörterbuch über das Alte Testament*, 3. Aufl., Leipzig 1828

—— , *Thesavrvs Philologicvs criticvs lingvae hebraeae et chaldeae veteris testamenti*, Tomi Primi, Lipsiae 1829

—— , *Hebräisches und chaldäisches Handwörterbuch über das Alte Testament*, in verbindung mit H. Zimmern, bearbeitet von F. Buhl, 14. Aufl., Leipzig 1905

—— , *Hebräisches und chaldäisches Handwörterbuch über das Alte Testament*, in Verbindung mit H. Zimmern / W.M. Müller / O. Weber, bearbeitet von F. Buhl, 15. Aufl., Leipzig 1910

—— , Kautzsch, E., *Gesenius's Hebrew Grammar*, Tr. A.E. Cowley, 2. Aufl., Oxford 1910

——, *Hebräisches und Aramäisches Handwörterbuch über das Alte Testament*, 18. Aufl., Hrsg. v. R. Meyer / H. Donner / U. Rüterswörden, 1. Lieferung א - ג, Berlin 1987

Gibson, J.C.L., *Canaanite Myths and Legends*, 2. Aufl., Edinburgh 1978

Glassner, J.J., L'hospitalité en Mésopotamie ancienne: aspect de la question de l'étranger, *ZA* 80 (1990) p. 60-75

Gonçalves, F.J., Isaie, Jérémie et la politique internationale de Juda, *Biblica* 76 (1995) p. 282-298

——, *L'Expédition de Sennachérib en Palestine dans la Littérature Hébraïque Ancienne*, PIOL 34, Louvain-La-Neuve 1986

Gordon, C., *Ugaritic Textbook*. AnOr 38, Rome 1965

Gorman, F.H., *The Ideology of Ritual. Space, Time and Status in the Priestly Theology*, JSOTSS 91, Sheffield 1990

Gray, G.B., *The Book of Isaiah*, ICC, 4. Ed., Edinburgh 1956

Greger, B., Beobachtungen zum Begriff (ger), *BN* 63 (1992) p. 30-34

Grelot, P., Art. Israël, in: X. Léon-Dufour (Éd.),*Vocabulaire de Théologie Biblique*, Paris 1962 p. 578-579

——, La dernière étape de la rédaction sacerdotale, *VT* 6 (1956) p. 174-189

——, Le Papyrus Pascal d'Éléphantine et le problème du Pentateuque, *VT* 5 (1955) p. 250-265

Griffith, F.L., *El Bersheh. Part II* (Special Publication of the EEF), London 1893-1894

Gröndahl, F., *Die Personennamen der Texte aus Ugarit,* Studia Pohl 1, Roma 1967

Gunkel, H., *Die Psalmen*, HK II/2, 5. Aufl., Göttingen 1968

Hanhart, R., *Sacharja*. BK XIV/7.2, Neukirchen-Vluyn 1991

Hardmeier, C., Erzählen-Erzählung-Erzählgemeinschaft. Zur Rezeption von Abrahamserzählungen in der Exilsprophetie, *WuD* 16 (1981) p. 27-47

Harl, M. / G. Dorival / O. Munnich, *La Bible Grecque des Septante. Du Judaïsme Hellénistique au Christianisme Ancien*, Paris 1994

——, *La Bible d'Alexandrie. LXX, I, La Genèse*, Paris 1986

Harlé, P. / D. Pralon, *La Bible d'Alexandrie. LXX, III, Le Lévitique*, Paris 1988

Hartog, F., *Le miroir d'Hérodote. Essai sur la représentation de l'autre*, Paris 1980

Hasel, G.F., Art. כרת, in: *TWAT* IV, Stuttgart-Berlin-Köln-Mainz 1986, col. 203-219

Haupt, P., Critical Notes on Esther. *AJSLL* 24 (1907-1908) p. 97-186

Havice, H.K., *The concern for the Widow and the Fatherless in the Ancient Near East: A Case Study in Old Testament Ethics*, Yale University diss., 1978

Hayes, J.H. / Prussner, F.C., *Old Testament Theology: Its History and Development,* London 1985

Heaton, E.W., Sojourners in Egypt, *ET* 58 (1946) p. 80-83

Helck, W., Art. Fremde, Verhältnis zur, in: *LÄ II*, Wiesbaden 1977 col. 311-312

——, Die Ägypter und die Fremden, in: *Saeculum* 15 (1964) p. 103-114

Hempel, J., *Die Schichten des Deuteronomiums. Ein Beitrag zur israelitischen Literatur und Rechtgeschichte*, Leipzig 1914

Hengel, M., *Judaism and Hellenism. Studies in their Encounter in Palestine during the Early Hellenistic Period*, 1/2, London 1974

Henton Davies, G., Art. Tabernacle, in: *IDB*, Vol. 4, New York 1962 p. 498-506

Hermisson, H.J., *Sprache und Ritus im altisraelitischen Kult. Zur "Spiritualisierung" der Kultbegriffe im A.T.*, WMANT 19, Neukirchen-Vluyn 1965

Hess, R.S., *Amarna Personal Names*. AASOR Diss. Serie 9, 1993

Hirsch, E.G., Art. Proselyte, in: *JewEnc*, Vol X, New York - London 1907 col. 220-224

Holladay, W.L., *A Concise Hebrew and Aramaic Lexicon of the Old Testament*, 1971

——, *Jeremiah 1/2*, Hermenia, Philadelphia 1986-1989

Horst, F., Art. Fremde, in: *RGG* 3. Aufl., II, Tübingen 1958 col. 1125-1126

Hossfeld, F.-L. / Zenger, E., *Die Psalmen. Psalm 1-50*, NEB, Würzburg 1993

Houten, C., *The Alien in Israelite Law*, JSOTSS 107, Sheffield 1991

Hulst, A.R., Der Name "Israel" im Deuteronomium, *OTSt* 9 (1951) p. 65 - 106

Imparati, F., *Le Leggi Ittite*. INCUNABULA GRAECA Vol. III, Roma 1964

In der Smitten, W.Th., *Esra. Quellen. Überlieferung und Geschichte*, SNN 15, Assen 1973

Jacob, B., *Das erste Buch der Tora. Genesis*, Berlin 1934

Jacobsen, T., *Towards the image of Tammuz and Other Essays on Mesopotamian History and Culture*, Cambridge 1970

Jagersma, H., *Leviticus 19 Identiteit - Bevrijding - Gemeenschap*, SSN 14, Assen 1972

Japhet, S., *The Ideology of the Book of Chronicles and its Place in Biblical Thought*, Frankfurt a. M. - Bern - New York - Paris 1989

Jenni, E., *Lehrbuch der hebräischen Sprache des Alten Testaments*, Basel - Stuttgart 1981

——, *Die hebräischen Präpositionen, Band 1: Die Präposition Beth*, Stuttgart-Berlin-Köln 1992

Jenson, P.P., *Graded Holiness. A Key to the Priestly Conception of the World*, JSOTSS 106, Sheffield 1992

Jepsen, A., *Zur Überlieferungsgeschichte der Vätergestalten*,
    Wissenschaftliche Zeitschrift der Karl-Marx-Universität Leipzig 3
    (1953/54) p. 139-155
Jeremias, J., *Jerusalem zur Zeit Jesu. Kulturgeschichtliche Untersuchung
    zur neutestamentlichen Zeitgeschichte*, 2 Aufl., Göttingen 1958
Joosten, J., *People and Land in the Holiness Code*, SVT 67, Leiden-New
    York-Köln 1996
Joüon, P. / Muraoka, T., *A Grammar of Biblical Hebrew. Subsidia
    Biblica* - 14/1-2, Roma 1993

Kaiser, O., *Der Prophet Jesaja Kapitel 13-39*, ATD 18, Göttingen 1973
——— , Die Ausländer und die Fremden im Alten Testament, in: *JRP* 14
    (1997) p. 65-83
Kaufman, S.A. / Sokoloff, M., *A Key-Word-in-context-Concordance to
    the Targum Neofiti. A guide to the Complete Palestinian Aramaic Text
    of the Thora*, Baltimore - London 1993
Kaufmann, Y., *The Babylonian Captivity and Deutero-Isaiah*, New York
    1970
——— , *The Religion of Israel*. Translated by M. Greenberg, Chicago 1960
Kautsch, E. / Bertholet, A., *Die Heilige Schrift des Alten Testaments*.
    Zweiter Band, 4 Auf., Tübingen 1923
Keel, O., *Die Welt der altorientalischen Bildsymbolik und das Alte
    Testament. Am Beispiel der Psalmen*, 3. Aufl., Neukirchen-Vluyn -
    Zürich 1980
Kellermann, D., Art. גּוּר, in: *TWAT* I, Stuttgart-Berlin-Köln-Mainz 1970-
    1973, col. 979-991
Kellermann, U., Erwägungen zum deuteronomischen Gemeindegesetz Dt
    23,2-9, *BN* 2 (1977) p. 33-47
Kilian, R., *Jesaja II*, NEB, Würzburg 1994
——— , *Literarkritische und formgeschichtliche Untersuchung des
    Heiligkeitgesetzes*, BBB 19, 1963
Kippenberg, H.G. (Hg.), *Seminar: Die Entstehung der antiken
    Klassengesellschaft*, stw 130, Frankfurt a. M. 1977
Kittel, R., *Die Psalmen übersetzt und erklärt*, KAT 13, 5.-6. Aufl.,
    Leipzig 1929
Kloppers, M.H.O., Die rol en funksie van die vreemdeling (*ger*) in
    Deuteronomium, *Fax Theologica* 6/2 (1986) p. 1-44
——— , 'n Verkenning van die wyse waarop die "vreemdeling" (ger) as
    teologiese term binne die ketubim funksioneer, met besondere verwysing
    na die Psalms. *NGTT* 23/3, 1978, p. 130-141
Knobel, A., *Die Genesis*, KeH 11, Leipzig 1852
——— , *Die Bücher Exodus und Leviticus*, KeH 12, Leipzig 1857

Koch, K., Die Entstehung der sozialen Kritik bei den Profeten, in: H.W.
Wolff (Hrsg.), *Probleme biblischer Theologie*. Festschrift G. v. Rad
zum 70. Geburtstag, München 1971 p. 236-257
—— , Sühne und Sündenvergebung um die Wende von der exilischen zur
nachexilischen Zeit, *EvTh* 26 (1966) p. 217-239
Kohler, J. / Peiser, F.E., *Aus dem Babylonischen Rechtsleben*. IV, Leipzig
1898
Köhler, L. / Baumgartner, W. / Stamm, J.J., *Hebräisches und Aramäisches
Lexikon zum Alten Testament*, Leiden 1967-1990
—— , / Baumgartner, W., *Lexicon in Veteris Testamenti Libros*, Leiden
1958
König, F.E., *Historisch-kritisches Lehrgebäude der hebräischen Sprache*.
Band II, Leipzig 1895
Kornfeld, W., *Levitikus*, NEB, Würzburg 1983
—— , *Studien zum Heiligkeitsgesetz*, Wien 1952
Koschaker, P., *Rechtsvergleichende Studien zur Gesetzgebung Hammurapis
Konigs von Babylon*, Leipzig 1917
Kramer, S.N., *The Sumerians. Their history, culture and character*, Chicago
1963
Krapf, T., Traditionsgeschichtliches zum deuteronomischen Fremdling-
Waise-Witwe Gebot, *VT* XXXIV 1 (1984) p. 87-91
Krašovec, J., Merism - Polar Expression in Biblical Hebrew, *Biblica* 64
(1983) p. 231-239
Kratz, R.G., Die Gnade des täglichen Brots. Späte Psalmen auf dem Weg
zum Vaterunser, *ZThK* 89 (1992) Heft 1 p. 1-40
Kraus, H.J., *Psalmen*. BK XV/1-2, 5. Aufl., Neukirchen-Vluyn 1978
Krebernik, M., *Die Personennamen der Ebla-Texte. Eine Zwischenbilanz*,
Berlin 1988
Kreuzer, S., Die Exodustradition im Deuteronomium, in: T. Veijola,
(Hrsg.), *Das Deuteronomium und seine Querbeziehungen*, Göttingen
1996 p. 81-106
Kuhn, K.G., Art. Proselyten, in: *RECA* Supp IX, Stuttgart 1962, col.
1248-1283
—— , Art. προσήλυτος, in: *TWNT* VI, 1959, p. 727-745
—— , Ursprung und Wesen der talmudischen Einstellung zum Nichtjuden,
FJF 3 (1939) p. 199-234
Kühne, C., *Die Chronologie der internationalen Korrespondenz von El-
Amarna*, AOAT 17, Neukirchen-Vluyn 1973
Kuli, H., Art. προσήλυτος, in: *EWNT*, Band III, 2. Aufl. 1992, Stuttgart -
Berlin - Köln col. 410-413

Labriolle, P., Paroecia, *RScR* XVIII (1928), p. 60-72
Lambert, W.G., *Babylonian Wisdom Literature*, Oxford 1960
Lang, B., Art. Fremder, in: *NBL*, 1, Zürich 1991 col. 701-702

Lanne, E., La "xeniteia" d'Abraham dans l'œuvre d'Irénée. Aux origines du thème monastique de la "peregrinatio", *Irénikon* XLVII (1974/1) p. 163-187

Le Déaut, R. / Robert, J., *Targum du Pentateuque. SC II, Exode et Lévitique*, Paris 1979

——, La Septante, un Targum?, in: R. Kuntzmann et J. Schlosser. *Études sur le Judaïsme Hellénistique*, LeDiv 119, Paris 1984 p. 147-195

——, / Lécuyer, J., Art. Exode, in: *DS* 4/2, Paris 1961 col. 1972-1990

Leahy, A., Ethnic Diversity in Ancient Egypt, in: *Civilizations of the Ancient Near East*, J.M. Sasson (Ed.), Vol. 1, New York 1995 p. 225-234

Lee, J.A.L., Equivocal and Stereotyped Renderings in the LXX. *RB* 87 (1980) p. 104-117

Leemans, W.F., *Foreign Trade in the Old Babylonian Period. As revealed by texts from Southern Mesopotamia*, Leiden 1960

Leeuwen, van C., *Le développement du sens social en Israël avant l'ère chrétienne*, SSN 1, Assen 1955

Leipoldt, J. / Grundmann,W., *Umwelt des Urchristentums I. Darstellung des neutestamentlichen Zeitalters*, 7. Aufl., Berlin 1985

Lesètre, H., Art. Étranger, in: *DBV*, X. 2°, Paris 1912 col. 2039-2042

——, Art. Prosélyte, in: *DBV*, V, Paris 1912 col. 758-764

Levine, B., *Leviticus*, JPS Torah Commentary, Philadelphia 1989

Levine, E., *The Aramaic Versions of the Bible*, Berlin - New York 1988

Levy, J. / Fleischer, H.L. / Goldschmidt, L., *Wörterbuch über die Talmudim und Midraschim*, III מ - ע, 2. Aufl., Darmstadt 1963

——, On Some Institutions of the Old Assyrian Empire. *HUCA* 27 (1956) p. 1-79

Liedke, G., *Gestalt und Bezeichnung alttestamentlicher Rechtssätze*, Neukirchen-Vluyn 1971

——, Art. שׁפט š p ṭ richten, in: *THAT* II, München 1971 col. 999-1009

Limet, H., L'Étranger dans la société sumérienne, in: *ABAW Phil.-hist. Klasse*, N.F. 75, München 1972 p. 123-138

Link, H.G., Art. ἱλάσκομαι, in: *TBNT*, 9. Aufl., Budapest 1993, p. 1304-1307

Lisowsky, G., *Konkordanz zum Hebräischen Alten Testament*, 3. Aufl., Stuttgart 1993

Liverani, M., Art. Nationality and Political Identity, in: *ABD*, Vol. 4, New York 1992 p.1031-1037

——, *Prestige and Interest. International Relations in the Near Eastern ca. 1600-1100 B.C.*, History of the Ancient Near/Studies I, Padova 1990

Lods, A., *Israël. Des origines au milieu du VIIIᵉ siècle*, Paris 1932

Loewenstamm, S.E. / Blau, J., *Thesaurus of the Language of the Bible*, II ב-ו, Jerusalem 1959

Lohfink, N., Das deuteronomische Gesetz in der Endgestalt-Entwurft einer Gesellschaft ohne marginale Gruppen, *BN* 51 (1990) p. 25-40

——, *Das Hauptgebot. Eine Untersuchung literarischer Einleitungsfragen zu Dtn 5-11*, AnBib, Roma 1963

——, Die Gattung der "Historischen Kurzgeschichte" in den letzten Jahren von Juda und in der Zeit des Babylonischen Exils, *ZAW* 90 (1978) p. 319-347

——, *Die Landverheissung als Eid, Eine Studie zu Gn 15*, SBS 28, Stuttgart 1967

——, *Die Väter Israels im Deuteronomium. Mit einer Stellungnahme von Thomas Römer*, OBO 111, 1992

——, Gibt es eine deuteronomische Bearbeitung im Bundesbuch?, in: *BEThL* 94 (1990) p. 91-113

——, Zum "kleinen geschichtlichen Credo" Dtn 26,5-9, *ThPh* 46 (1971) p. 19-39

——, Poverty in the Laws of the Ancient Near East and of the Bible, *TS* 52 (1991) p. 34-50

Löhr, M., *Das Asylwesen Im Alten Testament*, SKG.G 7/3, Halle (Saale) 1930

Lohse, E., *Die Texte aus Qumran*, Darmstadt 1971

Loprieno, A., *Topos und Mimesis. Zum Ausländer in der ägyptischen Literatur*, ÄA 48, Wiesbaden 1988

Lust, J. / Eynikel, E. / Hauspie, K., *A Greek - English Lexicon of the Septuagint I-II*, Stuttgart 1992-1996

Maarsingh, B., *Onderzoek naar de Ethiek van de Wetten in Deuteronomium*, Winterwijk 1961

Maier, J., *Die Texte vom Toten Meer*, Band II Anmerkungen, Basel 1960

Mandelkern, S., *Veteris Testamenti Concordantiae Habraicae atque Chaldaicae*, 9. Aufl., Tel Aviv 1971

Marti, K., *Das Buch Jesaja*, KHC 10, Tübingen 1900

Martin-Achard, R., Art. רוג gūr als Fremdling weilen, in: *THAT* I, München 1971 col. 409-412

——, Israël et les nations, Neuchâtel 1959

Mathys, Hans-Peter, *Liebe deinen Nächsten wie dich selbst*, OBO 71, 1986

Mayes, A.D.H., *Deuteronomy*, NCBC, Grand Rapids 1979

——, Deuteronomy 4 and the Litererary Criticism of Deuteronomy, in: *A Song of Power and the Power of Song*, D.L. Christensen (Ed.) SBTS 3, Indiana 1993 p. 195-224

McKane, W., *Jeremiah*, ICC, Edinburgh 1986

Mceleny, N.J., Conversion, Circumcision and the Law, *NTS* 20 (1974) p. 319-341

Meek, T., The translation of GER in the Hexateuch and its bearing on the Documentary Hypothesis. *JBL* 49 (1930) p. 172-180

Meier, G., *Die Assyrische Beschwörungssammlung MAQLŪ*, AfO 2, Osnabrück 1967

Meissner, B., *Babylonien und Assyrien*, Heidelberg 1920

Merendino, R.P., *Das Deuteronomische Gesetz*, Bonn 1969

Meyer, E., Die Entstehung des Judentums, Halle 1896

Michaeli, F., Livre de L'Exode, Neuchâtel 1974

Milgrom, J., Art. Priestly ("P") Source, in: *ABD*, Vol. 5, New York 1992 p. 545-461

──── , Leviticus 1-16, AncB 3, New York 1991

──── , Religious Conversion: the Revolt Model for the Formation of Israel, *JBL* 101/102 (1982) p. 169-176

──── , The Changing Concept of Holiness in the Pentateuchal Codes with Emphasis on Leviticus 19, in: J.F.A. Sawyer (Ed.), *Reading Leviticus. A Conversation with Mary Douglas* JSOTSS 227, Sheffield 1996 p. 64-75

Momigliano, A., *Sagesses barbares. Les limites de l'hellénisation*, (French translation from Alien Wisdom, 1976), Paris 1979

Monod, V., Le voyage, le déracinement de l'individu hors du milieu natal constituent-ils un des éléments déterminants de la conversion religieuse?, *RHPR* 3/5 (1936) p. 385-399

Moore, G.A., *Judaism*. 3 vols, Cambridge 1927-1930

Moraldi, L., *I Manoscritti di Qumran*, Torino 1971

Mosis, R., Das Babylonische Exil Israels in der Sicht christlicher Exegese, in: idem: *Exil-Diaspora-Rückkehr*, SKAB 81, Düsseldorf 1978 p. 55-77

Mowinckel, S., Zu Deuteronomium 23,2-9, *AcOr (L)* 1, (1922/3) p. 81-104

Müller, H.P., Phönikien und Juda in der exilisch-nachexilischen Zeit. *WO* 6 (1970) p. 189-204

Muntingh, L.M., *A Few Social Concepts in the Psalms and their Relationship to the Canaanite Residential Area*, Potchefstroom 1963 p. 48-57

──── , Die begrip 'Ger' in die Ou Testament, in: *NGTT* 3 (1962) p. 534-558

Nestle, E., Zur aramäischen Bezeichnung der Proselyten. *ZNW*, 5 (1904) p. 263-264

Neu, E., *Ein althethitisches Gewitterritual*, Wiesbaden 1970

Nicholson, E.W., *Preaching to the Exiles. A Study of the Prose Tradition in the book of Jeremiah*, Oxford 1970

Nielsen, E., *Deuteronomium*, HAT I/6, Tübingen 1995

Niederwimmer, K., Vom Glauben der Pilger. Erwägungen zu Hebr 11,8-10 und 13-16, in: S. Kreuzer / K. Lüthi (Hrsg.), *Zur Aktualität des Alten Testaments*, Festschrift G. Sauer zum 65. Geburtstag, Frankfurt am Main-Bern-New York-Paris 1992 p. 121-131

Nödelke, Th., Art. Fremde, in: *BiL*, D. Schenkel (Hrsg), Band 2, Leipzig 1869 p. 298-302

Noth, M., *Das Buch Joshua*, HAT I/7, 2. Aufl., Tübingen 1953

──── , *Das dritte Buch Mose. Leviticus*, ATD 6, Göttingen 1962

———, *Das vierte Buch Mose. Numeri*, ATD 7, Göttingen 1966

———, *Das zweite Buch Mose. Exodus*, ATD 5, Göttingen 1959

———, *Überlieferungsgeschichte des Pentateuch*, 2. Aufl., Darmstadt 1960

Nowack, W., *Lehrbuch der Hebräischen Archäologie*, Erster Band, Nachdruck der 1. Aufl. von 1894, Graz 1975

Oded, B., *Mass Deportations and Deportees in the Neo-Assyrian Empire*, Wiesbaden 1979

Ohana, M., Prosélytisme et Targum palestinien: Données nouvelles pour la datation de Néofiti 1. *Biblica* 55 (1974) p. 317-332

Oller, G.H., "Messengers and Ambassadors in Ancient Western Asia", in: *Civilizations of the Ancient Near East*, J.M. Sasson (Ed.), Vol. 1, New York 1995 p. 1465-1473

Olmo Olete, G. del, *Mitos y leyendas de Canaan según la tradición de Ugarit*, Fuentes de la ciencia bíblica 1, Madrid 1981

Orbe, P.A., *Parábolas Evangélicas en San Ireneo*, II, Madrid 1972

Osumi, Y., *Die Kompositionsgeschichte des Bundesbuches Ex 20,22b - 23,33*, OBO 105, 1991

Otto, E., "Das Heiligkeitsgesetz Leviticus 17-26 in der Pentateuchredaktion", in: P. Mommer / W. Thiel (Hrsg.), *Altes Testament - Forschung und Wirkung*, Festschrift H. Graf-Reventlow zum 65. Geburtstag, Frankfurt a. M. 1994 p. 65-80

———, *Theologische Ethik des Alten Testaments*, TW 3,2, Stuttgart - Berlin - Köln 1994

———, Sozial- und rechtshistorische Aspekte in der Ausdifferenzierung eines altisraelitischen Ethos aus dem Recht. *OH*, Schriftenreihe des FB 3, Bd. 9, 1987, p. 135-161

———, Hrsg., *ZABR* 1, 1995

Otto, E., *Die biographischen Inschriften der ägyptischen Spätzeit. Probleme der Ägyptologie* 2, Leiden 1954

Paton, L.B., *The Book of Esther*, ICC, 2. Impression, Edinburgh 1951

Patterson, R.D., The Widow, the Orphan and the Poor in the Old Testament and in the Extra-Biblical Literature, *SB* 139 (1973) p. 223-234

Pedersen, J., *Israel. Its life and culture*. I-II, London 1946

Perlitt, L., 'Ein einzig Volk von Brüdern' Zur deuteronomistischen Herkunft der biblischen Bezeichnung 'Bruder', in: D. Lührmann / G. Strecker (Hrsg.), *Kirche. Festschrift für Günther Bornkamm zum 75. Geburtstag*, Tübingen 1980 p. 27-52

———, Israel und die Völker, Erstpublikation in: *Allein mit dem Wort*, H. Spieckermann (Hrsg.), Theologische Studien, Göttingen 1995 p. 26- 66

———, *Vatke und Wellhausen. Geschichtsphilosophische Voraussetzungen und historiographische Motive für die Darstellung der Religion und*

Geschichte Israels durch Wilhem Vatke und Julius Wellhausen, Berlin 1965

Petit-Jean, A., *Les Oracles du Proto-Zacharie*, Paris - Louvain 1969

Pfeiffer, R.H., *Introduction to the Old Testament,* New York - London 1941

Pikaza, J., *La Biblia y la Teología de la Historia. Tierra y Promesa de Dios*, AB 28, Madrid 1972

Plöger, J.G., *Literarkritische, formgeschichtliche und stilkritische Untersuchungen zum Deuteronomium*, BBB 26, Bonn 1967

—— , *Aus der Spätzeit des Alten Testaments*, Göttingen 1971

Pons, J., La Référence au séjour en Égypte et à la sortie d'Égypte dans les codes de loi de L'Ancien Testament, *EThR* 63 (1988/2) p. 169-182

—— , *L'Oppression dans l'Ancien Testament*, Paris 1981

Pope, M.H., Art. Proselyte, in: *IDB*, Vol. 3, New York 1962 p. 921-931

Porten, B., *Archives from Elephantine. The life of an ancient Jewish Military Colony*, Berkeley 1968

Porton, G.G., *The Stranger within your gates: Converts and Conversion in Rabbinic Literature*, Chicago 1994

Powis Smith, J.M. / Meek, T.J., / Waterman, L., / Gordon, A.R., / Goodspeed, E.J., *The Complete Bible. An American Translation*, Chicago 1939

Preuß, H.D., *Deuteronomium*, EdF 164, Darmstadt 1982

Pritchard, J.B. (ed.), *Ancient Near Eastern Texts related to the Old Testament*, Third Edition with Supplement, Princeton 1969

Procksch, O., *Die Genesis*, KAT I, 3. Aufl., Leipzig 1924

—— , *Jesaja I*, KAT IX, Leipzig 1930

Quell, G., Jesaja 14,1-23, in: L. Rost (Hrsg.), *Festschrift Friedrich Baumgärtel zum 70. Geburtstag*, Erlangen 1959, p. 131-157

Rabenau, M., *Studien zum Buch Tobiah*, Berlin - New York 1994

Rad, G. von, *Das fünfte Buch Mose. Deuteronomium*, ATD 8, Göttingen 1964

—— , Das Gottesvolk im Deuteronomium (1929), in: ders., *Gesammelte Studien zum Alten Testament II*, TB 48, München 1973, p. 9-108

—— , *Gesammelte Studien zum Alten Testament I*, TB 8, 3. Aufl., München 1965

—— , *Deuteronomium Studien*, FRLANT 4, Göttingen 1947

—— , Verheissenes Land und Jahwes Land im Hexateuch (1943), in: ders., *Gesammelte Studien zum Alten Testament I*, TB 8, München 1965 p. 87-100

Ravasi, G., *Il Libro dei Salmi I/III*, Bologna 1981-1984

Reimer, D.J., Concerning Return to Egypt: Deuteronomy 17,16 and 28,68 Reconsidered, in: J.A. Emerton (Ed.),*Studies in the Pentateuch*, SVT 41, Leiden 1990 p. 217-229

Reiner, E., *ŠURPU. A collection of Sumerian and Akkadian Incantations*, AfO 11, Graz 1958

Rendtorff, R., *Die Gesetze in der Priesterschrift*, FRLANT NF 44, Göttingen 1963

Renger, J., Flucht als soziales Problem in der altbabylonischen Gesellschaft, in: Gesellschaftsklassen im Alten Zweistromland und in den angrenzenden Gebieten, *ABAW* NF 75, 1972: 167-182

Reventlow, H. Graf, *Das Heiligkeitsgesetz formgeschichtlich untersucht*, WMANT 6, Göttingen 1961

Rhode, E., *Psyche*, 2. Aufl., Darmstadt 1961

Roberts, A. / Donaldson, J. (Ed.), *The Ante-Nicene Fathers. Translation of The Writings of the Fathers down to A.D. 325*, Reprint of the Edinburgh Edition, 1962

Robertson Smith, W., *Kinship and Marriage in early Arabia*, 3. Aufl., London 1903

—— , *The Religion of the Semites*, 2. Aufl. 1894, Reimpression, New York 1972

Rofé, A., The laws of Warfare in the Book of Deuteronomy, *JSOT* 32, Sheffield 1985 p. 23-44

Roldanus, J., Le chrétien-étranger au monde dans les homélies bibliques de Jean Chrysostome, *Sacris Erudiri* XXX (1987-1988) p. 231- 251

—— , Références patristiques au "chrétien-étranger" dans les trois premiers siècles. *Cahiers de Biblia Patristica 1*, Strasbourg 1987 p. 27-52

Rose, M., *5. Mose*, ZB 1/2, Zürich 1994

Rosen, G. / Bertram, G., *Juden und Phönizier. Das antike Judentum als Missionsreligion und die Entstehung der jüdischen Diaspora*, Tübingen 1929

Ross, J.M.E., Art. Bunyan, in: *ERE* 2, Berlin - New York 1978 p. 897-901

Rost, L., *Die Vorstufen von Kirche und Synagoge im Alten Testament. Eine wortgeschichtliche Untersuchung*, BWANT 4/24, 1938, Nachdr., Darmstadt 1967

—— , *Studien zum Alten Testament*, Stuttgart - Berlin - Köln - Mainz 1974

Roth, M.T., *Law Collections from Mesopotamia and Asia Minor*. SBL Writings from the Ancient World Series 6, Roth 1995

Rouault, O., *MUKANNIŠUM. L'Administration et l'économie palatiales à Mari*, ARM ẊVIII, Paris 1977

Rücker, H., Die Begründungen der Weisungen Jahwes im Pentateuch, *EThSt* 30, Leipzig 1973 p. 28-37

Rupp, G., Art. Bunyan, in: *TRE* 7, Berlin - New York 1981 p. 416-419

Saporetti, C., *Le leggi Medioassire*, Malibu 1979

Schaeffer, C.F.-A. (Éd.), *Le Palais Royal D'Ugarit. III. Textes Accadiens et Hourrites des Archives Est, Ouest et Centrales*, traduction de J. Nougayrol, Paris 1955

Schäfer-Lichtenberger, C., *Stadt und Eidgenossenschaft im Alten Testament*, Berlin 1983

Schley, D.G., "Yahweh will cause you to return to Egypt in ships" (Deuteronomy xxviii 68), *VT* 35 (1985) p. 369-372

Schmid, H.H., *Altorientalische Welt in der alttestamentlichen Theologie*, Zürich 1974

Schmidt, K.L. / Schmidt, M.A., Art. πάροικος, in: *TWNT*, V p. 840-848

——— , Israels Stellung zu den Fremdlingen und Beisassen und Israels Wissens um seine Fremdlings- und Beisassenschaft, *Judaica* 1 (1945) p. 269-296

Schmitt, G., *Du sollst keinen Frieden schliessen mit den Bewohnern des Landes*, BWANT V/11, Stuttgart 1970

Schneider, T., *Asiatische Personennamen im ägyptischen Quellen des Neuen Reiches*, OBO 114, 1992

Schökel, L.A. (Ed.), *Biblia del Peregrino, Edición de Estudio, I/III*, Bilbao 1996-1997

——— , (Ed.), *Diccionario Bíblico Hebreo - Español*, Madrid 1994

——— , - C. Carniti, *Salmos I*, 2. Ed., Navarra 1992

——— , - C. Carniti, *Salmos II*, Navarra 1993

——— , - J.L. Sicre, *Profetas I/II*, Madrid 1980

——— , *Estudios de Poética Hebrea*, Barcelona 1963

——— , Jeremías como anti-Moisés, in: *De la Tôrah au Messie*. Mélanges Henri Cazelles. M. Carrez / J. Doré / P. Grelot Ed., Paris 1981 pp. 245-254

——— , Teología bíblica y lingüística, *Biblica* 43 (1962) p. 217-223

Schottroff, W., *'Gedenken' im Alten Orient und im Alten Testament. Die Wurzel zakâr im semitischen Sprachkreis*, WMANT 15, Neukirchen-Vluyn 1964

Schreiner, J., Art. Gastfreundschaft, in: *NBL*, 1, Zürich 1991 col. 730

Schreiner, J., Muß ich in der Fremde leben? *BiKi* 42 (1987) p. 50-60

——— , Gastfreundschaft im Zeugnis der Bibel. *TThZ* 89 (1980), p. 50-60

Schürer, E., *The History of the Jewish People in the Age of Jesus Christ (175 B.C. - A.D. 135)*, A New English Version revised and edited by G. Vermes et al, I/III.2, Edinburgh 1973-1987

Schwartz, J., Remarques Littéraires sur le roman de Tobit. *RHPR* 67 (1987) p. 293-297

Schwienhorst-Schönberger, L., "... denn Fremde seid ihr gewesen im Land Ägypten". Zur sozialen und rechtlichen Stellung von Fremden und Ausländern im Alten Israel, *BuL* 63, (1990) p. 108-117

——— , *Das Bundesbuch (Ex 20,22-23,33)*, BZAW 188, Berlin 1990

Seebaß, H., Art. בחר, in: *TWAT* I, Stuttgart-Berlin-Köln-Mainz 1973 col. 592-608

Seitz, G., *Redaktionsgeschichtliche Studien zum Deuteronomium*, BWANT V/13, Stuttgart 1971

Seters, J. van, *Abraham in History and Tradition*, New Heaven - London 1975

——— , Confessional Reformulation in the Exilic Period, *VT* 22 (1972) p. 448-459

Seux, M.-J., *Hymnes et prières aux dieux de Babylonie et d'Assyrie*. Littératures Anciennes du Proche Orient 8, Paris 1976

Sicre, J.L., *Con los pobres de la tierra. La justicia social en los profetas de Israel*, Madrid 1984

Siebert-Hommes, J.C., Mozes-'vreemdeling' in Midjian, *ACEBT* 10 (1989) p. 16-20

Simon, M., Sur les débuts du prosélytisme Juif, in: A. Caquot / M. Philonenko (Éd.), Hommages a André Dupont-Sommer, Paris 1971 p. 509-520

Smith, M., *Palestinian Parties and Politics that shaped the Old Testament*, New York 1971

Snaith, N.H., *Leviticus and Numbers*, NCBC, London 1977

Snijders, L.A., *The meaning of* זר *in the OT, an Exegetical Study*, OTS 10, 1953

Soden, W. von, *Akkadisches Handwörterbuch*, Wiesbaden 1959-1981

Soisalon-Soinenen, I., Der Infinitivus constructus mit ל im Hebräischen, *VT* 22 (1972) p. 82-90

Sokoloff, M., *A Dictionary of Jewish Palestinian Aramaic of the Byzantine Period*, Ramat Gan 1990

Solignac, A., Art. Pèlerinages, in: *DS* 12/1, Paris 1984 col. 887-894

Spencer, J.R., Art. Sojourner, in: *ABD*, Vol. 4, New York 1992 p.103-104

Spicq, C., *Notes de Lexicographie Néo-Testamentaire*. Tome II (OBO 22/2), 1978

——— , *Vie Chrétienne et pérégrination selon le Nouveau Testament*, LD 71, Paris 1972, p. 59-76

——— , *Les Épitres de Saint Pierre*, SBi, Paris 1966

Spieckermann, H., Die Stimme des Fremden im Alten Testament, *PTh* 83 (1994) p. 52-67

Spina, F.A., Israelites as *gerim*, 'Sojourners' in Social and Historical Context, in: C.L. Meyers / M.O. Conner (Ed.), *The word of the Lord shall go forth*, Festschrift D.N. Freedman, Winona Lake 1983

Stade, B., *Lehrbuch der hebräischen Grammatik*, Leipzig 1879

Stählin, G., Art. ξένος, in: *TWNT* V, Stuttgart 1954 col. 5-36

Stählin, O., *Des Clemens von Alexandreia*. BKV zweite Reihe, Band XVII, München 1936

Stamm, J.J., *Die akkadische Namengebung*, Leipzig 1968
—— , "Fremde, Fluechtlinge und ihr Schutz im Alten Israel und in seiner Umwelt", in: *Der Flüchtling in der Weltgeschichte* (Hg. A. Mercier), Bern - Frankfurt a. M. 1974 p. 31-66
Steck, O.H., *Israel und das gewaltsame Geschick der Propheten. Untersuchungen zur Überlieferung des deuteronomistichen Geschichtsbildes im Alten Testament, Frühjudentum und Urchristentum*, WMANT 23, Neukirchen-Vluyn 1967
Steuernagel, C., *Das Deuteronomium*, HK I/3/1, 2. Aufl., Göttingen 1923
—— , Die jüdisch-aramäischen Papyri und Ostraka aus Elephantine und ihre Bedeutung für die Kenntnis palästinensischer Verhältnisse, *ZDPV* 1912
Stipp, H.-J., *Jeremia im Parteienstreit. Studien zur Textentwicklung von Jer 26,36 - 43 und 45 als Beitrag zur Geschichte Jeremias, seines Buches und judäischer Parteien im 6. Jahrhundert*, BBB 82, Bonn 1992

Talmon, S., Jüdische Sektenbildung in der Frühzeit der Periode des Zweiten Tempels, in: W. Schluchter (ed.), *Max Weber Sicht des antiken Judentums*, Frankfurt a. M. 1985 p. 233-280
Tcherikover, G., 'Natives' and 'Foreigners' in Palestine, in: *The Age of the Monarchies: Culture and Society*, A. Malamat (Ed.), vol. 4, Jerusalem 1979 p. 87-95
Thiel, W., *Die deuteronomistische Redaktion von Jeremia 1 - 25*, WMANT 41, Neukirchen-Vluyn 1973
—— , *Die soziale Entwicklung Israels in vorstaatlicher Zeit*, 2. Aufl., Berlin 1985
Thompson, J.A., *Deuteronomy*, TOTC, London 1974
Tigay, J. H., *Deuteronomy*, JPS Torah Commentary, Philadelphia-Jerusalem 1996
Toorn, K. van der, *Sin and Sanction in Israel and Mesopotamia. A comparative study*, SSN 22, Assen 1985
Tov, M., Three Dimensions of LXX Words. *RB* LXXXIII (1976) p. 528-544

Vaulx, J. de, Art. Refuge, in: *DBS* 9, Paris 1979 col. 1480-1510
—— , *Les Nombres*, SB, Paris 1972
Vaux, R. de, *Les institutions de L'Ancien Testament*, I/II, Paris 1958-1960
Vermeylen, J., *Du Prophète Isaie à l'Apocalyptique. Isaie I-XXXV*, Tome I, Paris 1977
Vesco, J.L., Les lois sociales du Livre de l'Alliance. *RThom* 6 (1968) p. 241-264
Vincent, A., *La Religion des Judéo-Araméens d'Éléphantine*, Paris 1937
Vink, J.G., The date and origin of the Priestly Code in the Old Testament, in: *The Priestly Code and seven other studies*, OST XV, 1969

Virolleaud, Ch., Textes administratifs des Ras Shamra en cunéiforme alphabétique, *RA* XXXVII (1940) p. 34-44

Vries, J. de, art. Gastfreundschaft, in: *RGG* 3. Aufl., II, Tübingen 1958 col. 1205

Waltke, B.K. / O'Connor, M., *An Introduction to Biblical Hebrew Syntax*, Winona Lake 1990

Weber, M., *Das antike Judentum. Gesammelte Aufsätze zur Religionssoziologie III*, Tübingen 1921

Weiler, I., Zum Schicksal der Witwen und Waisen bei den Völkern der Alten Welt, *Saeculum* 31 (1980) p. 157-193

Weimar, P., *Untersuchungen zur Redaktionsgeschichte des Pentateuch*, BZAW 146, Berlin 1977

Weinfeld, M., *Deuteronomy and the Deuteronomic School*, Oxford 1972

Weippert, H., *Palästina in vorhellenistischer Zeit. Handbuch der Archäologie. Vorderasien II/1*, München 1988

Weiser, A., *Die Psalmen*, ATD 14/15, 9. Aufl., Göttingen 1979

Wellhausen, J., *Die Composition des Hexateuchs und der Historischen Bücher des Alten Testaments*, Berlin 1899

Welten, P., Art. Jerusalem I, in: *TRE* 16, Berlin - New York 1987, col. 590-609

—— , Zur Frage nach dem Fremden im Alten Testament, in: E.L. Ehrlich / B. Klappert (Hrsg.), *"Wie gut sind deine Zelte, Jaakow ..."*, Festschrift R. Mayer, Gerlingen 1987 p. 130-138

Westerbrook, R., *Studies in Biblical and Cuneiform Law*, CahRB 26,1988

Westermann, C., *Das Buch Jesaja Kapitel 40-66*, ATD 19, Göttingen 1966

—— , *Genesis*, BK I/2, Neukirchen-Vluyn 1981

Whitaker, R.E., *A Concordance of the Ugaritic Literature*, Massachusetts 1972

Wiesehöfer, J., "Reichsgesetz" oder "Einzelfallgerechtigkeit"? Bemerkungen zu Peter Freis These von der achaimenidischen "Reichsautorisation", in: *ZABR* 1 p. 36-46

Wijngaards, J.N.M., *Deuteronomium*, BOT 256, II/3, 1971

Wilcke, C., *Das Lugalbandaepos*, Wiesbaden 1969

Wild, H., Art. Fremde in Agypten, in: *LÄ* II, Wiesbaden 1977, p. 306-310

Wildberger, H., Art. בחר bḥr erwählen, in: *THAT* I, München 1971 col. 275-300

—— , Die Neuinterpretation des Erwählungsglaubens Israels in der Krise der Exilzeit, in: *Gesammelte Aufsätze zum Alten Testament*, TB 66, München 1979, p. 192-209

—— , Israel und sein Land. *EvTh* 16 (1956) p. 404-422

—— , *Jesaja*, BK X/1-3, Neukirchen-Vluyn 1972-1982

Williamson, H.G.M., *1 and 2 Chronicles*, NCBC, Grand Rapids 1982

—— , *Ezra, Nehemiah*, WBC 16, Waco 1985

Winer, G.B., *Lexicon Manuale Hebraicum et Chaldaicum in Veteris Testamenti Libros*, Lipsiae 1828
Wolff, H.W., *Dodekapropheton 1. Hosea*, BK XIV/1, 3. Aufl., Neukirchen-Vluyn 1976

Zeitlin, S., Proselytes and Proselytism during the second Commonwealth and Early Tannaitic Period, in: Idem., *Studies in the Early History of Judaism*. Vol II, New York 1974 p. 407-417
Zimmerli, W., Die Eigenart der prophetischen Rede des Ezechiel. Ein Beitrag zum Problem an Hand von Ez 14, 1-11, *ZAW* 66 (1955) p. 1-26
—— , *Ezechiel*, BK XIII/1-2, Neukirchen-Vluyn 1969
Zobel, H.-J., "Israel" in Ägypten, in: S. Kreuzer / K. Lüthi (Hrsg.), *Zur Aktualität des Alten Testaments*, Festschrift G. Sauer zum 65. Geburtstag, Frankfurt am Main-Bern-New York-Paris 1992 p. 109-117
—— , Das Recht der Witwen und Waisen, in: P. Mommer / W.H. Schmidt / H. Strauß (Hrsg.), *Gottes Recht als Lebensraum*, Festschrift H.J. Boecker zum 65. Geburtstag, Neukirchen-Vluyn 1993 p. 33-38
Zorell, F., *Lexicon Hebraicum Veteris Testamenti*, Roma 1961
—— , *Lexicon Graecum Novi Testamenti*, Paris 1961

Index of Authors

Index of References

I. Old Testament

Genesis

Synoptic Concordance

A Greek Concordance to the First Three Gospels in Synoptic Arrangement, statistically evaluated, including occurrences in Acts

Paul Hoffmann, Thomas Hieke, Ulrich Bauer

In four volumes; Volume 1 (Introduction, A − Δ). 1999. 31 x 23,5 cm.
LXXIII, 1032 pages. Cloth. DM 298,–/öS 2175,–/sFr 265,–/approx.US$ 175.00
• ISBN 3-11-016296-2

The *Synoptic Concordance* is a major new research tool for the analysis of the first three Gospels, providing an extensive mass of data that greatly facilitates literary and linguistic examination.

The advantages of a concordance are combined with those of a synopsis: each occurrence of a word in the synoptic Gospels, along with a section of text that provides its context, is displayed in three columns. The result is that one sees not only the occurrences of a certain word in one Gospel, but also the parallels in the other two Gospels.

Prior to the availability of this new scholarly tool, it was necessary first to check the concordance for the occurrences of a certain word, then to look up each reference individually in a syn-opsis, and finally to take notes, before moving on to the next entry in the concordance, and so on. The *Synoptic Concordance* presents the whole synoptic situation at one time: all of the differences and similarities are obvious at a glance, so that the first three Gospels can easily be compared according to their divergent terminology and syntax. On the two-document hypothesis, one can see, for example, how Matthew or Luke takes over and changes his Markan source, or how they differ in the redaction of their Q text.

The Synoptic Concordance will appear in four volumes, with a total size of about 5,000 pages.

Price is subject to change

WALTER DE GRUYTER GMBH & CO KG
Genthiner Str. 13 · D–10785 Berlin
Tel. +49 (0)30 2 60 05–0
Fax +49 (0)30 2 60 05–251
Internet: www.deGruyter.de

de Gruyter
Berlin · New York